Critical Acclaim for *REALITY, A Plain-Talk Guide to Economics, Politics, Government and Culture*

Mike Rosen is a fellow supply-sider whom I've known since the Reagan days, and I have been on his radio show many times. It's been said that it's not the things you don't know that get you in trouble, it's the things you think you know that aren't so. In this book Mike debunks numerous false claims and misconceptions with his trademark knack for explaining a wide range of complicated economic and public policy issues in terms everyone can understand. It's an enlightening and entertaining read.

Arthur B. Laffer, Ph.D. CEO, Laffer Associates. Served on President Reagan's Economic Policy Advisory Board. Best known for the "Laffer Curve," illustrating how a reduction in excessive tax rates can produce greater revenues

****

Renaissance men are hard to come by these days, but after reading Mike Rosen's *REALITY*, I think we found one. Rosen is a conservative, for sure – the smart, upbeat, optimistic kind who writes with intelligence and wit about all sorts of things, from Dr. Zhivago and Ayn Rand to – ready for this? – Hostess Twinkies. My old *CBS News* colleague Dan Rather even gets a mention. And Rosen's tale about the time he tried to trip up William F. Buckley with a long-winded question that had more big words that nobody ever heard of is laugh out loud funny. *REALITY* is really worth your time.

Bernard Goldberg *CBS News, Fox News* and author of: *Bias: A CBS Insider Exposes How the Media Distort the News*

****

From Brooklyn to broadcasting is a simple description of Mike Rosen's career, but it doesn't begin to convey the knowledge and wisdom he has accumulated on his journey from New York's largest borough to the continental United States' highest mountain range. For that you need to consult *REALITY*, his plain-talk guide to economics, politics, government and culture. Enjoy.

Michael Barone *Washington Examiner*; American Enterprise Institute; Co-author: *The Almanac of American Politics*

D0179966

****

Brilliant, humorous and informative! Mike Rosen enlightens the world.

Hank Brown former U.S. Senator (CO) and President of the University of Colorado

****

Jewish kids from Brooklyn are supposed to move to Vermont and become socialists (at least this election season anyway). Mike Rosen ended up a conservative in Colorado. The story of how this happened is both engaging and instructive. Beyond the personal odyssey, *REALITY* is a model of how to bridge the range from radio to print journalism, which Mike does with unparalleled skill.

Steven Hayward Ronald Reagan Distinguished Visiting Professor, Pepperdine University

****

Mike Rosen has been a voice of sanity and common sense on the radio for decades. But much of his lasting impact has been in print. In this book, Mike assembles his most enduring columns that have real lessons for us today. But the real treat is an introductory chapter in which Mike lets us in on the pivotal events in his life that made him a master communicator. This book is chock full of words to live by and insights on all the issues.

John Fund Commentator, columnist, author, national affairs columnist for *National Review Online* and a senior editor at *The American Spectator*

REALITY

A Plain-Talk Guide to
Economics, Politics, Government and Culture

Mike Rosen

Mark L. Swanson, Editor

Deer Track Publishing
Centennial, CO

First Edition

Library of Congress
  Control Number: 2015947089

ISBN: 978-0-9823520-8-3

Published by: Deer Track Publishing
                 Centennial, CO

Email: deertrackpublishers@comcast.net

Cover: A.Duffy Design, Denver, CO

An Unconventional Dedication

Two Irreplaceable Minds
March 28, 2008

It may be true that no one is indispensable. That is, people come and go, and the world goes on. Perhaps irreplaceable, then, is a better word. Individuals whose unique persona, contributions and impact on events make them one of a kind.

In the past several months, we've seen the passing of two such people, both of whom were my intellectual heroes and mentors. In November, Nobel laureate economist Dr. Milton Friedman died, and earlier this month we lost William F. Buckley, Jr. Friedman described himself as a libertarian; Buckley was a conservative. Friedman was Jewish; Buckley, Catholic. They had different specialties, different agendas and different styles, but had much in common and often overlapped on matters of policy and politics.

I read and was greatly influenced by their writings and ideas, and I had the distinct privilege of knowing them personally. They were kind enough to appear on my radio show on several occasions. Those interviews were always an honor and a special treat.

Friedman restored respectability and stature to free-market economics and had a rare gift for explaining economics in common-sense terms that laymen could understand. (My copy of *Free to Choose* has the unique distinction of being autographed by Milton *and* his wife and co-author, Rose.)

The *Economist* magazine of London named him "the most influential economist of the second half of the twentieth century." His work on monetarism revolutionized the field and earned him a Nobel Prize. He was a brilliant and articulate critic of Keynesian government policies. Friedman was a pioneer in advocating for choice and competition in public education through vouchers. A key advisor to Ronald Reagan, he was described as the president's economic guru. As a champion of limited government and a critic of central government planning he once quipped that, "If government were put in charge of the Sahara Desert, within five years there'd be a shortage of sand."

Buckley, more than any other figure, redefined, reshaped and restored conservatism in the second half of the 20th century. I first subscribed to his signature magazine, *National Review*, in the late 1960s. I haven't missed an issue since. It's been my primer and my undergraduate and ongoing post-graduate course in refined conservative thought.

In a column written in 1984, he boldly addressed the use of force as a foreign policy option. In response to the question of whether he would deny that the use of force is only a last resort, he answered: "I not only deny it, I denounce it as a mischievous, dangerous cliché. People who utter it mean, or ought to mean, something else. Force should be resorted to when the absence of force does not effect an imperative national objective and should always be used when less force guards against the use of more force at a later time. A lesser force used against Hitler in 1937 would have prevented the need for greater force used against him beginning in 1941. The difference between the two modes of force is measured by about 45 million lives. Lives lost by using force too late."

Buckley often quoted Willi Shlamm, an ex-communist who profoundly observed, "The trouble with communism is communism. The trouble with capitalism is capitalists." Buckley recognized that capitalism was an imperfect system practiced by imperfect beings but was, nonetheless, far superior to the evil and inherent incompetence of communism or to any other practical alternative.

Acknowledging human fallibility in any endeavor, he conceded that, "To believe that capitalists will behave honorably just because they are engaged in capitalism is akin to believing that no priest will engage in pedophilia simply because he is a priest."

In a debate on Buckley's *PBS Firing Line* show in the 1970s, feminist Germaine Greer, denying the fundamental differences between the sexes, argued that, "Some women are stronger than some men," to which Buckley countered, "Yes, and some apes are smarter than some people."

Finally, in one of my radio interviews with Bill, in 1983, I sought to parody his legendary vocabulary with a painstakingly contrived (in advance, with much dictionary assistance) tongue-in-cheek question self-consciously laden with multi-syllabic words, to wit: "Mr. Buckley, your supporters regard your style as epideictic, gnomic, perhaps even profluent or perspicuous. Your detractors, however, might contend that your approach leans toward the pleonastic, periphrastic or euphuistic and, in any event, is obstruent to luculent communication. How do you feel about that?" Without hesitation, his modest reply was, "I'm not sure what obstruent means."

****

We Love You J.T. – and We're Going to Miss You

September 4, 1985

I lost a good friend last week. More than a good friend, a man who was a major influence in my life, and the lives of many others. I think there's at least one thing you don't get any better at with practice: handling the death of someone you love.

John T. McCarty left this world last Monday. We had a grand send-off for "J.T." on Thursday. He would have loved the party – good talk, dear friends and all the Coors beer you could drink.

His ashes are now blessing, equally, the Colorado Rockies and the California coast, two of J.T.'s favorite places on this earth. I'll miss his physical presence, but spiritually he's sitting right next to me as I write this remembrance. As a matter of fact, there's a large measure of J.T. in most of what I write.

J.T. was a man who cared. He cared about people, and he cared about ideas. He understood that ideas move the world. I think it was J.T. who first introduced me to Richard Weaver and his book, *Ideas Have Consequences*. (With the possible exception of the Library of Congress, J.T. was the world's champion book-passer-arounder.)

Wherever J.T. stopped, he moved people. A lot of people. His little black book was approximately the size of the Manhattan telephone directory. In it was a veritable *Who's Who* of international movers and shakers. J.T. was a force; a perpetual motion machine. I don't ever remember him doing less than three things at the same time. At his memorial service, Dr. John Howard of the Rockford Institute described J.T. as "an inexhaustible, benevolent atomic energy pile, radiating cheerfulness and friendship, confidence and hope."

I know J.T. moved me. As a matter of fact, I probably wouldn't be doing what I do today were it not for his help and inspiration. Mentors play a great role in the lives they touch. J.T. was mine. When we first met, I was a corporate financial executive on a fast track, making good money with a pretty secure future. It was a nice way to make a living, but personally, it wasn't very rewarding. My real love was issues, politics and economics. J.T. was my recruiting sergeant in the war of ideas.

There's a great commonly held myth that most businessmen are conservative. That might be true if one describes conservative as: risk-averse, pragmatic, tied to the status quo, hedging your bets by supporting both the Democratic and Republican candidates in a race for a given seat in the House, looking to government for regulatory protection from the rigors of competition. That's not my definition of conservative, nor was it J.T.'s. Conservatism is a philosophy based on clear economic and moral principles, centered on individual rights and responsibilities, free choice, and traditional values. J.T. was a principled conservative and a businessman, a rare combination.

He was a success in academia at Rockford College and Pepperdine University; a success in business at General Electric and at Coors; and an overwhelming success in his personal life. Witness to that are his wife – and principal co-conspirator – Carol, his sons Tom, Michael, Peter and Justin, and anyone else who was privileged to have known J.T.

J.T. had a profound understanding of the way the world works. Liberals indulge their compassion; J.T. balanced his with reason. As he surveyed the damage done to our economy and public institutions by the well-intentioned but wrong-headed enthusiasts of the welfare state, J.T. zeroed in on the essential biological malfunction of the liberal condition. "The trouble is," J.T. would say, "they think with their hearts. You don't pump blood with your brains. You can't *think* with your heart." J.T. had an extraordinary brain and a heart well-endowed with compassion. He used each appropriately.

There's an old Jewish proverb that says, "Be sure to send a lazy man for the angel of death." For J.T., they sent a sprinter. Cancer took him in the blink of an eye. But, oh, what he accomplished in his 63 years. And what a legacy he's left behind. J.T. survives a thousand times over in all those he's touched.

In the words of William Faulkner, "Between grief and nothing, I will take grief." The more someone means to you, the more painful it is when he goes away. We love you J.T. And we'll miss you.

****

Contents

III. Politics

IV. Government   179

Providing for the Common Defense –
War and Peace

The State of Welfare, Social Security
and Health Care

Educational Reform against the Monolithic
Establishment

The Relentless Contortion of the Constitution

V. Culture 275

Reality Is Not an Abstraction

A Schism in World Views

Liberal Guilt on Parade

A Medley of Rosenosophy

I. From Brooklyn to Broadcasting

As Groucho Marx once said, "Outside of a dog, a book is your best friend." He then added, "Inside of a dog, it's too dark to read." (That's Groucho.) For many years, people have been urging me to write a book. My excuse has always been that I just don't have the time. And unlike other authors in politics and the media, I don't have a ghost writer. But it's occurred to me that I've already written one in the body of my 1,600 columns in the *Denver Post, Rocky Mountain News* and other publications over more than three decades. Many have stood up to the test of time and are as relevant today as when I first wrote them. Others are valuable as historical benchmarks to set the record straight and as a correction and rebuttal to revisionist history from the usual suspects. It was Mark Twain who profoundly observed that, "History doesn't repeat itself but it rhymes."

Rather than reinvent the wheel, I've assembled a collection of these columns, with some modifications and updates, and grouped them into general subject categories. As a personal legacy, I'd be proud and gratified if you, dear reader, can make good use of this volume not only as a walk down memory lane but, more importantly, as a reference source and as ammunition for your own daily battles in the war of ideas.

<u>Where I came from and how I got into the Media.</u>

I'm frequently asked about my roots and my background, and how and why I got into the media. I often start by saying, "I may be in the media but I'm not of the media." It's a vital distinction that I'll expand upon shortly. I don't believe my life story merits a full-blown memoir (I didn't think Barack Obama's did either when he was merely a freshman senator from Illinois, although it got him elected president), but it's been an interesting and fulfilling journey for me and helps explain how I reached my own conclusions about the way the world works. It's also my personal story of the American dream from humble beginnings. So, I'll apply to myself a variation on a question I regularly put to my radio callers, and I'll tell you where I've sat so you can better understand where I stand.

Reality

Let's begin at the beginning. I don't mean the Big Bang or the Book of Genesis; my humble beginning. Technically, I'm not a Baby Boomer. Those are people who were conceived and born after World War II when the troops came home. I was born in 1944 in Brooklyn, New York. My dad, Robert Rosen, was in the U.S. Army, then stationed stateside. My mom, Corinne, was a 20-year-old petite beauty with movie star looks. After the war, my father, who had not attended college, took a clerical job with Montgomery Ward and Co., a catalog retailing competitor to Sears. About forty years later, he retired from that same company. (I still have the gold watch he was given after 25 years of faithful service.) Bob, as he was called, was steady, hard-working, responsible and low key. He never reached a management level or made much money. As the understated old Jewish saying goes, "he made a living." He put bread on the table and made ends meet.

My mom was the polar opposite: outgoing, gregarious, loquacious, fashion conscious, a social butterfly. She never had a career, per se, although she worked for many years as a part-time saleswoman in the women's clothing department at B. Altman & Co., a Fifth Avenue department store in Manhattan. She spent a good portion of what she made at Altman's buying fashion items at bargain prices made available to employees. It was a different, simpler era. Bob worked for one company his entire career, and my folks were married until my father died after they retired in Florida.

I was an only child, perhaps because my parents didn't think they could afford another. I never thought of our family as poor. Most of my friends in the neighborhood were in the same socio-economic stratum. From an income standpoint, one might say we were lower-middle-class. That sounds more respectable. There wasn't much in the way of government public assistance programs in those days – not like the cornucopia of today's welfare-state "entitlements" – and my parents would have been ashamed to accept that kind of thing anyway. There was a stigma to that back then. During my years living at home, we had a small one-bedroom apartment in Brooklyn. As a little boy, I slept in my parents' bedroom. (I did have my own bed, starting with a crib.) For the rest of my time at home, including my first unsuccessful pass at college, I used a sleeper sofa in the living room.

In New York City, elementary schools were known by their number. Mine was PS 130 (PS stood for public school), a neighborhood school just a few blocks away, which I attended in the early 1950s. I was a smart kid and did well in school. I got good grades on my report card, except for sometimes in "conduct." Not that I was some kind of JD (that was the period's nomenclature abbreviation for "juvenile delinquent," which will be familiar to those who remember the Broadway play "West Side Story" or the movie "Blackboard Jungle.") I was just a little restless.

Social life for kids was neighborhood life. You played tag, stoopball, roller-hockey in side streets, stickball in the street or in schoolyards, baseball on sandlots, basketball in playgrounds and football almost anywhere. We had lots of balls. Carrying a rubber bounce ball in your back pocket was standard equipment. A "Spalding" (pronounced: "Spawl-DEEN") was the premium brand and cost 25 cents, much preferred to the lower grade "Pennsylvania Pinky." There were no soccer moms since most moms didn't drive. (No one played soccer anyway.) There were not a lot of organized after-school "activities" like ballet lessons, tennis lessons or gymnastic classes. They cost money. Kids just got together on their own and had fun.

The social divisions fell into religious and ethnic categories, with some overlap. In my neighborhood, there were mostly Jewish kids and Catholic kids, the latter group dominated by Irish and Italians. We mixed fairly well. I socialized comfortably across the lines. "Multiculturalism" and "diversity" weren't part of the politically correct vocabulary back then.

My parents were loving and devoted and we did things together, including some vacation trips by car – once to Niagara Falls. There were parts of some summers spent at a bungalow colony in "the country," the Catskill Mountains, a few hour's drive north of New York City. But I was an independent self-reliant kid, spending a lot more time with my friends. And I was a born entrepreneur, the first kid on the block to start a lemonade stand, which was a great introduction to Free Market Economics 101. I had all kinds of summer and part time jobs, from picking corn to walking dogs, all necessary to supplement my modest allowance.

In high school a friend and I started a record magazine called *New Disc Data* which we copied on a mimeograph machine. We didn't have any paid subscribers, but it gave us an excuse to knock on the doors of all the record company offices headquartered in Manhattan.

3

Most of them thought it was cute, and we'd come away with hundreds of "Not for Sale" DJ samples of 45 rpm records and 33-1/3 rpm albums. I still have a lot of them, except for the ones we sold. Hey, it's not like we were dealing drugs!

Later on, as a teenager in college, I worked summers at a number of hotels in those same Catskill Mountains as a busboy, waiter, car hop, bell hop and bartender. You worked hard and for long hours but you got free room and board, the tips added up and the social life for hotel staff was great. The 1987 movie *Dirty Dancing* with Patrick Swayze, Jennifer Grey and Jerry Orbach delivered a good sense of it.

When I started junior high school (JHS 62), there was an optional program called "SP" (for "special progress"). To qualify, students took an IQ test. Those with exceptionally high scores were accelerated, completing 7th, 8th and 9th grade in two years instead of three and moving on to high school a year early. My parents thought this was a good idea. I think they were proud that their son had a high IQ. In retrospect that was unwise. My brain was a little ahead of my maturity. And that caught up to me in high school and college. I got good but not great grades (B's and a few A's) in high school without working very hard. I graduated from high school and started college at the age of 16, and I looked about 14.

I had applied to some out of town schools and got some acceptances, but my folks couldn't afford it. Today's option of obtaining a student loan and the prospect of government later relieving your obligation wasn't available then. The alternative was one of the city colleges that were part of the University of the City of New York, where tuition was free. I had even scored well enough on the New York Regents exam to win a small cash scholarship. So in September of 1961, I enrolled in Hunter College. It was in the north Bronx; we lived in Brooklyn, and I was a commuting student living at home. By foot, subway and bus, the journey was over an hour and-a-half each way. The trip was an ordeal, and studying on the noisy NYC subway was not pleasant.

Even worse, this was the soon-to-be politically turbulent 1960s and I quickly discovered that I was a fish out of water. With only a little exaggeration of the ideological culture of the student body and faculty, I was the only non-communist at Hunter College in the Bronx. I was instinctively conservative from as far back as I can remember. To say

4

the least, I was not happy with the college atmosphere or my lifestyle — and my academic performance reflected that. Perhaps cutting off my nose to spite my face, so to speak, I just coasted, skipped classes and didn't study much. Academic standards were high at this school, as today's brand of grade inflation hadn't set in yet. For a kid with a high IQ, my grades were terrible, with a rare B in academic courses here and there (I also got an A in tennis and a B in basketball) amidst plenty of C's, D's and even a couple of F's, along with a bunch of "incompletes" from courses I dropped.

I wasted the next three years in this mode, in and out of school, with semesters on academic probation. While in school, I had a part-time job in the mail room of an advertising agency on Madison Avenue in Manhattan (not the one Don Draper worked at in *Mad Men*). They liked me and offered me a regular job. Who knows where or what I might have been today had I taken it? During one out-of-school period, I worked as a showroom salesman for a furniture company. Finally, in early 1965, I packed it in and quit college — or maybe flunked out; it would have been a close call. This was during the peak of the Vietnam War. I was 20 and knew all too well that losing my college deferment would almost certainly get me called up. I took off for Florida to escape the New York winter. I bummed around for a while, did odd jobs and waitered, mostly in upscale Miami Beach hotels like the Americana. I then came back to New York and spent the next six months working at an auto dealership in Brooklyn selling British Triumphs, MGs and Austin Healys. (I had a Triumph TR-3 and then a TR-4 myself.)

My First Pivotal Life Event

In August 1965, I finally got my draft notice, which did in fact start with, "Greetings from the President of the United States." Frankly, I was kind of looking forward to it. I wasn't part of the anti-war movement, and supported our cause. Also, I wanted a change of pace in my life. Rather than join (which was a three-year hitch rather than two in the draft), I was going to let fate take its course. And it did. In retrospect, this was a turning point, the first of four pivotal events in my life and one of the best things that ever happened to me.

I matured in the Army. I learned a lot about myself physically and mentally. And I did very well, being a lot more motivated than I was in college. After basic combat training at Fort Gordon, Georgia, I was sent to Fort Bliss, Texas for training as a Hawk missile crewman. This was a ground-launcher-based anti-aircraft missile system for defense against low- to mid-altitude aircraft.

From a graduating class of about 100, all but two of us got orders for Vietnam. I was one of the two sent to Germany. Just random chance. We had about 400,000 troops serving among the NATO forces in Europe as a forward defense and deterrent against the Soviet Union and the Warsaw Pact. Somebody had to go there. As it turned out, it was great duty. Shortly after my assignment to a Hawk battery in Landshut, about 40 miles northeast of Munich, our First Sergeant pulled me off the missile site to Battery Headquarters and offered me an administrative job. With some college and good verbal, written and analytical skills, I apparently had a competitive edge over the competition. Also, the "Top Kick" (First Sergeant) and the Battery Commanding Officer had noted from my personnel file that during basic training orientation I scored in the top percentile on the General Intelligence Test (the Army's equivalent of the IQ).

I capitalized on that opportunity and made myself, if not indispensable, at least a valued resource. So much so that I attained the rank of Specialist E-5 in only 18 months from my enlistment date. Normally, you'd have to stand out in combat to make rank that fast. I got to travel all over Europe on leave. I made some life-long friends as Army buddies, along with a good number of Germans in town, and had a beautiful German girlfriend.

When I was rotated back to the states and honorably discharged in late 1967, I moved back in with my parents in Brooklyn. Ultimately I took an entry level job in the customer service department of General Cable Corporation's national headquarters in Manhattan. The company was a fabricator of insulated copper wire and cable. From there I was promoted to assistant manager of product planning in the company's magnet wire division. We produced that very thin wire you'd see in electric generators or radios back in the day. This will be relevant information in a moment.

After just a year, my boss left the company and I was named acting manager. I seized on that opportunity as well, introducing innovations refining a computerized system (yes, there were computer systems back then, huge mainframes into which you fed old-fashioned punch cards) for inventory reporting and control, and optimizing production schedules that improved manufacturing efficiency in the plants that I worked with around the country. That led to the removal of "acting" from my title. I recall that I got a raise to something like $190 a week, and I had the nerve to ask my boss to round it up to $200 so I could finally hit five figures a year and qualify for an American Express card. He did.

Over the next couple of years as I travelled to our plants and learned more about our product, I discovered that magnet wire was a losing proposition for us. We were middle-men competing with companies like Phelps Dodge and Anaconda that were vertically-integrated operations that fabricated insulation over copper that they mined and refined themselves and sold to us at an elevated price. We were only fabricators hopelessly dependent on our competitors for copper supplies. And there wasn't much insulation coating the magnet wire so there wasn't much value added on our part.

With more principle and courage than career pragmatism, I made this argument within our division in some written reports. It wasn't favorably received by my senior superiors who had a career stake in the status quo. And I was just a kid in my twenties and a college dropout to boot who suddenly became understandably unpopular with my higher ups. Fortunately, I had the support of our vice president of corporate Human Resources. But the damage to my future in the division was already done.

My Second Pivotal Life Event

One life lesson I've learned is to roll with setbacks and turn a problem into an opportunity. This was my second pivotal life event. Knowing that my career prospects at General Cable were limited, I decided it was a good time to take advantage of my military benefits and go back to college on the GI Bill. My Human Resources VP sponsor arranged for me to take a leave of absence and for a company contribution to my tuition. As providence had it, I had seen an ad in a newspaper about a University of Denver admissions officer who was taking appointments in his Manhattan hotel room for applicants.

I was getting sick of New York: the politics, the unions, the traffic, the weather and a good many New Yorkers, and I loved to ski —

even with long lift lines, boiler-plate ice, freezing temperatures and a four-hour drive to Vermont on weekends. Denver sounded like an adventure. But there was the problem of my puny grades at Hunter College. I met with him anyway and we clicked. He saw some potential in me and liked the idea that I was a veteran. It was 1971, I was 26 and ten years removed from my first entry into college. The deal was, I'd be accepted to the business school at DU, could transfer only some of my college credits and, given my feeble grade point average, would start out on academic probation.

My office romance, Nancy Baker, was an executive secretary at General Cable. We got married, put most of our worldly possessions in my VW Beetle and took off for Denver. We moved into off-campus married student housing ($110-a-month, furnished.) She got a job as the administrative assistant to the Executive Director of the Sports Car Club of America, headquartered in Denver. She took our VW for commuting and I bought a 175cc Honda motorcycle to get to school. Now fully motivated and obliged to send my grades to General Cable, I became a serious Dean's List A-student. By my second quarter at DU I was off academic probation and on a fifty percent academic scholarship. I took an extra-heavy course load, finished up my undergraduate degree and completed a Masters Degree in Business Administration, all in three years.

As for General Cable, I hadn't been forgotten. A new CEO had taken command and had been told by our Human Resources VP about this Rosen guy in Denver who was on a leave of absence attending college and had some unorthodox views about the magnet wire division. The CEO's secretary contacted me, made a date to for me to meet with him and sent me a plane ticket to New York. I spent several hours with him in his office and made my case. He thanked me and I returned to Denver. Not long after, there was a story in the *Wall Street Journal* announcing that General Cable was abandoning its magnet wire operations.

By the time I got my MBA, we had fallen in love with Denver. General Cable had offered me a job, but Nancy and I didn't want to move back to New York or anywhere else, and we were soon to start our family. General Cable was gracious about my decision and even forgave the payments they had made toward my tuition at DU. (Since I helped them save millions when they eliminated their magnet wire division, I figured I earned that.)

I looked for a company that was headquartered in Denver. Samsonite was a perfect match. The chairman and president was King Shwayder whose father, Jesse, had pioneered the company. King was keen on bright, young MBAs with cutting edge ideas. In 1973, I became a member of that team, as did many others who went on to highly successful careers. It was a great place to work and I learned a lot.

By 1979, I was in corporate finance as Manager of Business Development, Strategic Planning and Financial Systems. Unfortunately, with King Shwayder's retirement, Samsonite was acquired by Beatrice Foods Co., which had become one of those 1970s conglomerates expanding into manufacturing and consumer products. The Beatrice strategic management and corporate officers, located in Chicago with a food and dairy industry mentality, made for a poor match. This led to the gradual exodus by many of the Samsonite whiz kids.

My Third Pivotal Life Event

Once again, it was time to turn a problem into an opportunity. And providence again intervened. Beatrice Foods had agreed to participate in a White House program run by the President's Commission on Executive Exchange, that sent federal executives to private sector companies and private sector executives to the federal government for temporary assignment to better appreciate how the other side works and offer some useful assistance from a novel perspective.

Beatrice Foods committed to host an executive woman from the U.S. Civil Service Commission, and they sent her to Denver where she spent part of her time shadowing me at Samsonite. Since I was already considering other career options, this program intrigued me as an interim bridge. So I decided to offer myself to represent Samsonite and Beatrice Foods in the coming year to fulfill their part in the exchange. They agreed and I went through the Commission's screening and selection process, was accepted and became one of a select group of 25 private-sector executives, nationally, to take a position with the federal government. The job I took was as Special Assistant for Financial

Management to the Assistant Secretary of the Navy. That was a GS-15 grade, the approximate civilian equivalent of a Navy Rear Admiral, quite a promotion from a former U.S. Army enlisted man.

It was 1979. Nancy and I rented out our home in Parker, Colorado, packed up the family, got in the car and drove cross country to Great Falls, Virginia where we were renting a house. Our family then included two wonderful daughters, Lynn, four, and Jill, fourteen months. (Jill is now the mother of Jenna Lynn, my 4-year-old granddaughter.) By the way, some years later, they both graduated from the University of Colorado and managed to do so without being transformed into left-wingers. So that's possible. I like to think the influence of their conservative dad had something to do with it.

This was my third pivotal life event. Life has so many crossroads. You never know how a change in direction will turn out. I've been very fortunate; how much of my good fortune was due to luck and how much to smart choices, I'll never know. My experience with the Department of the Navy, the Washington environment and other elements of this exchange program was fantastic and, as it turned out, ultimately led me into talk radio.

I wasted no time diving into my Navy duties. In studying the intricacies of Navy finances and its budget process, I learned that the stiff competition for limited funding within the shipbuilding budget favored warships. But the Navy was sorely in need of ice-breaking capable ships which never seemed to make the cut. It occurred to me that funds might be more easily attainable from what's called the O&M appropriation for operations and maintenance. In the private sector, companies short on capital funds for plant and equipment sometimes engage in build and lease-back arrangements with contractors who provide the financing. If the Navy followed that model, it could contract with private shipbuilders and lease these vessels that otherwise wouldn't be built. This led to my involvement with a Build and Charter Program along with several other high impact special projects.

By the end of my tenure, I was proud to be awarded the Department of the Navy Superior Civilian Service Medal. This is the citation as written by my boss, George A. Peapples, the Assistant Secretary:

The Assistant Secretary of the Navy for Financial Management takes great pleasure in presenting the NAVY SUPERIOR CIVILIAN SERVICE AWARD to MICHAEL W. ROSEN in recognition of distinguished service as set forth in the following CITATION:

For exceptional meritorious service in the position of Special Assistant for Financial Management to the Assistant Secretary of the Navy for Financial Management while participating in Interchange X (1979-1980) of the President's Executive Interchange Program.

Since assuming his duties in September of 1979, Mr. Rosen has distinguished himself through his accomplishments. His gifted facility for penetrating objective analysis together with his ability to articulate complicated problems has proven of great value to the Navy Secretariat. In this regard, Mr. Rosen conducted an in-depth review of the financial and legislative considerations associated with the Navy's Build and Charter Programs. This exceptional effort resulted in proposed shipbuilding financing alternatives for the acquisition of vitally needed naval vessels. Mr. Rosen also conducted a detailed analysis of the organization of the Comptroller of the Navy. Based on the application of strategic planning concepts, his recommendations for functional realignment demonstrated an incisive and intuitive grasp of the role of financial management in the Navy and provided authoritative guidance to achieving a more effective and efficient Comptroller organization.

Mr. Rosen has continually and aggressively applied his considerable professional talents and management expertise to enhancing financial management in the Department of the Navy. His impressive performance has reflected great credit on himself, and his personal qualities have been in keeping with the highest traditions of the United States Naval Service.

Fringe Benefits

Through this experience, I also learned about the overall federal budget process and its intricacies, becoming something of budget wonk. It's served me very well in my talk radio career when analyzing matters of government finances, public policy and politics.

Along with my technical work, the Navy Department also allowed me to get some first-hand exposure to their primary function through some seagoing adventures. I spent two days on the aircraft carrier *USS Independence*, landing on its deck and getting a catapult shot off its bow and, in between, observing operations and flight qualifying. Three days were spent aboard the *USS Sea Devil*, a nuclear attack submarine, observing war games exercises at the Navy's Atlantic Undersea Test and Evaluation Center off of Andros Island in the Bahamas. And I even went to the Panama City, Florida Naval Base for a ride on a Navy LCAC, the air-cushioned landing craft that flies over the waves at about fifty knots and transports tanks and Marines to beachheads.

During the course of my exchange assignment I learned my way around Washington and sat in on dozens of Congressional committee meetings and hearings. Our exchange executives as a group met with President Carter at the White House and regularly had formal sessions with members of his cabinet and staff, executive branch officials, Congressional leaders, the CIA and FBI, top business CEOs, lobbyists, journalists, jurists and foreign ambassadors. We also spent two weeks in Great Britain, France and Germany meeting with high government officials and business leaders, and with the NATO high command in Belgium.

My Fourth Pivotal Life Event: The Media Crossover

All this was heady stuff. And along the way I had an inspiration. How could I leverage my background and what I'd learned to influence public policy? Running for political office? Perhaps, but even better: the media. My catalyst was a daily radio talk show on *WRC*, an *NBC*-owned local station in Washington, D.C., co-hosted by the conservative Pat Buchanan and the liberal Tom Braden. It aired each evening during drive time from 4:00-7:00 p.m. Everyone who followed politics listened to it. And political talk is to Washington as Broncos talk is to Denver. I thought to myself: "I could do that."

The conventional pathway into the media starts with self-selected college students majoring in journalism. They tend to be the liberal kids. More conservative students major in things like business, engineering or mathematics – or join the ROTC. Journalism students are taught by liberal journalism instructors. When they graduate and find a job at a newspaper, magazine, radio or TV station they're greeted, mentored and reinforced in that liberal media culture by others who followed the same path before they did.

It occurred to me that someone with my knowledge, experience and an interest in business, economics, finance, politics and the military – and, particularly, with a conservative philosophy and perspective – needed to break the liberal mold and bring all that with him into the media. But how many business people would desire or even think to do something like that? I say, "I may be in the media but I'm not of the media" because I came into this domain from a different place, with a different vision and with a different agenda than the liberals who still dominate it. Conservatives have made great gains in media presence, but we're still a minority. When I invaded the media in 1980, we were a tiny minority but I did my part to establish our beachhead.

It frustrates me that conservatives use the label "mainstream media" when they refer to what I prefer to call the DLEMM, that is, the "dominant liberal establishment mass media." I know my term doesn't roll easily off the tongue but it's precise, and every one of the words is necessary to describe it for what is. (By the way, I intentionally use DLEMM in the singular sense as a collective institution, not the conventional grammatical treatment of media as the plural for medium.) "Mainstream media" conveys the false impression that the DLEMM reflects the mainstream of public opinion, which it doesn't, and which conservatives don't mean to convey. The DLEMM is well left of America's political mainstream.

So a crossover into the media became my objective and my calling. At the end of my Presidential Exchange assignment, our family returned to Colorado and I to my job at Samsonite. On the side, I knocked on some Denver radio station doors and explained what I wanted to do: a talk show patterned after that Buchanan-Braden show in D.C. I'd be the conservative, pair me up with a liberal. The first question I was asked was, "What experience have you had in radio?" My answer was, "none," which was exactly my point. This was a crossover; I'm bringing something unique to the medium. Not surprisingly, I was turned down by the bigger stations (including *KOA*) in my first attempts. Until I knocked on the door of *KWBZ*, "The Nifty 1150."

The station had a weak radio signal and remote dial position but a pretty talented lineup that included Alan Berg, Woody Page and Irv Brown, Bill Barker, Judy Muller and Peter Boyles, who had the 6:00-10:00 a.m. slot. And Peter Boyles, at that time, fit the liberal role. John Mullins, Jr. who owned the station and Van Kyrias, the general

13

manger, signed me up and I was introduced to Peter as his new co-host. He wasn't happy about the arrangement and who could blame him.

I left Samsonite and took a huge pay cut to embark on my radio career, but I was intent on giving this a shot and figured I could always go back to a corporate finance career if I had to. Peter and I became a duo in December 1980, shortly after Ronald Reagan was elected. Supply-side economics, taxes and federal spending were the hot topics and that was right in my wheelhouse, if not Peter's. I took to talk radio like a fish to water. After five weeks and feeling good about it, I was driving to the station one morning at about 4:30 a.m. to prepare for the 6:00 show. I turned on the radio expecting to hear our overnight host but instead was treated to 1950s rock and roll music. Huh? When I arrived there, I was informed that the format had been changed and the talk show hosts, myself included, were no longer employed. As I was to discover, that's the radio business.

So what was I to I do now? I'm out of work and have a family to support. That's when the phone rang. It was Joe Coors, the brewer, a fellow conservative Republican whom I had known from some of my political activities. He asked me if I'd come to his office in Golden for a chat. Sure. He and his brother Bill actually shared an office side by side. I sat down with both of them. They said they had been listening to my radio show, really appreciated what I was doing and encouraged me to continue. I explained that there weren't any other radio offers. And they said, "Why don't you come work for us as an economic consultant while you explore other options?" That was the bridge that enabled me to keep my talk radio ambitions alive. It's not the kind of thing a typical corporation would do, but Joe and Bill Coors weren't typical businessmen. They were principled conservatives committed to the war of ideas, and they owned the company.

My relationship with Coors later led to a position as vice president of the Shavano Institute, a start-up Colorado-based conservative public policy center affiliated with Hillsdale College, a remarkable conservative school in Michigan that the Coors family also supported.

The next radio break came in 1982 when Sandusky Broadcasting converted a Denver music station to a talk format and rechristened it *KNUS*. They offered me a daily 7:00-10:00 p.m. slot. I took it and worked two jobs: days at Shavano, nights on radio.

By 1986, I realized that if I wanted to make a big impact on radio, *KOA*, "the 50,000 watt blowtorch," was the place to be. So I visited with Lee Larsen, *KOA*'s general manager, and offered my services. He was agreeable but didn't have a prime time slot open just yet. So we worked out an arrangement. I'd do a regular Saturday night show, for the time being, along with recorded drive-time commentaries, fill-ins for other hosts and one day a week I'd be a guest co-host with their regular morning guy, Gary Tessler, from 9:00 a.m.-noon. Gary was a dyed-in-the-wool liberal and a good match for my conservative-liberal dichotomy concept. Just as was the case with Peter Boyles at *KWBZ*, Gary wasn't wild about this arrangement, but that's radio.

In 1988 the radio Gods struck again. One day when Tessler was out of town, I substituted for him on his show. As fate had it, a programming executive from *KOA*'s parent company, Jacor Communications in Cincinnati, was visiting for a meeting with Lee Larsen. He had been listening to me filling in for Gary, and during his meeting with Lee suggested that I might be a better choice for the show. Gary's audience ratings were soft and, presto-chango, soon after that Gary was gone and it became the Mike Rosen Show. That's radio; 27 years later, I'm still here.

Flashback — Becoming a Newspaper Columnist

Rewinding a bit, while working at *KNUS* in 1984, I frequently had Chuck Green on my show as a guest. Chuck, at that time, was the editorial page editor of the *Denver Post* and a left-of center guy, so it made for a dynamic point/counterpoint and we had some good exchanges. We were friends and had even played golf together. On the air with Chuck, one day, I mentioned the *Post's* imbalance of liberal op-ed columnists compared to conservatives. Chuck disagreed and said he thought it was pretty even handed.

Over the next month, I kept track of every op-ed contributor in the *Post* and categorized their opinion pieces on a scale from left to right. I did my best to be objective. The next time Chuck was on my show, I presented my evidence to him, allowing for the possibility that he might disagree with my evaluation. On my scorecard, of the paper's last 105 bylined opinion columns, 67 had been written by liberals and only 10 by conservatives. In fact, he agreed. I had written a number of guest opinion columns in the *Post* and other publications so Chuck was familiar with my work. To my surprise, he asked, "Why don't we try you out as a regular weekly columnist on the *Post*'s opinion pages?" Shortly thereafter, the *Post* introduced me to readers with an ad that read: "Meet Colorado's 'Mr. Conservative' on Wednesday." (I should note that as the years went by, Chuck eventually came over to our side and became an articulate spokesman for conservative ideas.)

My run as a token conservative at the reliably liberal *Denver Post* lasted fifteen years, through a succession of editorial page editors, that included some rocky passages. On several occasions, editors would simply "spike" one of my columns with which they disagreed or didn't like for whatever reason, sometimes claiming it violated the paper's often vague or arbitrary editorial policy. ("Spike" is newspaper jargon for "kill.")

The last straw for me was a series of run-ins with Dennis Britton, the *Post*'s editor-in-chief in 1998. Britton was farther left than his predecessors and had a particularly disagreeable, overbearing personality. Even the liberals at the *Post* didn't like him, triggering an online "Dennis Britton Go Home!" page. In the run-up to that year's election, he imposed an irrational policy barring columnists from offering their opinions – *on the opinion pages* – regarding candidates or ballot questions. The whole point of commentary pages is to present private viewpoints in the hope, and perhaps the expectation, of shaping public opinion. It makes no sense to withhold the opinions of bylined columnists just before an election. This is like barring the Broncos from the playoffs after the regular season. At the same time, the *Post*'s liberal editorial board published its own endorsements of these same candidates and took sides on the ballot questions. Even worse, the paper's *news* pages spun stories and contrived headlines to favor liberals.

After Britton spiked two of my pre-election columns I had had enough. And that's when I moved over to the *Rocky Mountain News*, the *Post's* competitor. Incidentally, the *Post* dumped Britton later that year. A story in the *American Journalism Review* described him as having been "abruptly dismissed." I wrote for the *Rocky* for the next 10 years until it ceased publication in 2009. That left the *Denver Post* as the sole major daily in town. Not one to hold a grudge, I called Dean Singleton, chairman of the Media News Group, the *Post*'s owner, with whom I had a friendly relationship and said I'd be willing to return. He was happy to have me. So, I've been back in the *Post* for the last 6 years. That's the newspaper business.

Where I Sit

My development of a personal philosophy on human nature and the way the world works began early. I was always instinctively independent, individualistic, capitalistic and meritocracy orientated. It started to formalize when I read Ayn Rand's *Atlas Shrugged* at the age of fourteen in 1958. I've reread it since then as an adult along with many other of Rand's fiction and non-fiction works. Her larger-than-life heroes like John Galt, Hank Rearden, Dagny Taggart and Howard Roark (in *The Fountainhead*) are ideals. Unfortunately, very few people in real life are up to those admirable, uncompromising, courageous standards of personal principles, ethics, self-reliance and courage. But what made a more visceral impression on me were her villains. Despicable characters like Wesley Mouch, James Taggart, Floyd Ferris and Robert Stadler. They're all too believable and every bit as petty, smug, vindictive and dictatorial as real-life government bureaucrats and politicians in real life with too much power can be – even more so today.

While I was inspired by Rand, I never became a full-fledged Randian or an Objectivist. Similarly, I've been inspired by many libertarian ideals but can't subscribe to the dogmatic version of that ideology either. I'm glad those ideals are part of the war of ideas and hope they have some influence in tugging public policy marginally in that direction of freedom and self-reliance, but the demands of doctrinaire libertarians for uncompromising ideological purity is simply impractical and doesn't appeal to very many in the great majority of mere mortals who breathe and vote. When it comes to public policy and governing, I'm less about preening and posturing and more about practical political reality. Ideology is about ideas; politics is about winning elections.

When U.S. forces deposed Saddam Hussein in Iraq and ran into roadside bombs, also known as IEDs (improvised explosive devices), that wreaked havoc on insufficiently armored vehicles, Defense Secretary Donald Rumsfeld responded to complaints by frustrated troops about inferior equipment, explaining that, "You go to war with the army you have, not the army you might want or wish to have at a later time." I'm constrained by the reality that you craft public policy, practice politics and go to the voters with the electorate you have, not the one you imagine or wish you had. In the words of William F. Buckley, Jr., "Idealism is fine, but as it approaches reality the cost becomes prohibitive."

I believe in limited government, a constitutional republic, a relatively free-market economy, individual rights and responsibilities, peace through strength, nationalism, patriotism and a raft of other conservative principles. But I know that I'm outvoted in the imperfect democratic process and that my vision of a more perfect union isn't on the menu of what today's electorate is willing to bestow. So you settle for what you can get in the fickle winds of politics. The best shouldn't be the enemy of the merely good if the best is unattainable.

I'm an advocate, but I'm also an analyst, not just a cheerleader. There's a great public divide in our nation, with irreconcilable differences and no clear permanent majority on either side. It's an endless battle with elections decided at the margins, often by people who spend little time becoming informed about policies, politics or politicians. They're sometimes referred to as "low information voters." I'm committed to the conservative side of that battle, but I have no illusions. I can't be certain our side will prevail, but neither am I defeatist about our prospects. Hopefully we'll muddle through. What's the alternative? Surrender isn't an option. I wish I had a grand plan for victory but I don't. As T.S. Elliot put it, "There are no lost causes, because there are no gained causes."

My objective when I made my crossover into the media 35 years ago was to inform and influence public opinion and public policy. There's no right or wrong way to do talk radio. Just different ways that appeal to different audiences. For some in this business, which isn't exclusively about politics, it's just a job and the goal is to beat the competition and make a good living. For me, talk radio is first and foremost one of several channels available to engage in the war of ideas with the ultimate goal of winning elections and governing with a conservative agenda. My style may be too intellectual for some who will respond better to a more simplistic argument or gut-level appeal by a different kind of conservative. I welcome any approach or style that adds followers to our cause.

As I've often explained, the only practical vehicle for conservatives to govern in our two-party system at this time is the Republican Party, imperfect as any major party must necessarily be. And in order for us to be a majority party, it's essential to cobble together a broad coalition that includes those who are right-center, right-wing, practical libertarians (not always an oxymoron), squishy "moderate" swing voters with no coherent ideology and even an occasional Democrat.

On the air, I've always been myself. I rely on facts, reason and logic. I have a dry and often wry sense of humor and I can be quick with a quip. I like to debate with people who disagree. But I don't pander to people on my side who make rash claims and just want to vent. I'm not a screamer and I'm slow to anger, but sometimes a caller can exasperate me. Most of the time I'm reasonably calm. It's important to be entertaining as well as informative in this medium, but I stop short of being contrived, overly theatrical or intentionally over the top, although that style has paid off handsomely for some – on both the left and the right. I'm comfortable with my approach and have found that it can be more effective in swaying people who are on the fence and in winning converts from the other side. Some of the most gratifying comments I get are from people who tell me they're recovering liberals who have been won over by superior conservative ideas.

Preaching to the conservative choir isn't a waste of time when it reinforces that choir and arms them with better arguments with which to do battle in the war of ideas. That's part of my mission. Most people with careers, families, friends and hobbies don't have the time to read voluminously on public policy and current events. But that's my vocation and my avocation. It's why I love what I do. So I perform something of a digest service. I do the legwork and analysis, with many hours of research and show prep for every hour on the air, and streamline the message for my audience's consideration.

The columns and essays that follow are the product of that effort. I hope you find them interesting, thought provoking and entertaining. In selecting those with the greatest impact, in the interest of space, it was painful for me to have to "kill a number of my darlings," as the old editing saying goes. I should prepare you for some of the repetition you'll see. I wouldn't just relegate this to the Department of Redundancy Department. In over thirty years of writing about public policy, the same general topics come up time and time again, with only slight variations in the details or that overlap. You'll find the same statistics and profound quotes offered by me in more than one place. You'll also recognize some arguments I've perfected over many years reiterated in rebutting leftist claims and assertions that, themselves, come up time and time again. I've always considered that this may be the first time for new readers and listeners, while serving as reinforcement for old timers. So, I'll fall back on a memorable justification I learned from my mentor William F. Buckley, Jr., "Repetition is the price of mastery." And as George Will once observed, "The problem with the younger generation is that they haven't read the minutes of the last meeting."

I hope you'll make use of this book as a sort of Army field manual in the war of ideas. Don't treat it as a museum piece. Mark it up with a yellow highlighter. Underline passages. Annotate it with comments in the margins. Dog-ear the pages. Make this your personal weapon of mass instruction.

II. Economics

An economic system is the process that determines what and how goods and services will be produced and provided, how they will be priced and distributed, and how incomes and profits will be taxed. The two basic types are "demand" economies, in which market forces shape those decisions and "command" economies in which government makes those decisions. The term "political economy" describes the combination of an economic system with a political system.

The former Soviet Union was a command economy married to a communist one-party totalitarian political system. The U.S. is a demand economy but not a pure free-market economy given the significant intervention of government laws, regulations and policies. Conservatives advocate for capitalism and freer markets in the name of equal opportunity, property rights, individual liberty, economic efficiency and a meritocracy. Liberals advocate for socialism and more government controls in the name of collectivism, "social justice," income equality and security.

It's been said that capitalism is the economic dimension of liberty. Capitalist systems have produced history's greatest measure of prosperity and freedom, elevating multitudes out of poverty. Its market incentives reward excellence and its market disciplines punish inefficiency. Although still governed by a one-party Communist dictatorship, it's instructive to note that the dramatic economic gains of the People's Republic of China are the direct result of its adoption of a quasi-capitalist system within its political economy.

The basic tenet of President Ronald Reagan's highly successful supply-side economic reforms of the 1980s was the concept that "What you tax you get less of and what you subsidize you get more of." Left-wing Keynesians like Paul Krugman tinker with demand-side government policies to artificially stimulate consumer spending. Through reductions in excessively high tax rates, overburdening regulations, and counterproductive government spending, supply-siders focus on policies that increase productive output by elevating the prospect of greater after-tax returns on work, savings and investment. As French economist Jean-Baptiste Say explained, "Supply creates its own demand."

Reality

The columns that follow in this section deal with a range of subjects on political economy that include philosophy, the mechanics of taxation, the mentality of welfare-state entitlement, income inequality and the debunking of several economic myths. This is all in the service of a broader understanding of how economic principles are applied to effective public policy in the world we live in today.

Capitalism Works

Greed, Ambition and Covetousness
November 3, 2011

Over the years, I've written versions of this column as far back as 1989. With the politics of envy in full bloom once again, it's time for an update. *Plus ca change, plus c'est la meme chose.*

Leftists in general, and today's Occupy Wall Street crowd in particular, are obsessed with the word "greed" to the point of irrationality.

They just don't get it. A market economy is based on incentives. The prospect of financial reward is what motivates most people to work and invest. There's nothing particularly ingenious about a system that recognizes this. It's intuitive. More than 200 years ago when Adam Smith wrote *The Wealth of Nations*, he didn't invent an economic system; he merely observed and analyzed what people do naturally when left to their own devices.

Socialism, on the other hand, fancies itself as an ingenious system, an invention of coercive economic utopians, based on the notion that human nature can be elevated to a collective, altruistic plane. Its myriad failures in the real world include places like the former Soviet Union, North Korea and Cuba. The European socialist democracies are rapidly proceeding down that road, with Greece leading the procession. Ironically, the recent economic rise of Communist China is directly related to its increasing embrace of at least some elements of good old-fashioned capitalism, a system that has ably served its Asian neighbors in Taiwan, South Korea and Japan.

What leftists brand as greed is what conservatives call *ambition*. Ambition and reward are what fuel prosperity in a market economy. When you impose penalties and restrict rewards on economic activity – with excessive taxation and overbearing regulations – however noble your motives, there are consequences. You get less work, investment and output. That's why we can't tax ourselves rich. The fatal flaw of socialist economies is their inability to sufficiently reward excellence, so, inevitably, they get less of it. It's that fundamental conflict with human nature that guarantees socialism's ultimate failure.

To a leftist, greed is when someone makes too much. But how much is too much and who makes that judgment for others? This is an intriguing individual moral dilemma and may make for an interesting discussion with your priest, rabbi or favorite philosopher, but a market economy doesn't ask that question, which, in any event, is impossible to objectively define. One farmer produces twice as much as another. Is he greedy, more efficient or a harder worker? It doesn't really matter. The one who produces more should be suitably rewarded.

Adam Smith also observed that in a market economy, people pursuing their own prosperity are inadvertently moved as if by an "invisible hand" to promote the interests of society as a whole. This is precisely what Steve Jobs did. Whether his motive was entrepreneurial gratification, a quest for fame and fortune, serving humankind, or some combination of these, what matters most is that he put people to work, served consumers, elevated productivity and expanded societal wealth. In the process, he became wealthy himself. Perhaps the geniuses who are occupying Wall Street can tell us at what level of net worth Jobs crossed the line that made him evil.

Yes, there are greedy people in this world. There are also lazy people. There are producers and there are parasites. But it's a futile moralistic exercise to calculate where ambition ends and greed begins. The virtue of a market economy is how it maximizes human energy for the private and public good. Leftists have little regard for the creation of wealth. They simply take that for granted. It's the redistribution of wealth that excites their passions.

It may be difficult to define greed, but it's easy to define covetousness. That's the greed of leftists for governmental power to control the lives and confiscate the property of others.

Spring in the Food Court
February 28, 1992

Let's set the record straight. There is no nationwide recession. There was one, but it's over. Objectively, the technical definition of a recession is two consecutive quarters of decline in real gross domestic product. That occurred between the third quarter of 1990 and the first quarter of 1991. Since then, we've had modest, but positive growth. Another recession – a double-dip – may be imminent and may not. I think not. But that's a question about the future.

Does that mean that prosperity reigns throughout the land? Of course not. There are still industries and regions – the car business in Michigan comes immediately to mind – that remain depressed. But there's enough health and vigor in other sectors of our economy to offset the pockets of malaise, yielding the positive figures. Today's unemployment rate of 7.1 percent is considerably better than the 10.7 percent rate we hit during the 1981-1983 recession, with 17 million more Americans now employed.

Look at Colorado. We had our recession during the mid-1980s, after the oil crash, when other parts of the country were booming. Now we're doing relatively well and some other places aren't. That's life. National economic policy wasn't tailored to Denver's peculiar difficulties in 1985, and it shouldn't have been, just as today's policies shouldn't be tailored to Detroit or New Hampshire.

I can speak frankly because I'm not a politician.

If George Bush were to candidly declare that there is no national recession, he'd be accused of rank insensitivity to the unemployed auto workers in Detroit. So he he'll say what politicians say.

To contestants in the Democratic Party's presidential sweepstakes, a sluggish economy is a target of opportunity. The worse they can make the economy sound, the more they can promise better results. They can't necessarily deliver, but they can sure promise. Many voters want desperately to believe those promises.

When you get right down to it, with the deficit at $400 billion and interest rates already low, the federal government has no fiscal or monetary tricks left in its bag to stimulate this fledgling recovery. It can, however, make things worse with misguided, interventionist policies designed primarily to give the impression of doing something in an election year. The economy runs in cycles. It has its ups and downs. During the '80s, we had an unusually long up. We started the '90s with a relatively short and not very deep down, from which we're now emerging.

I was walking through the Food Court at a downtown shopping mall the other day, noting the changes since I had last been there. Some eating establishments had folded; others had taken their places. This is a volatile, high-risk industry, like our market economy in microcosm.

Businesses that meet the market test prosper; others don't and are replaced. Economist Joseph Schumpeter called this process the "creative destruction" of capitalism.

In the movie, *Being There*, Peter Sellers played a likable but addle-pated gardener who was mistaken for an economic sage. Although he was simply describing the effects of the seasons on his garden, his remarks were recognized as a profound metaphor for the economy. As he explained it, first comes the spring, a period of rebirth; followed by the growth of summer; the harvest and graying of autumn, and; finally, the cold and decline of winter; after that, the process repeats itself. Simple wisdom.

There you have it: The business cycle. During the winter we work off the fat. Come spring, we're in better shape. Government can, up to a point, blunt the winter cold by providing blankets. It can't prevent the change of seasons, and it can do a lot of harm when it mistakes spring for winter.

It's a Wonderful Service
June 27, 2008

"Did you ever think what a bank earns on home loans over the life of a loan? What real value have they added to the economy by making the true cost of a house the cost of a lifetime for most of us? Isn't that a subtle brand of servitude? We never ask questions like that because questioning the system would look capitalism straight in the eye and capitalism is not a fan of fundamental questions."

Actually, such questions might be asked by an innocent young child or a student taking his first class in basic economics. It's how they learn. In this case the questioner was presumably an adult (and probably a "progressive" Democrat) whose letter was published in the *Rocky Mountain News*. That's embarrassing. This is beyond ideology. Your typical Marxist college professor might not like capitalism but he certainly understands how market economics works. The letter was a public display of ignorance on stilts. The writer may be beyond help, but it's a good object lesson for others.

Think of the ever-lovable Jimmy Stewart as George Bailey, the friendly banker in Frank Capra's heartwarming, perennial Christmas-season classic, *It's a Wonderful Life*. The Bailey Building and Loan Association was a financial intermediary, a middleman between savers and borrowers. Rather than keeping their hard-earned savings hidden under a mattress, depositors entrusted their cash to George.

He kept it safe and also paid them rent, in the form of an interest rate for the use of their money. George, in turn, would make that money available to borrowers in the form of a mortgage so that they could buy a home.

He'd charge the borrowers interest for the use of capital provided by the depositors at a rate marginally above the interest rate he was paying those depositors. That differential enabled George to recover his operating costs (payroll for Uncle Billy and others, utilities, rent, maintenance, taxes, etc.) with, he hoped, something left over for profit. That was his business and livelihood.

George's value to the community and the service he provided to the good people of Bedford Falls was to enable them to live the

American Dream, to enjoy the benefits of owning their own home sooner rather than later. Had they not been able to borrow money from the building and loan, they'd have had to defer the purchase and save for a lifetime to cover the full price of a home.

This is most definitely not "a subtle brand of servitude." The interest a borrower pays on his mortgage is compensation for the use of someone else's money for as much as 30 years, recognizing that the lender could have earned a return on that money in some other investment. If you want to pay less interest over the life of the loan, pay it off faster. What could be fairer and how could it be otherwise?

It should also be noted that George's loans enable developers to put people to work building those homes.

The same type of transaction happens millions of times every day when people borrow money from financial institutions to purchase cars, refrigerators, televisions or buy something on their credit card.

The reason even kind-hearted George Bailey might sometimes have to foreclose on a delinquent mortgage is that he has an obligation to be a responsible steward of the money entrusted to him by his investors and depositors. The same obligation applies in real life to Wells Fargo, Chase or FirstBank.

Not every capitalist is as honorable and compassionate as George Bailey. So, who will protect us from the likes of George's avaricious competitor Mr. Potter? Yes, there's a role for prudent and reasonable government regulation. But the most efficient and effective influence is competition in the marketplace and due diligence by depositors and borrowers. An economy can't function without financial intermediaries. Show your appreciation and hug your local banker.

Meaning of Laissez Faire
April 8, 2010

In response to my column on dunderheaded legislation pouring out of the state legislature, one self-described executive replied that he was unable to "make sense" of my criticism of Senate Bill 28. This was a proposed "work share" program that would avoid prospective layoffs by cutting back the hours worked by other employees and paying them all "underemployment insurance." He couldn't understand why this would cost more than just laying off a smaller number of workers.

As I explained to the confused businessman, if two people were laid off and paid unemployment insurance, they'd have an incentive to quickly find new jobs and replace their full pay. Conversely, if rather than laying off two workers, 20 would have their hours reduced by 10 percent each, they'd likely stay at their jobs and collect the offsetting underemployment allowance. This would result in a greater total outlay of underemployment insurance payments from Colorado's already bankrupt trust fund.

Additionally, in the absence of this work-sharing program, an employer would be inclined to lay off his two least-efficient workers. By "sharing" the burden among all 20, he's getting fewer hours worked and less productivity out of his best employees.

The confused businessman must be a Democrat.

The common delusion of all these counterproductive bills is that Democrats in government somehow imagine they have the brilliance to restore the economy with their meddling. This is a longstanding conceit. As legend has it, during the reign of Louis XIV in France, his finance minister, Jean-Baptiste Colbert, sent for the kingdom's leading merchants. In order to win their allegiance, he asked what he could do for them. Their unanimous answer was, "Pray sir, *laissez nous faire,*" which translates to: "Let us do for ourselves." That, purportedly, is the derivation of the term "laissez faire" economics.

Whether or not it happened exactly this way is beside the point. You get the idea. Government can't give anything to anybody without taking it away from someone else.

An international market economy with trillions of economic

transactions every day is far too complicated for any collection of bureaucrats to understand or control. Of course, since the invention of government, there's never been a truly laissez-faire economy and never will be. That's why economists use the term "political economy" to describe the confluence of politics and economics.

The debate is always about the degree of government involvement, with conservatives arguing for less and liberals arguing for more. The debate this time around is in the name of "economic stimulus." After the expenditure of hundreds of billions and the commitment of trillions in debt, President Obama and Democrats at the federal and state level have accomplished pitifully little in the short run while laying the groundwork for devastating economic consequences when the debt and inflation bill comes due in the long run.

Here's another example: A press release from former Governor Bill Ritter's office heralded a federal government grant to Colorado's Tri-County Health Department of $10.5 million (that the U.S. Treasury doesn't have) under the American Recovery and Reinvestment Act to promote "healthy eating and physical activity" in Adams, Arapahoe and Douglas counties. Seventy percent of this is allocated to school districts, municipalities and other community organizations. This was Colorado's share of $372 million, nationally. However nice it may be to promote healthy eating and physical activity, who in his right mind can believe that this will stimulate the economy and that it justifies additional deficit spending?

It's been said that the private sector is that part of our society under government control, while the government is the part that's out of control. This is a good time for politicians to do nothing more and get out the way of economic recovery.

Deflating the Inflation Myth
July 5, 1996

My contract with *The Denver Post* allows me to write one boring, although necessary, column on economics every three years. This is it. Be warned. You may not enjoy today's piece, but it'll be good for you. This is *National Public Radio* mentality.

It was announced that the Denver Nuggets were increasing their ticket prices an average of 10 percent. My purpose isn't to complain about that. Nuggets ticket prices are still among the lowest in the league.

Nobody's forced to go to the games. When the team's ticket prices become too high in the highly competitive entertainment market, their customers will let them know by not filling seats. Explaining the price increase, the president of Ascent Sports, the Nuggets' parent company, cited "the *inflationary* (my italics), cost-driven industry of sports." I don't disagree that player payrolls have skyrocketed in recent years and that this leads to higher ticket prices (assuming the fans are willing to pay them). But I do object to the use of the term "inflation."

I'll give you another example. In the debate between Republicans and Democrats over government spending on medical care, both sides propose spending increases. The GOP is resigned to increases of about 7 percent a year; the Democrats want to spend 10 percent more per year. The Dems claim this is necessary because of *inflation* in medical costs. They call anything less than a 10 percent increase a cut. Once again, I object to the use of the term "inflation." It has a precise meaning, and this isn't it.

Inflation is strictly a monetary phenomenon. It has only to do with the relationship of the things we buy and the dollars we buy them with. Inflation is nothing more and nothing less than a decline in the purchasing power of the monetary unit. It's caused by an increase in the money supply greater than the overall increase in the supply of goods and services produced. That's it. Inflation *isn't* higher prices. Higher average prices are the *result* of inflation. They're how we measure inflation. The cause is excessive money supply growth. This can be controlled by the Federal Reserve.

Increases in the price of basketball tickets or brain surgery are *relative* price increases. The rate of inflation is measured by *general* price increases. To do this, The Bureau of Labor Statistics tracks prices for a market basket of goods and services. Some prices may go up, some may go down. The overall weighted average of the items in this basket is the measure of inflation. We call this the Consumer Price Index (CPI). If money supply and overall output were held constant, an increase in relative prices in one area would have to be offset by a decrease in prices in another. If people continued to buy basketball tickets at higher prices, their demand for some other item, say, vacations to Hawaii, would diminish, influencing a drop in prices for that.

If this were a barter economy and you traded for other things with corn that you grew, a huge increase in the supply of corn relative to other things would cause you to have to offer relatively more corn in exchange for, say, basketball tickets. It works the same way with the money supply: If that grows faster than the things we buy with it, those things will cost more when denominated in dollars. That's inflation.

If Nuggets tickets are going up 10 percent this year, 3 percent can be attributed to an increase in the general price level, as measured by the CPI. The other 7 percent is a relative price increase.

There's a practical application to this concept when we look at the political debate over medical costs. These soaring costs are not inevitable.

Medical prices have been growing faster than general prices because of extremely high demand in this sector. Demand is high in large part because medical consumers aren't particularly price-conscious, with third-party payers – insurance companies, employers and the government – picking up the tab. This leads to wasteful use of finite medical resources. The GOP remedy is to make medical consumers more cost-conscious.

This would be achieved through catastrophic insurance for major illnesses, combined with medical savings accounts through which consumers would more judiciously manage their medical needs.

The Democratic alternative is to socialize medical delivery, spend more taxpayer money and blame it on "inflation."

Obama's Roanoke Rant
July 19, 2012

The teleprompter must have been out of commission when president Obama, speaking off-the-cuff, stuck his foot in his mouth at a campaign rally in Roanoke, Virginia last Friday. You know someone is in trouble when his flacks, in damage-control mode, are forced to explain "what the president meant to say." Despite the best efforts by campaign spokesman Ben LaBolt to recast Obama's remarks, he said what he said.

"If you were successful, somebody along the line gave you some help. There was a great teacher somewhere in your life. Somebody helped to create this unbelievable American system that we have that allowed you to thrive. Somebody invested in roads and bridges. If you've got a business, you didn't build that. Somebody else made that happen."

The hell they did! You made it happen. It's true that no man is an island and, of course, government is a factor. If it weren't for the U.S. military in World War II, we might all be speaking German or Japanese now. And, yes, there's infrastructure paid for with taxes, and a legal system to enforce contracts. Although there were many kids in that great teacher's classroom, you may be the only entrepreneur who emerged, the one with the inspiration and talent to build your own business; to risk a second mortgage on your home for startup capital; to work countless hours to get it off the ground; to run the obstacle course of government bureaucrats to get the required permits and licenses; and to take the job home with you every night.

What Obama called our "unbelievable American system" was founded on individual liberty, private enterprise and limited government. That was the engine that propelled our economy to world dominance from the 19th century industrial revolution onward. Government was miniscule then by today's standards. Even by the roaring 1920s, federal outlays were a mere 3 percent of economic output. Today, big government has grown to 25 percent of GDP and we're deeply in debt.

Henry Ford mass-produced automobiles long before the infrastructure of paved highways. The likes of Thomas Edison,

Alexander Graham Bell, Andrew Carnegie, John D. Rockefeller, Bill Gates and Steve Jobs are those who rise above the crowd. Their contributions were the result of individual initiative that ultimately created more wealth for the collective than it did for themselves.

This is all a blind spot for Barack Obama, the student, community organizer, law-school-lecturer and politician. He's had no life experience in the world of commerce. In his mind, business is something to be mistrusted, regulated and taxed. He takes the production of wealth for granted. His joy is in the redistribution of it. And he sees government as the utopian solution to all our problems.

That mentality came through in the wording of his non-scripted populist rant in Roanoke where he portrayed government as the mainspring of human progress. It's not. I wouldn't call government a "necessary evil." It is necessary but not necessarily evil, as long as it's kept under control as our founders intended. In places like Nazi Germany, the former Soviet Union, North Korea and far too many others, when government controls society it does become evil.

Intrinsic in the trajectory of Obama's political agenda is the expansion of government in everything from healthcare to energy to business – everything but defense. And his flawed vision equates society with the state. But the state isn't society. It's a subset of society.

This nation is much more than our government. In the words of Arthur Shenfield, "A society cannot be free if it is synonymous with the state. For if it were, all human activity would not only be governed by law, it would also be prescribed and licensed by law, which is the meaning of totalitarianism."

"Atlas" Flogged Yet Again
April 3, 2009

For nearly 60 years, Ayn Rand's philosophical masterpiece, *Atlas Shrugged*, has been a perennial best-seller. This prescient warning about the excesses of intrusive government and arrogant bureaucrats has seen a resurgence in sales of late as the agenda of the Obama administration and the Democrat-controlled Congress continues to unfold. The unprecedented scope of government intervention in the economy, proposed regulations and planned expansion of social spending programs has made Rand's prophecy ever more topical.

One byproduct of this has been a counterattack from the left. *Comedy Central's* Stephen Colbert ridiculed Rand and *Atlas* on a recent program to the delight of his studio audience, who couldn't have reacted as they did if they had ever read the book. Colbert's attack was long on misrepresentation, demagoguery and cheap laughs, but short on accuracy or reason.

Some liberals have condescendingly dismissed Rand's objectivist philosophy as an adolescent flirtation that sophisticates like them soon grow out of. They've belittled the contributions of Rand's "producers," arguing that individualistic excellence in innovation and discovery is highly overrated with the glib assumption that if John Galt or Albert Einstein hadn't stumbled on some revolutionary technological or scientific breakthrough someone else would have inevitably done so.

Really? And how much later might that have been and at what cost to society? Suppose Hitler had come up with the atomic bomb first. Or how many children would have died from polio in the years between Jonas Salk's development of the vaccine and the next guy to come along?

That blind spot is typical of so many on the left who ignore the first law of economics: Production must precede consumption. Liberals don't want to be bothered with the heavy lifting of producing something; their joy comes in "equitably" redistributing what others have created. And they're deaf, as well, to the indispensability of incentives. Even if the contribution of a singular great person would have inevitably been duplicated, why not create incentives and rewards for many more thousands of singular great persons to add to societal wealth?

35

The left's counterattack on Ayn Rand is rooted in its disdain for individualism and its preference for collectivism. They prefer the forced communitarianism, security and order of a beehive or an ant colony to the freedom and unequal rewards of a market economy.

Atlas Shrugged isn't a practical blueprint. It's a warning and an inspiration. Rand's capitalist icons – John Galt, Francisco d'Anconia, Ragnar Danneskjöld, Hank Rearden, and Dagny Taggart – are the larger-than-life ideal. They're superheroes whose uncompromising standards of excellence, rugged individualism and courage are offered as lofty goals to which mere mortals can only aspire, not actually attain.

Conversely, Rand's villains are much closer to real-world bureaucratic meddlers, nannyists and flighty utopians with whom we've become all too familiar. These are egalitarians, social levelers not satisfied with equality of opportunity, but intent on imposing equality of *outcome* at all costs, preferring the equality of a relatively poorer society to the inequality of a richer one that rewards individual excellence.

Today's producers can't actually find safe haven in Galt's Gulch. The looters, to use Rand's term, won't allow it. They can't stand the competition. The social engineers, bureaucrats and tax collectors dependent on our life-blood would hunt us down. Besides, I'm not yet willing to concede to them the battle for our way of life.

Enviro-Socialism
February 23, 2007

One of my favorite films is the 1965 movie version of Boris Pasternak's *Doctor Zhivago,* with Omar Sharif and Julie Christie. One scene, in particular, made an indelible impression on me.

After his service as a medical officer in the Russian Army during World War I, Zhivago returns to his wife and son who had been living with his in-laws, the Gromekos, in Moscow. By this time, the Russian army had largely disintegrated, the czar had been overthrown and the Bolsheviks had taken control following the revolution. Arriving at the Moscow townhome of Alexander Gromeko, a retired professor, Zhivago is greeted by a burly woman in semi-military garb. She's an overbearing, petty party official, a "comrade," who acidly instructs him that the home has been confiscated by the government in the name of the people; that the rooms have been redistributed to other tenants; and that his extended family has been relegated to one room on the second floor.

I can imagine petty professors and the local chapter of the Young Socialists League at the University of Colorado in the People's Republic of Boulder, standing up and cheering that scene, but as one who's always preferred Ayn Rand to Karl Marx, I found it revolting (pun intended).

This memory was stimulated by a recent guest column in *The Denver Post* ("A sense of entitlement,") by one F.R. Pamp, an environmental lawyer and anti-war activist from Salida. Pamp singled out John Elway's ex-wife, Janet, and her 17,000 square-foot house as an example of "wretched excess," as he put it. Pamp is one of those sanctimonious enviro-scolds, outraged that materialistic Americans consume an inequitable share of the world's resources. As you'd expect, he also disapproves of SUVs and second homes. In his parting shot, he dreams of the day when: "Thirty years from now, maybe the Elways' giant house will have been turned into 10 apartments."

Really? By whom and how? Shades of *Zhivago*. Maybe Pamp could find that brutish Bolshevik bureaucrat to divvy up the space. Or maybe he would appoint himself commissar of a new Federal Bureau of Residential Square Footage and Unneeded Second Homes, RVs, SUVs,

Snowmobiles, Campers, Motorboats, Yachts, Pickup Trucks and Harleys for Middle-Aged Guys, arrogating to himself the power to decide what each of us "needs" and what we don't?

Better yet, Comrade Pamp, what others do with their after-tax income and savings is none of your business. You're a glaring example of the enviro watermelon: green on the outside and red on the inside, a coercive utopian who wants to dictate lifestyles. Americans consume more than others simply because we can afford to. It's called freedom. And we can afford to because we've produced so much more of the world's wealth. People work, invest or buy lottery tickets because they hope to buy things with the proceeds and to secure financial independence.

Doomsayers have always been with us from Thomas Malthus – who predicted mass starvation as population growth would overwhelm food production in the 18th century (it didn't) – to Al Gore and global warming alarmists today. The world has survived ice ages, global warming, global cooling, meteor collisions, volcanic eruptions, plagues, droughts, floods and more. We'll adjust and survive this, too.

Throughout human history, new energy sources have replaced old. It'll happen again. We solve today's problems with tomorrow's technology. I like cars, planes, air conditioning and indoor plumbing. I have no interest in joining the Birkenstock Brigade in reverting to a primitive lifestyle. I don't believe we're doomed to ever-shrinking resources. But if that's our unalterable fate, then it's only a question of time. In which case we might as well enjoy ourselves while we can.

The Reality of Twinkienomics
November 23, 2012

If you're a longtime gourmet of Hostess Twinkies, fear not. Although the company, Hostess Brands Inc., is going under, as long as there remains consumer demand for the Twinkie, it or a reasonable facsimile thereof will live on. As the company liquidates its marketable assets, among them is the Twinkie brand and recipe, which may be appealing to a competing baker and marketer.

When Twinkie makes its comeback, it would be in defiance of the health food police who frown on such sugary confections and disapprove of scofflaw Americans who enjoy them. It's a wonder New York's nannyist mayor Michael Bloomberg hadn't already slapped a ban on the 92-year-old Twinkie, a senior citizen of delicious but unwholesome "junk food." Al Gore has probably blamed it for global warming.

A larger lesson in the demise of yet another troubled American enterprise is the irrational, intransigent and suicidal behavior of a labor union representing a sizable contingent of Hostess workers; in this case, the AFL-CIO-affiliated Bakery, Confectionery, Tobacco Workers and Grain Millers International (that's quite a labor conglomerate).

Hostess had been in financial distress for some time, filing for bankruptcy in 2004 and again in 2009, at which time it was rescued from oblivion by a team of hedge fund and private equity investors. In January 2012, it filed for bankruptcy yet again, citing an operating loss of $341 million, declining market share and increases in uncontrollable costs for ingredients and fuels.

Even more crippling were counter-productive work rules, unsustainable labor costs and $2 billion in unfunded pension liabilities, the consequences of having to deal with no fewer than 12 different unions representing its employees.

The Wall Street Journal reported that Hostess had 372 separate collective bargaining agreements for various categories of workers that required it "to maintain 80 different health and benefit plans, 40 pension plans and mandated a $31 million increase in wages and health care and other benefits in 2012."

Inflexible union work rules "required cake and bread products to be delivered to a single retail location using two separate trucks. Drivers weren't allowed to load their own vehicles, and the workers who loaded bread weren't allowed to load cake."

You get the picture.

After carefully analyzing Hostess' financials, the bankruptcy court scaled back union contracts and imposed other economies in an effort to help the company and its 18,500 employees nationwide survive. Even the normally pugnacious Teamsters union went along. But not the bakers, who wanted to have their Twinkie and eat it, too.

Speaking for their union, AFL-CIO president Richard Trumka served up the usual demagogic clichés, blaming the company's dire financial condition on "Bain-style Wall Street vultures" making "themselves rich by making America poor." These so-called vultures are otherwise known as investors, who came in after the 2009 bankruptcy and poured an additional $60 million into the company last year alone to keep it afloat. When the 5,000 unionized bakers balked at the court-ordered settlement and went out on strike, the company called it quits. So, yet another self-absorbed suicidal union has cost its members their jobs.

Operating a company isn't a hobby or a charitable exercise for managers or investors. It's a business proposition in a competitive market economy that has to earn profits as measured by a return on invested capital to justify its existence. The alternative is a socialist system that subsidizes inefficient businesses, the model for which was the former Soviet Union – where they had countless "Solyndras" that weren't allowed to fail.

Like so much of our society today, too many unionists have an entitlement mentality regarding their jobs, their pay and their benefits that exceeds the value they add to what they produce. They don't care about consumers, investors, management or taxpayers. Twinkienomics is a reality check.

Where Did it All Go?
January 2, 2009

The recent meltdowns of financial markets have afflicted, either directly or indirectly, just about everyone in the world economy (with the exception of short sellers). Upwards of $10 trillion of paper wealth has vaporized on Wall Street, venerable investment banks have folded and high-flying hedge funds have simply disappeared. Multi-billionaire Warren Buffett, a sophisticated investor if ever there was one, has dropped about $14 billion, leaving him with a meager net worth of barely $50 billion. Pension funds – like Colorado's government-employees' PERA, off 25% – are being ravaged. Prestigious universities have seen the value of their endowments plunge. And, of course, tens of millions of ordinary citizens have watched their 401-k plans shrink, stock market investments tank and home values erode.

So where did all the money go? Some of it was stolen. The perfidy of hedge-fund con men like Bernie Madoff is reprehensible. But those sensationalistic incidents represent only a fraction of the tens of trillions of dollars of market capitalization. The bulk of the paper investment losses is in money that was never really there. Yes, part of a company's valuation is based on its net worth, the amount by which its assets exceed its liabilities. But financial markets look to the future. The value of a company's stock, today, is mostly a function of its prospects, tomorrow, as perceived by current and prospective investors appraising future cash flows and appreciation. That's why a company's stock might sell for large multiples over its earnings per share or book value. Google's stock, for example, was selling at lofty premiums long before it was turning a profit. An oil lease is worth a lot more before drilling starts than after a few dry holes.

Think of it this way: let's say you were in Las Vegas last July before the start of the NFL season, and you bought a $100 ticket on the Broncos to win the Super Bowl. The odds on that bet might have been 30-1 back then. Although a Super Bowl victory months away would win you $3,000, the market value of your ticket in July was just the $100 you paid for it. After the Broncos' 4-1 start, the odds might have dropped to 10-1. A potential buyer might have paid you, say, $300, for your ticket in August with the prospect of a possible $3,000 payoff. After last

Sunday's loss to the Chargers, that ticket is now worth zero. Its earlier value was tied purely to future prospects.

Near-term prospects for economic growth, employment, retail sales, personal income, home values, corporate profits and government deficits are dim. Hence, the future isn't worth what it used to be and market valuations are consequently depressed. Call it the business cycle or market gravity. What goes up eventually comes down, if not all the way down. Between 1985 and 2005 household net worth quadrupled from $14 trillion to $57 trillion. We were exuberant then, perhaps irrationally so, as Alan Greenspan termed it.

The economy is retrenching now as it has periodically in the past. When all the dust settles, we'll still be relatively well off. This isn't Somalia. I have great faith in our market economy and our people. This downturn, too, shall pass.

There are those on the left who would seize on our current predicament as an opportunity to turn our economy over to the government, as if the imperfections and corruption of capitalists would not be exceeded by the imperfections and corruption of politicians and bureaucrats, compounded by their monopoly power and the influence of special interests. Recall the corrupt former Illinois Gov. Rod Blagojevich.

A Conflict of Economic Visions

True Measure of Society
April 27, 2007

A core belief of "progressives" goes something like this: *"The true measure of a society is how it treats the weak and needy."* This is a superficially noble and nice-sounding platitude. Politically, it's the foundational justification for the cradle-to-grave welfare state and its perpetual expansion. It's heard so often, I suspect many people who have never paused to critically appraise its validity simply accept this bromide as a truism.

I don't. It's simplistic and absurdly narrow. You might say that *one* measure of a society is how it treats those in need. Fair enough. But that's hardly the only "true measure" of a society's values, merits or contribution to the world – or even its most significant.

The promise of Marxism, after all, is: "From each according to his ability, to each according to his need." While this might sound seductive to the collectivists among us, its incompatibility with human nature dooms it to failure as a system of political economy. We've seen the destructive results of this ideology, inevitably leading to totalitarianism and bankruptcy in places like the former Soviet Union, North Korea and Cuba. Even the vaunted Israeli kibbutz, a voluntary, altruistic commune, is rapidly sliding into oblivion.

Rather, there are manifold measures of one society's relative greatness compared to all others in the *real* world – as opposed to nonexistent utopian visions in some imagined world. These include, but are not limited to, its systems of governance, justice, law and commerce. Its commitment to freedom and individual rights. Its achievements in science, engineering, industry, technology and exploration. Its military strength. Religion and philosophy. Literature, art, music, culture. Medicine and health. Education, scholarship, intellectualism. Economic growth, wealth creation and standard of living. All of these things, and more, are measures of a society.

Humanitarianism and philanthropy, of course, have their place in any good or great society, but they're not the exclusive province of government, funded by taxation. The state is not society; it's a subset of society. We are more than our government. Who says government handouts are nobler than private charity?

And while compassion is commendable, it, too, is not the one "true measure" of an individual. Mother Teresa did good work in her specialty. But so did Socrates, Thomas Jefferson, Albert Einstein and Dwight Eisenhower in theirs. We could debate which of these people made the greatest contribution to their societies and the world.

As Tevye mused in *Fiddler on the Roof,* there may be no shame in being poor, but it is no great honor, either. Poverty is nothing to be revered. The poor want it least of all. That's why President Lyndon Johnson declared war against poverty in 1964. Democrats and Republicans alike have vowed to eradicate what passes for poverty in America, where the poor live better than most of the world's population.

For all their well-intentioned efforts, it hasn't been social workers who have elevated the poor; their job is to minister to them. Ironically, many social programs create dependency, perpetuating poverty. In fact, it's been capitalists, entrepreneurs and technicians driving our productivity and creating jobs that have produced a rising economic tide lifting even the poorest of boats. It should be obvious that a wealthy society is best able to tend to the welfare of those in need. Compassion is limited to the fruits of success.

Perhaps a truer measure of a society is to observe which way the guns are pointed: inward to keep captive subjects from escaping (e.g., the old Berlin Wall) or outward to keep too many hopeful immigrants from entering (U.S. border security – if we had any). That's the objective market test. And by that standard, America must truly be the greatest society of all.

Concentrated vs. Diffused Interests
June 2, 1995

Concentrated vs. *diffused* interests. This is the dichotomy described by economist Milton Friedman in explaining why it's so difficult to cut, or even restrain, government spending in our society.

The concentrated interest is represented by those who benefit from a given program. The diffused interest is everyone else. In this case, ironically, there's a weakness in numbers. The diffused interest, though in the majority, isn't as engaged, interested or organized as groups whose rice bowls are at stake.

Friedman used the example, some years ago, of merchant marine and shipbuilding subsidies. Six hundred million dollars from the Treasury (a pittance today) was being dispensed to a few large companies, benefitting the owners and their 40,000 employees. Benefits to the industry were worth about $15,000 per employee. That's the concentrated interest. The cost to taxpayers was less than $3 apiece. That's the diffused interest. If you're in the shipping industry, a nice donation to your trade association, so it may hire lobbyists to protect your rice bowl, is an investment that figures to pay handsome dividends. If you're an individual taxpayer, how involved will you get for three bucks?

The problem is, all those individual programs, small and large – from tobacco subsidies to Urban Development Action Grants, to Social Security and Medicare – add up to an unbroken stream of federal budget deficits and spiraling national debt. The concentrated interests are out there working the system and fighting like hell to protect their piece of the pie, while the diffused interest does little more than telling pollsters of a wish for a balanced budget.

In a vacuum, almost any government program has merits. In the aggregate, we can't afford them all. Something must be cut – perhaps everything. Here's an example of a current dispute. Trying for a balanced budget by 2002, House and Senate Republicans have proposed, among other things, economies in the college student loan program. Nothing drastic, not eliminating the program or even restricting eligibility requirements, just reforms that would save about $2 billion per year. Under current policy, students can borrow up to

$17,125 over four years. They don't begin to repay the loan until they graduate and get a job. While they're in college, interest on the loan is picked up by taxpayers. Postgraduate students can go 10 years without accruing any interest. The GOP proposal asks that students repay the interest that accrued on their loan while they were attending school. As in the current program, those interest payments wouldn't commence until the student graduated.

A student who borrowed the maximum amount over four years, repaying his loan over the next 10 years, would see his monthly payment increase $42, from $207 to $249. That's about $1.40 per day, the equivalent of a Super Gulp at 7-Eleven, where some guy without a college degree, who's been subsidizing these loans, is working for a lot less money than our college graduate.

College grads today earn, on average, 1.9 times what high school grads do. That's up from 1.45 times in the late 1970s. Postgraduates include doctors, lawyers and MBAs who pull down big bucks – earning, on average, $56,000 a year more than high school graduates – over long, lucrative careers. Why in the world should middle-class taxpayers and lower-paid people with less-marketable educational credentials subsidize them?

Sure, a well-educated citizenry is a benefit to society. But it's even more to the benefit of those individual, well-educated citizens. In pursuing their own self-interest, they'll also serve the national good. What could be better? They have more than enough incentive now to seek a college degree without this interest subsidy. It's unrealistic to contend that this relatively minor change will significantly affect their behavior.

College students don't like this proposal; neither do Democratic big spenders like Ted Kennedy. Hey, this subsidy is worth more than 5 million votes. Also lobbying against it are groups like the American Council of Education, representing 2,000 colleges and universities. They're paranoid that anything that increases the effective cost to their customers, even after graduation, might reduce demand. They could offset it by restraining tuition hikes, but that would come out of their pockets. What other reaction would you expect from concentrated interests?

Income Inequality is Inevitable

December 15, 2011

The injustice of income inequality has long been a passion of the left and the centerpiece of its condemnation of economic freedom.

The raw data in this area can be more inflammatory than enlightening. To exaggerate the "inequities," leftist demagogues torture the statistics, comparing the pre-tax income of the rich with the understated incomes of the poor, ignoring trillions of dollars in transfer payments, social programs and subsidies.

Income inequality is the inevitable consequence of the unequal distribution of skill, intelligence, ambition, dedication, parental involvement, market valuation, risk taking and just plain luck, to name only a few variables. Government intrusion to equalize individual income inevitably reduces aggregate income and wealth creation in a society.

The demise of the middle-class has been greatly exaggerated – as evidenced by the post-Thanksgiving shopping binge – although many have been cutting back on vacations and brand-new Harleys these days. Of course, this is small consolation to some in the middle-class who have lost their jobs and can't find new ones of equal value.

The middle-class is an eclectic mixture. Unskilled workers in some heavily unionized industries, like automobile manufacturing, traditionally enjoyed premium compensation packages well in excess of the value they added to their employer's product. This was largely thanks to the power of their labor union cartel and the compliance of shortsighted management. The same shift to a highly competitive international economy that brought down compensation to unionized workers also brought down the cost of automobiles to consumers, especially when considering the improvement in their quality and features. Premiums paid for productivity, education and refined skills in some middle-class job categories today have been offset by reductions in other categories lacking those attributes.

In recent decades, government workers have leveraged the political power of their unions to add jobs, pay and benefits for their rank and file at the expense of private-sector middle-class workers.

Further muddling the middle-class metrics is immigration. Millions of lower-paid Latino immigrants, both legal and illegal, have brought down the

U.S. national wage average while ironically elevating the living standard of those immigrants well above what they could have earned in their native countries.

Yes, this surely is a sluggish economy, job creation is seriously lagging, and the housing market has a long way to come back – but it's nothing like the Great Depression. The current 8.6 percent unemployment rate is hardly the same as 1933's 25 percent. And trillions of dollars in social programs that didn't exist during the 1930s are most certainly there today to cushion the blow.

Piggybacking on the emotionally charged but misleading statistics on income inequality, left-wing opportunists like *New York Times* columnist Paul Krugman are taking it to the next level, claiming the economic power of the wealthy is undermining our democratic institutions. "Can anyone deny that our political system is being warped by the influence of big money?" he asks.

Krugman's irrational premise seems to be that the "warping influence" of the wealthy has driven income inequality. This is absurd. Does he imagine the wealthy speak or spend with one voice?

The biggest spender among the super-rich is George Soros, the capitalist billionaire who funds every anti-capitalist cause from Occupy Wall Street to electing Democrats. And the so-called Gang of Four, Colorado's cabal of liberal fat cats, has lavishly funded an expansive network of left wing activism dwarfing any efforts by well-heeled conservatives.

Other major centers of influence include private and public labor unions, think tanks, foundations, the K-12 education establishment, higher education, the media, Hollywood, TV and the pop culture. Their influence on public policy extends far beyond the money they spend, and their ranks are overwhelmingly dominated by "progressives," to use the fashionable label of the day.

This is what's "warping" our political system – and they're philosophically in bed with Krugman! So what's his beef?

Prosperity isn't an Entitlement

November 10, 2011

From London to Greece to Occupy Wall Street, angry, indignant mobs have taken to the streets in protest. They imagine they've been deprived of what they're "entitled" to: a well-paid, gratifying job; forgiveness of their student loans; a bigger share of other people's wealth; a world without war, and so on.

This notion of entitlement and the belief that government can deliver happy endings is a delusion. Their actual argument is with economic reality.

From its beginnings, America was blessed with abundant natural resources, wide open spaces, a free market economy, individual liberty, limited government, class mobility, and generous rewards for individual enterprise. These attributes propelled waves of immigrants to personal success and the nation to world economic dominance for generations.

That was then; this is now. Natural resources are in greater demand and more expensive. And foreign competition has gotten tougher. We import relatively more and export relatively less. Americans continue to enjoy a standard of living that's among the highest in the world. There's no abject poverty in this country, only *relative* poverty. That's a very different thing. Americans who fall below the government's official poverty level live better than three-quarters of the world's population and better than the middle-class in most countries.

But we don't dominate the world economically to the degree we once did. Advances in communications technology and international transportation have given rise to a global economy where the rules have changed and we've lost much of our comparative advantage. Now, the task is to regain it.

Labor in less developed nations and rapidly expanding ones like China and India is cheaper than ours for a variety of reasons. But protectionism, tariffs and trade wars aren't the answer. That would only raise consumer prices. Foreign labor has long been cheaper. In the past, we've trumped that by being smarter. To reassert ourselves, the U.S. needs dramatic advances in productivity and economically viable

49

new technologies. Failing that, our overall standard of living will inevitably decline.

We're not entitled to high wages and an elevated standard of living simply because we're Americans. The world doesn't work that way. Throughout history, wealthy empires have come and gone. National prosperity must constantly be earned.

In a market economy, employers pay wages based on the expected value that a worker adds to a product or service. That applies at all pay levels, from NFL quarterbacks to movie stars to CEOs to the take-out window at McDonald's. The decline of the U.S. auto industry was largely a consequence of a labor union cartel extracting compensation for its rank and file greatly in excess of their value added. Ultimately, economic reality intervened. The middle-class can't long be prosperous at the expense of their employers, consumers or the government. And "eating the rich" is a one-time feast that wouldn't feed 300 million Americans for very long.

The Occupy Wall Street movement is more a self-indulgent temper tantrum of underachievers than a realistic economic alternative. Wall Street is only the symbol of their animus. Capitalism is the real target, and their imagined remedy is some vaguely understood notion of socialism.

Among them are many unemployed college grads, including one (or perhaps a counterdemonstrator making a sardonic point) who was holding a sign: "$96,000 for a BA in Hispanic, Transgender, Gay and Lesbian Studies, and I can't find a job." The unemployment rate for college grads is a mere 4 percent, less than half the overall rate.

But all degrees aren't created equal.

Graduates with degrees in science, technology, engineering and math are in high demand. That's called market feedback. Unless daddy can foot the bill and support you afterwards, it may not be wise these days to go in hock for a degree in theater. Oh wait; Occupy Wall Street also wants the government to forgive their college loans.

Socialists Seduce Gullible to Survive
December 10, 1999

Why do socialists persist? That question was put to me recently by someone expecting a profound answer. You might as well ask why mosquitoes persist. It's what they do. Socialists are driven by a combination of ideological fervor and animus towards capitalists. It's a philosophy based on envy and resentment, dressed up as "social justice."

Once upon a time, socialist doctrine called for government ownership of the means of production. As we move into the 21st century, the rhetoric of socialism has become more sly and euphemistic. As long as government controls the terms of production through regulations and mandates, and the fruits of production through taxation and redistribution, ownership of the means of production is a mere formality. As a matter of fact, the appearance of private ownership provides a wonderful cover for Big Brother when conservatives throw around inflammatory terms like "socialism." The "S" word is out of fashion these days. Contemporary socialists are now called liberals or, as they prefer, "progressives."

During the 1980s, champions of market economics, lower taxes and limited government, like Margaret Thatcher and Ronald Reagan ushered in a dynamic new era. Conservative governments were elected even in traditional bastions of democratic socialism. Carried away with their enthusiasm, some conservative true believers went so far as to announce the imminent death of socialism. This was wishful thinking.

Socialism will never die simply because capitalism will never deliver utopia. In the words of Irving Kristol, capitalism may not be the best of all imaginable worlds, only the best under the circumstances, of all possible worlds.

Socialism is, at its core, utopian. Socialists can't deliver utopia either; but they can always outbid conservatives in the auction for desirable political outcomes. Periodic economic recessions are inevitable. When one occurs on a conservative watch, socialists need only seduce a sufficient number of gullible voters with the promise of joy. It happens.

51

Socialists operate on an idealistic notion of human nature that imagines individuals will work as hard for the benefit of others as they will for the benefit of themselves and their families. Socialists are egalitarians in the worst sense of the term. While conservatives believe in equality of opportunity, socialists would dictate equality of outcome. Since socialism fails to reward individual excellence, it gets much less of it. By undermining incentives, socialism undermines prosperity. Socialism is a perfect system for perfectly self-sacrificing human beings. It cannot and does not work with the imperfect, real world species that we are.

There is no "Third Way" in politics, just as there are no new ideas. Absolute capitalism and absolute socialism have never existed and never will. Even in the former Soviet Union there were pockets of underground capitalism – about the only place in that dismal economy where some measure of efficiency could be found. The pendulum continually swings back and forth from left to right. If Tony Blair and Bill Clinton, representing parties of the left, have appeared to forge a middle ground in recent years, it's only because the political environments in England and the U.S. aren't conducive to a more aggressive from of socialism at this moment in time.

But the agenda of American leftists remains unchanged. Since they couldn't get socialized medicine in one fell swoop, they'll take it in smaller doses. Higher minimum wages are just a step along the way to guaranteed employment and guaranteed incomes. Taxes can never be too high on the rich or benefits too generous for the poor. Socialists will never stop demanding more socialist programs while their impossible dream is unmet. In the process they would cost us both our prosperity and our freedom.

But they'll persist. And by and large they'll do it where the political environment is most hospitable: within the Democratic Party.

Lower Rates, Higher Revenues
August 18, 2011

During last week's Iowa debate, panelist Byron York and *Fox News* moderator Bret Baier sought to put the eight Republicans on record about tax hikes and spending cuts. To a person, all eight believe massive federal deficits are the product of excessive government spending and a raft of bad policies from the Obama administration and congressional Democrats that have discouraged business investment and stunted economic growth.

Since Democrats control the Senate and the White House while Republicans have only a majority in the House, the GOP debaters were presented with a hypothetical political compromise. In order to make a budget deal with Democrats, the Republicans on that Iowa stage were asked, by a show of hands, if any of them would walk away from a deal involving tax increases in exchange for spending cuts even if the ratio of spending cuts to tax increases were 10 to 1.

Every candidate raised a hand. Liberal pundits pounced on this, as did Barack Obama on his Midwest campaign tour, to brand the GOP field as intransigent ideologues, pandering to their base. In fact, the candidates were on solid ground, and the critics reveal their lack of understanding of fundamental economics. If not that, they're hopeless Keynesians or partisan Democrats – which tends to be one and the same.

The question itself was a false dilemma with no simple yes or no answer. The short-form Iowa debate format didn't permit the appropriate response which could have clarified the confusion between tax *rate* increases and tax *revenue* increases. While long-overdue spending cuts are essential to head off national bankruptcy, revenue increases must also be part of the plan to close the deficit. At 25 percent of GDP, federal spending is well above our tax capacity, hence the need to reduce spending. At 16 percent of GDP, tax revenues are currently below our tax capacity of about 20 percent. So let's work on balancing the budget at that level. A balanced budget amendment limiting spending would certainly help.

The path to increased tax revenues, however, is not through

higher tax rates, especially on middle-and-upper income taxpayers and businesses. (People with lower incomes don't pay income taxes. After exemptions and tax credits, the bottom 45 percent currently pays zero in federal income taxes.) Incentives matter, and higher tax rates on individuals and businesses reduce the prospect of after-tax returns on work and investment, discouraging both. Such a policy is suicidal in an already anemic economy. Instead, Republicans, led by Rep. Paul Ryan, have proposed the elimination of numerous deductions to broaden the tax base, then reducing tax rates to provide a real stimulus to private sector growth. The fruits of a sharply expanding economy, not the burden of higher tax rates, is what will drive up federal revenues.

It's worked historically. Tax-rate reductions led to revenue increases under Presidents Coolidge, Kennedy, Reagan and George W. Bush. Yes, the economy expanded and tax revenues rose during the Clinton presidency. But that wasn't because of his tax-rate increases. It was in spite of them. Tax rates are an important economic variable, but not the only one. The post-Cold War peace dividend, productivity gains, the tech boom, dot-com boom and stock market boom that all, coincidentally, occurred on Clinton's watch mitigated the drag of higher income-tax rates – offset, let's not forget, by his reduction in capital gains tax rates, which produced higher capital gains tax revenues.

When Obama and progressive Democrats insist on soaking the rich, it's not really about economic policy. You can't finance leviathan government on the backs of the rich, and they already pay more than their fair share. It's about leftist ideology, punitive class warfare, redistribution of income and political pandering to their progressive base. As Austrian economist Ludwig von Mises observed, "Socialism is nothing but a grandiose rationalization of petty resentments."

Envy Driving Tax Hikes
September 30, 2010

Economic conditions can never be so bad – or so good, for that matter – that liberal Democrats don't want to raise taxes on "the rich." This is partly motivated by their socialist ideology but mostly by raw, political calculus: There are more votes in the bottom 98 percent of the population than in the top 2 percent. So, the scheduled expiration of the Bush-era tax-rate cuts at the end of 2010 is an opportunity for leftist demagogues to strut their stuff.

In 2001, marginal tax rates were lowered across the board. The bottom rate was slashed immediately from 15 percent to 10 percent, a 33 percent reduction. The top rate was shaved from 39.6 percent to 35 percent, a 13 percent reduction phased in over five years. Other deductions, exemptions and credits further favored those with lower incomes. Nonetheless, the liberal media – conveniently ignoring the percentage differentials – falsely claimed that these reforms benefitted the rich more than the poor and the middle-class because the rich would have greater dollar savings. Duh! This was obviously because the rich pay more in taxes.

Democrats have proposed that the Bush tax cuts be extended to all but "rich" Americans; defined as $200,000 for individuals and $250,000 for families. That's about the top 2 percent. In addition to their soak-the-rich mentality, the Dems claim this will reduce projected deficits. But that assumes taxpayers are indifferent to increases in marginal tax rates, that incentives and disincentives don't matter. If that were true, why not raise rates to 50 percent or 70 percent or 100 percent?

It's obviously because incentives do matter, to say nothing about the injustice of that degree of property theft. Workers and investors care about their after-tax income. The higher one's marginal tax rate, the more sensitive one is to tax rates. This is Laffer Curve/Supply Side Economics 101.

As for the effect on the deficit – even if you blithely assume that higher tax rates have no negative consequences – the revenues from soaking the rich are dwarfed by the revenues from soaking everyone else. The Democrats' own estimate claims $675 billion in additional taxes over 10 years by singling out the rich compared to $3.7 trillion in additional taxes if rates were raised for everyone.

The Bush tax reforms were given the milk-carton, expiration-date treatment because of Democratic opposition. So, they've been called "temporary" tax rates. But all tax rates are temporary. They can be changed at any time by new legislation. Why label the Bush tax rates a cut just because they scaled back the Clinton tax-rate increase? In the 1980s, Ronald Reagan was able to take the top rate from an outrageously confiscatory level of 70 percent down to 28 percent, and all other marginal rates down with it. The economy boomed as a result. By 1993, under Clinton, it was pushed back up to 39.6 percent. Who says that's the optimum rate?

On last week's *CBS News Sunday Morning*, Linda McGibney branded conservative economist and actor (you've seen him in movies and in "Shaq and Stein" Comcast commercials) Ben Stein "greedy" and uncaring about the financial suffering of other Americans. Stein's crime was describing how much he already pays in taxes and explaining that no known economic theory – monetarist or Keynesian – advocates raising taxes in the midst of a severe recession. This is fiscal policy suicide.

The rich don't pay their "fair share" of the income tax burden. They pay far more than that. The top 1 percent, with incomes over $400,000, accounts for more than 40 percent of total income-tax collections, about twice their share of individual income. The bottom 50 percent provides less than 3 percent.

Stein is right. Raising taxes only on the rich at this time isn't motivated by sound economics, just envy and punishment.

Populists Equalize Poverty
January 19, 2007

With the Democrats back in power in Congress and with the 2008 election campaign already upon us, you'll be hearing much more about "income inequality." This is a major issue for "progressives" (when you hear that word, think "socialists") like Speaker of the House Nancy Pelosi. Populism is back in fashion.

By populism, I mean the exploitation of the uninformed, angry impulses and unfiltered passions of the masses. That anger and resentment has historically been directed at the usual villains and cardboard stereotypes: bankers, insurance companies, "big pharma" (that means drug companies), agri-business, "the military-industrial complex," free trade, free markets and, of course, "the rich." This mentality feeds on conspiracy theories and simplistic fantasies about the way the world works. It seeks to impale the minority of "haves" on the pitchforks of the more numerous "have nots." When you do the political calculus, it can seem like a seductive winning formula for many politicians.

Complaints of income inequality are nothing new. Will Durant traces its history to ancient Rome. He observes that: "The concentration of wealth is a natural and inevitable result of the concentration of abilities in a minority of men and regularly recurs in history...Despotism may for a time retard the concentration; democracy, allowing the most liberty, accelerates it."

Along the way, societies have dealt with income disparities, as Durant puts it, through "legislation redistributing wealth or by revolution distributing poverty." Alexis de Tocqueville, writing *Democracy in America* in the 1830s, cautioned that democracy could be taken too far, noting that "there exists in the human heart a depraved taste for equality, which impels the weak to attempt to lower the powerful to their own level, and reduces men to prefer equality in slavery to inequality in freedom."

The French Revolution consumed itself on populist excesses and atrocities on persons and property in the name of "egalitarianism." The difference between a prosperous free society like ours and impoverished, collectivist despotisms is the difference between our notion of equality of *opportunity* and the self-destructive egalitarian notion of equality of *outcome*.

To be sure, there are some very rich people in America who earn and possess hundreds of thousands of times what poorer people earn or possess. But the poor in this country are only *relatively* poor. We have no *abject* poverty. On the contrary, America's "poor" have cars, TVs, appliances, computers, $200 basketball shoes and own their own homes. Their lifestyle would be the envy of most of the world's population.

As long as there's relative wealth, there will always be relative poverty. The only alternative is an impossible one: absolute income and wealth equality. In a market economy like ours, the state of the economy will never be good enough for some and never bad enough for others. In a dynamic economy, there will always be relative winners and losers. Some industries will be ascendant and others will be in decline. For the vast majority of Americans, today's income disparities are mostly related to differing levels of education and skills of marketable value.

Be wary of misleading economic statistics glibly tossed around by populist politicians. A flood of low-skilled immigrants, many illegal, has had a downward influence on average wages. Increases in nonwage compensation – like employer-provided health insurance or deferred compensation in the form of generous defined-benefit pension plans for government employees – are frequently ignored in the wage data. Then there's the discrepancy between reported incomes and consumption, with consumption data – a much better measure of living standards – showing far less inequality.

Politicians and the U.S. government have long been in the business of redistributing income through progressive taxation (the top 10 percent of Americans pay two-thirds of all income taxes; the bottom 50 percent pay only 3 percent) on the one hand, and transfer payments to the poor and middle-class on the other. Remarkably, the official income-distribution figures don't subtract income taxes paid by heavily-burdened net tax *payers*. Compounding the distortion, cash transfers and the cornucopia of government services and subsidies obtained by net tax *receivers* are also ignored. Even though we spend hundreds of billions on this, it's like those benefits don't exist.

Individual incomes are determined objectively in the marketplace. When politicians or labor unions don't like the results, they meddle in people's lives and businesses in pursuit of power while invoking the name of "social justice," today's name for egalitarianism. Excessive concentration of income and wealth can destroy a society politically. We're nowhere near that point. Excessive *redistribution* of income, and wealth – without regard for talent and productivity – can destroy a society economically. That's the more tangible danger.

Beware of False Profits
June 23, 2011

The E.F. Schumacher Society is a left-wing, anti-capitalist advocacy group that radically exploits the cause of environmental sustainability to advance a decidedly socialist agenda. Recently, it changed its name to the New Economics Institute.

One of its leaders, Gar Alperovitz, author of *America Beyond Capitalism*, has outlined his vision of the new-economy movement, "one that is based on rethinking the nature of ownership and the growth paradigm that guides conventional policies." In his judgment, "new-economy efforts will ultimately pose much more radical systemic challenges than many have contemplated."

This is the way these people talk, but you get the idea.

Alperovitz heralds the creation of so-called "B" Corporations, "allowing a company to subordinate profits to social and environmental goals." Initially, Alperovitz and his ilk would "allow" companies to organize as non-profits. Later, they'd likely hope to mandate it. An Alperovitz colleague at the New Economics Institute, Gus Speth, has indicted our market economy as incompatible with "ecological imperatives." In their "new economy," private enterprise capitalism would be transitioned to state capitalism, an oxymoron that's the practical equivalent of socialism.

Unfortunately, given the feeble state of today's economy and the high level of unemployment, many for-profit companies find themselves mired in unintended and involuntary non-profit condition. We don't need more non-profits; we need fewer.

There are about 1.5 million non-profit organizations currently registered with the IRS, representing less than one-tenth of our market economy. They include churches; charities; hospitals; think tanks on the right and left; trade associations; labor unions; and advocacy groups like the ACLU, NAACP and NRA. Organizations are sometimes formed as non-profit enterprises to perform public services outside of what would be provided by investors seeking economic returns.

Organizing as a non-profit also confers numerous tax

advantages and exemptions. Some non-profits do good things. Others, in my view, don't, although they believe they do. "Good," in this case, is subjective.

But let's not lose sight of the reality that, in our capitalist system, all of the capital invested in non-profit organizations is initially derived from the profit and wealth created in the for-profit sector, the source of benevolence and what drives the engine. It all begins with entrepreneurs and investors who risk their capital in a profit-seeking venture. If it's not for profit, it's not a business; it's a charity.

In a market economy, profits are an instrument of the price mechanism, providing market feedback from customers about which products or services are desired, how they should be priced, and what their production costs must be limited to in order to deliver them at a market-clearing price. In a competitive market, companies are price-takers, not price setters. Thus, cost is determined by selling price, not the other way around. Only companies that meet the test of competition will survive. Profits are like a report card.

On average, profits are about 5 percent of sales. Profitable businesses flourish, unprofitable ones perish (as they should), and their assets are put to better use by others. This is what Joseph Schumpeter called the "creative destruction" of capitalism. Most of a successful, growing business' profits are reinvested in that business. Of the remainder, payments to shareholders or creditors are the cost of capital.

The self-anointed geniuses at the New Economics Institute aren't smart enough to override the trillions of economic decisions made every day by millions of individual participants in our market economy. No one is, especially a panel of government central-controllers. That was the grand conceit of the failed, former Soviet Union.

By the way, if all businesses were organized as non-profits, how would liberals collect the corporate income tax?

The Incredible Bureaucracy Machine
March 20, 1998

Bill Gates isn't the first businessman to run afoul of jealous competitors, whining busybodies, opportunistic politicians and petty bureaucrats.

In his ballad, *Tom Smith and His Incredible Bread Machine*, R.W. Grant chronicled the apocryphal plight of the man who single-handedly ended world hunger with a miraculous invention. That, as it turned out, was the easy part. Satisfying the whims of federal regulators, however, proved to be a mission impossible. Herewith, the lyrical highlights of Grant's epic poem:

The way to make bread he'd conceived
Cost less than people could believe.
And not just make it! This device
Could, in addition, wrap and slice!
The price per loaf, one loaf or many:
The miniscule sum of under a penny.

Although Smith had succeeded in feeding millions at unprecedented low prices, he ran into trouble when, in response to an increase in the business tax, he was forced to raise the price of his bread to one full cent.

"What's going on?" the public cried,
"He's guilty of pure plunder.
He has no right to get so rich
On other people's hunger!"

(A prize cartoon depicted Smith
With fat and drooping jowls
Snatching bread from hungry babes
Indifferent to their howls!)

Well, since the Public does come first,
It could not be denied
That in matters such as this,
The Public must decide.

So, antitrust now took a hand.
Of course, it was appalled
At what it found was going on.
The "bread trust," it was called.

And this was Tom Smith's dose of justice as explained by a government anti-trust lawyer:

"The rule of law, in complex times,
Has proved itself deficient.
We much prefer the rule of men!
It's vastly more efficient.

Now, let me state the present rules.
The lawyer then went on,
These very simple guidelines
You can rely upon:

You're gouging on your prices if
You charge more than the rest.
But it's unfair competition
If you think you can charge less.

A second point that we would make
To help avoid confusion:
Don't try to charge the same amount:
That would be collusion!

You must compete. But not too much,
For if you do, you see,
Then the market would be yours
And that's monopoly!"

Price too high? Or price too low?
Now, which charge did they make?
Well, they weren't loath to charging both
With Public Good at stake!

In fact, they went one better
They charged "monopoly!"

No muss, no fuss, oh woe is us,
Egad, they charged all three!

"Five years in jail," the judge then said.
"You're lucky it's not worse.
Robber Barons must be taught
Society Comes First!"

Now, bread is baked by government.
And as might be expected,
Everything is well controlled;
The public well protected.

True, loaves cost a dollar each.
But our leaders do their best.
The selling price is half a cent.
(Taxes pay the rest!)

For the sake of computer users everywhere, consumers in general, unborn generations of would-be entrepreneurs, and the economic well-being of civilization, let's wish Bill Gates a better fate than Tom Smith.

Taxes, Government Spending and Supply-Side Economics

Permanent State of Entitlement?
March 6, 2009

A common refrain among populists is that the rich don't pay their fair share of the income tax burden. In fact, the top 10 percent of income earners in the U.S., who account for 39 percent of total individual income, pay fully 70 percent of all individual income taxes, while the bottom 50 percent pay barely 3 percent.

About a year ago, someone who shared my frustration about this widespread misconception emailed me with a seemingly practical remedy: "I've come to the conclusion that we should drop the tax rate of the lower 50 percent to zero," he said. "What's a lousy 3 percent increase for the rest of us if it shuts up those that complain about tax cuts for the 'rich.' It might remove the smoke screen and make tax reform/simplification that much easier."

While I understood his logic, I thought it would more likely be trumped by politics and human nature. My reply was as follows: "After you've removed the bottom 50 percent from the income tax rolls, the next 10 percent would want to be removed, then the next 10... Then the bottom 50 percent would want to be excused from paying Social Security taxes; etc. Then they'd want direct payments from existing taxpayers.... They'd never shut up."

He recently reminded me of our exchange in a very brief email: "I guess you were right," he noted.

Welcome to the Obama era. Alexander Tytler was a Scottish historian who lived in the 18th century, a student of the rise and fall of Athenian and Roman democracy. I first learned of him about 30 years ago when this quote attributed to Tytler caught my imagination: "A democracy cannot exist as a permanent form of government. It can only exist until the voters discover that they can vote themselves largesse from the public treasury, with the result that a democracy always collapses over loose fiscal policy, always followed by dictatorship."

65

Tytler further observed: "The average age of the world's greatest civilizations has been two hundred years. These nations have progressed through this sequence: From bondage to spiritual faith; from spiritual faith to great courage; from courage to liberty; from liberty to abundance; from abundance to complacency; from complacency to apathy; from apathy to dependence; from dependence back again into bondage."

Tytler's prophesy is making the rounds on the Internet. I've heard there are some who question whether Tytler actually said precisely this. But it doesn't matter. What is disturbing is its relevance to modern forms of democratic governance, including our own and our accelerating march toward Euro-socialism.

Once upon a time there was something known as the American dream. And no, it's not winning the Powerball lottery. That's just a windfall. More than any other place on Earth, an individual in this land of opportunity could achieve success and even greatness through ingenuity, hard work, personal responsibility and deferred gratification. This was historically in an environment of limited govern- ment. As government has expanded, the American dream has increasingly morphed into the American entitlement, with government assuming the role of benefactor, redistributing income – "sharing the wealth," as President Obama has put it – to improve the lot of some at the expense of others; rewarding dependency while punishing productivity.

Rather than enriching a society through policies and incentives that promote the creation of wealth, this is a formula that would erode societal wealth in the name of compassion, collectivism and "social jus- tice." The current economic recession has provided an excuse for the greatest expansion of government intervention and control of our market economy and individual freedom in this nation's history.

It remains to be seen whether this will be a temporary or permanent condition.

"Trickle-Down" is a Democratic Epithet
December 2, 2010

Unless Congress acts in this lame-duck session, a massive tax increase will automatically go into effect across all income levels on January 1st. Given the state of our economy, Republicans and moderate Democrats realize this would be fiscal-policy insanity. Nonetheless, liberal Democrats are holding a universal rescue plan hostage to their obsession with soaking "the rich."

Supply-side economics recognizes that prosperity is ultimately dependent on productivity and output. The way to stimulate more of that is to create incentives for productive enterprise. Lower rates of taxation on savings, investment, work and production encourage these very things; higher tax rates discourage them. Contemptuously misrepresenting supply-side economics as "trickle-down" has been a standby of Democrats for years. The pedigree of that epithet dates back to William Jennings Bryan's infamous "Cross of Gold Speech" in 1896 in which he declared, "There are those who believe that if you will only legislate to make the well-to-do prosperous, their prosperity will *leak through* on those below."

"Leak through" or "trickle down" – same snide sentiment. Bryan was a pompous, populist demagogue, a practitioner of the politics of envy, which latter-day Democrats have raised to an art form.

A rare exception was Democratic President John F. Kennedy, who persuaded Congress to cut income tax rates across the board, including the top rate, then more than 90 percent, down to a mere 70 percent. In a speech to the Economic Club of New York in 1962, JFK explained: "In short, it is a paradoxical truth that tax rates are too high today and tax revenues too low – and the soundest way to raise revenues in the long run is to cut tax rates now." Under the Kennedy tax-rate cuts, as predicted, revenues grew.

Twenty years later, when tax rates were cut even more under Ronald Reagan, federal tax revenues again soared, with the "rich" paying an increasingly greater share of the income tax burden. Since it was now a Republican initiating this policy, Democrats branded it "Reaganomics" and mocked it as half-baked, "trickle-down" economics.

In fact, it's simply common sense. It applies to all facets of commerce. Think of a department store, for example. When it wants to make more money, it doesn't raise its prices; it advertises a sale and cuts them. The store might make less money per unit sold, but by stimulating the volume of economic activity, it increases its profits. Lower tax rates are a sale on economic enterprise.

The concept was understood as far back as the 14th century, when the Arabic philosopher, Ibn Khaldun, observed, "The strongest incentive for cultural activity is to lower as much as possible the amounts of individual imposts levied upon persons capable of undertaking cultural enterprises."

In *Federalist No. 21*, Alexander Hamilton echoed this same theme, arguing that taxes "prescribe their own limit; which cannot be exceeded without defeating the end proposed – that is, an extension of the revenue .... If duties are too high they lessen the consumption; the collection is eluded; and the product to the treasury is not so great as when they are confined within proper and moderate bounds."

It's ironic that liberals smugly ridicule this proposition when John Maynard Keynes, economic guru of FDR's New Deal, endorsed it in his 1933 tract, *The Means to Prosperity*. Keynes observed that "taxation may be so high as to defeat its object, and that, given sufficient time to gather the fruits, a reduction of taxation will run a better chance, than an increase, of balancing the budget."

The left's simple-minded notion of capital formation is not of entrepreneurs creating jobs but of fat cats getting rich and throwing a few crumbs at exploited laborers. They don't much understand or care for capitalism, and like capitalists even less – except for George Soros, who gives them money.

The Truth about Reaganomics
March 25, 1994, August 16, 1996

Criticizing the financial assumptions built into Bill and Hillary's health care plan, Rich Thomas, *Newsweek* magazine economics writer, couldn't resist making the following inept comparison: "But from a financial standpoint, it is the biggest exercise in wishful thinking since President Reagan promised to cut taxes, increase defense spending and balance the budget more than a decade ago..." Thomas may be an economics "writer," but he's obviously not much of an economics student.

In liberals' never-ending campaign to discredit the Reagan years, their most enduring myth is the 1980s tax cut. That and huge hikes in defense spending caused all of those budget deficits. I don't care how many times you've heard that, it simply isn't true. I'll keep correcting that claim as long as libs keep falsely asserting it.

Taxes were not cut during the 1980s. Tax *rates* were. The theory was that lower tax rates would produce higher incomes and increase tax revenues to the Treasury. Just as lowering prices on things people buy boosts revenue by stimulating demand, lower income tax rates offer incentives that stimulate economic activity. The theory worked. In 1980, federal receipts were $517 billion; by 1989, they had grown to $990 billion (exceeding inflation by $220 billion). What's more, IRS data irrefutably show an inordinate share of the income tax hikes was borne by upper-income taxpayers.

Liberals, preferring the stick to the carrot, argue that higher tax rates on income would have produced even greater revenues. This confuses the arithmetic effect of tax rate increases with the economic effect. Yes, on paper; you can arithmetically calculate greater tax revenues from a *given* level of economic activity by raising tax rates. But that's not how the *real* world works. The level of economic activity is not a given. Higher tax rates erode incentives; they're an economic drag. If that weren't so, we could tax ourselves rich by simply raising rates until we had all the revenues we wanted. Budgeting would be a snap. Only an economic imbecile could believe that.

The essence of supply-side theory is very simply that *incentives matter*. That human energy responds better to the carrot than the stick. That the key to prosperity is encouraging producers to produce more by offering them the prospect of greater rewards for their efforts. You do that by letting them keep more of the fruits of their labor by reducing the share that government confiscates. Demand-side economics, conversely, seeks to soak the productive through high taxes and inflation, redistributing the proceeds to net tax receivers who will then spend us all to economic Utopia.

Okay, so if taxes rose in the 1980s, why did we have the huge budget deficits? Because spending increased even more and mostly on non-defense items. In 1980, defense spending was $134 billion. In 1989, it was $304 billion. In 1980, non-defense spending was $457 billion. In 1989, it was $840 billion. That's why we had deficits.

We have a deficit when we spend more than we collect in taxes. You can close it by spending less or taxing more. Taxing more isn't the answer. Misguided attempts to do so may produce less revenues, not more, if they push the economy into recession. Besides, at more than 19 percent of Gross Domestic Product, federal taxes are at their practical limit. They've exceeded 20 percent of GDP only twice since World War II, and both those years (1969 and 1981) preceded recessions.

That leaves only the obvious choice – what we should have done a decade ago. Cut spending. Bring it down to our tax capacity, about 19 percent of GDP, and prioritize within that ceiling. The breakdown might look like this: Spend 3 percent of GDP to pay the interest on the national debt (we're stuck with that), 4 percent for defense (40 percent less than our 1980s peak), and that leaves 12 percent for everything else, on which we're now spending about 15 percent. That 3 percent of GDP differential represents about $200 billion in reduced federal spending. It would have to come out of an array of popular programs including Social Security, Medicare, Medicaid, farm subsidies, education, transportation, etc.

That's it. The deficit dilemma is at once that simple and that complicated. We must cut spending on programs we like. Families and businesses do it every day. They prioritize. There's no logical reason our elected representatives in Washington can't do it – they just don't want to.

Lowdown on High Taxes
April 22, 2005

With April 15 having just passed, the scars are still fresh. I hope you're not one who rejoiced over your tax refund as if the feds were presenting you with some kind of gift. Generally, if you're getting a refund check it's only because excessive taxes were withheld from your paychecks all year. What you'll be getting back is your own money, the return of principal on the interest-free loan you were kind enough to extend to the U.S. Treasury in the prior year.

Molly Ivins, the late, folksy, sassy socialist from Texas (by way of *The New York Times,* where she once worked as a *reporter,* which speaks volumes about the leftist bias of *Times* reporters) has her own views on taxes. Good golly, Miss Molly's nationally syndicated diatribe on the subject was headlined, "Tax system favors the super-rich." This, of course, is nonsense on stilts. Those who make over a million dollars a year – that's 169,000 tax returns out of about 130 million – constitute one-tenth of 1 percent of all tax filers, earn 8 percent of aggregate individual income, and pay 17 percent of the nation's total income tax bill all by themselves. Federal income taxes average 28 percent of their adjusted gross income.

On the other hand, the bottom 50 percent of tax filers – those 64 million Americans making less than $29,000 – earn 14 percent of aggregate individual income and pay a mere 3.5 percent of the nation's total individual income tax bill. Federal taxes average about 3 percent of their adjusted gross income. A typical family of four with just under $40,000 of income, after exemptions, deductions and credits, pays zero federal income taxes.

So how can Ivins say such things? She cites her "favorite authority on taxes," Davis Cay Johnston of the *New York Times* (there's that paper again), author of the book, *Perfectly Legal: The Covert Campaign to Rig Our Tax System to Benefit the Super Rich – and Cheat Everyone Else.* Doesn't sound like there's any political agenda in that title.

Says Johnston, "People making $60,000 paid a larger share of their 2001 income in federal income, *Social Security and Medicare* (italics mine, see "clever trick," below) taxes than a family making $25 million ..." Well, duh, of course they do. They also spend a larger share of their income than do millionaires on food, clothing, shelter, iPods, automobiles, vacations, toilet paper and candy bars.

You see, the super-rich have more disposable income, much of which is reinvested in our economy, adding to the capital stock and creating jobs. That's what capitalists do. Moreover, the super-rich derive a much larger portion of their income from capital gains and municipal bonds than do wage earners. Capital gains are taxed at a lower rate because the principal invested has already been taxed. And interest on municipal bonds is exempt from federal taxes because the Supreme Court ruled in 1895 that it would be unconstitutional to treat it otherwise.

But notice Johnston's clever trick. Since those who make under $60,000 pay only about 20 percent of the nation's income taxes, he combines income taxes with Social Security and Medicare taxes to muddy the waters and inflate their relative tax burden.

In exchange for the modest taxes they pay, those who make less than $60,000 benefit to a much greater extent from various social spending programs than do the super-rich who don't qualify for day care, food stamps, housing subsidies, Medicaid, etc. In the final analysis, upper-income earners are net tax *payers* while lower-income earners are net tax *receivers*. The payment of Social Security taxes is a requirement to qualify for Social Security benefits regardless of one's income, rich or poor. The Medicare tax is dedicated to Medicare spending. The rich pay a smaller portion of their income on Social Security taxes precisely because there's a cap on income subject to the Social Security payroll tax. And the reason there's a cap on that tax is because there's a cap on benefits, too. If there weren't, this so-called "social insurance" system would be just another bald-faced redistribution-of-income scheme – which is exactly what the Democrats hope to make it.

Income taxes are progressive. Upper incomes are subject to a higher marginal rate than lower incomes. That's why poor people in this country pay nothing in income taxes and the well-to-do pay the lion's share. Other taxes, like sales taxes, property taxes and payroll taxes aren't progressive, that is, everyone pays the same rate regardless of income. We have that mix so that most people pay at least some tax. Otherwise the tax users would pick the taxpayers clean. That's called socialism.

ADDENDUM: I wrote this column in 2005. Since then, I have repeatedly addressed this topic and debunked the false claim put out by demagogues like President Obama that "the rich don't pay their fair share of the taxes."

The latest data issued by the IRS provide the figures for 2012 on income distribution and tax incidence — what I call, "Who makes what, and who pays what." The following charts and a table illustrate this graphically and dramatically. If anything, the rich pay far *more* than their fair share of the income tax burden, a share that has risen steadily since 1981 when President Ronald Reagan succeeded in reducing their marginal income tax rates along with everyone else's. This is a historic lesson in supply-side economics.

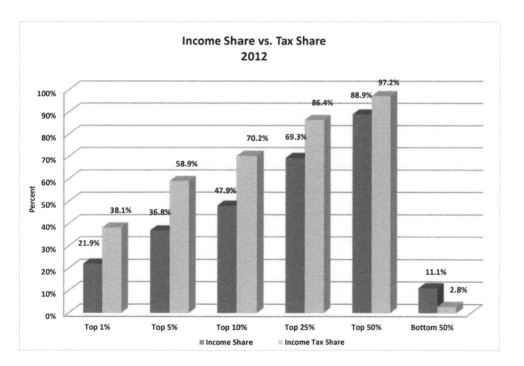

73

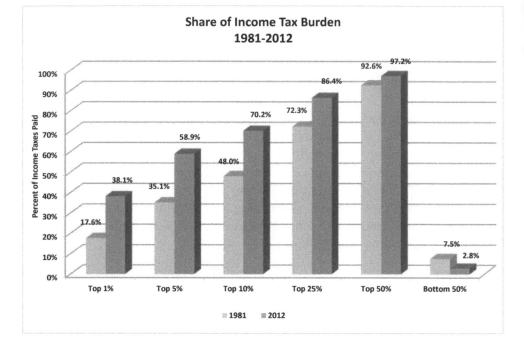

Share of Income Tax Burden 1981-2012

	Top 1%	Top 5%	Top 10%	Top 25%	Top 50%	Bottom 50%
1981	17.6%	35.1%	48.0%	70.2%	92.6%	7.5%
2012	38.1%	58.9%	70.2%	86.4%	97.2%	2.8%

■ 1981 ■ 2012

		Income and Tax Shares 2012				
	Number of Tax Returns (000)	Adjusted Gross Income ($000,000)	Income Tax ($000,000)	AGI as a Percent of Total AGI	Income Tax as a Percent of Total Income Tax	Income Split Point
Top 1%	1,361	1,976,738	451,328	21.9%	38.1%	Above $434,682
Top 5%	5,443	3,330,944	698,543	36.8%	58.9%	Above $175,817
Top 10%	13,608	4,327,899	831,445	47.9%	70.2%	Above $125,195
Top 25%	34,020	6,261,677	1,024,046	69.3%	86.4%	Above $73,354
Top 50%	68,040	8,037,800	1,152,063	88.9%	97.2%	Above $36,055
Bottom 50%	68,040	1,003,944	32,915	11.1%	2.8%	Below $36,055
Total	136,080	$9,041,744	$1,184,978	100.0%	100.0%	

Source: Internal Revenue Service (Preliminary Data); The Tax Foundation, December 2014

INDIVIDUAL INCOME TAXES

2012

Adjusted Gross Income Category	% of Tax Returns	% of Income	% of Tax	Avg Tax Rate	Tax % of AGI
Lower: Under $30,000	46.7%	8.3%	1.8%	10.7%	1.7%
Middle: $30,000-75,000	30.6%	23.7%	12.5%	12.4%	6.6%
Upper Middle: $75,000-100,000	8.4%	11.5%	8.2%	13.6%	9.4%
Upper: Over $100,000	14.4%	56.5%	77.4%	22.3%	17.9%
TOTAL	100.0%	100.0%	100.0%	19.0%	13.1%
Getting Rich: $200K+	3.6%	33.4%	55.1%	25.5%	21.5%
Near Rich: $500K+	0.8%	20.4%	35.6%	26.3%	22.8%
Kinda Rich: $1,000,000+	0.3%	15.2%	26.0%	25.7%	22.4%
Rich: $2,000,000+	0.10%	11.5%	19.2%	24.9%	21.7%
Really Rich: $5,000,000+	0.03%	8.0%	12.7%	23.8%	20.7%
Super Rich: $10,000,000+	0.012%	6.0%	9.1%	22.8%	19.8%

OTHER GROUPINGS

	% of Tax Returns	% of Income	% of Tax	Avg Tax Rate	Tax % of AGI
Under $10,000	16.9%	-0.8%	0.1%	10.5%	0.4%
$10,000-50,000	47.2%	20.0%	6.3%	11.3%	4.1%
Over $50,000	35.9%	80.9%	93.6%	18.7%	13.8%
Total	100.0%	100.0%	100.0%	19.0%	13.1%
Under $10,000	16.9%	-0.8%	0.1%	10.5%	0.4%
$10,000-20,000	16.7%	4.0%	0.5%	9.7%	1.5%
$20,000-50,000	30.5%	16.0%	5.9%	11.5%	4.8%
$50,000-75,000	13.1%	12.8%	7.9%	12.9%	8.1%
$75,000-200,000	19.1%	34.6%	30.6%	15.9%	11.5%
Over $200,000	3.6%	33.4%	55.1%	25.5%	21.5%
Total	100.0%	100.0%	100.0%	19.0%	13.1%

Source: IRS Pub. 1304(Rev 08-2014)

Buffett's Tax Fraud
February 2, 2012

Perched next to Michelle Obama at President Obama's State of the Union campaign speech, in full view of the TV cameras, was Warren Buffett's secretary, the woman who Buffett tells us pays more taxes than he does, her multibillionaire boss. She served as a convenient prop for Obama's latest round of class warfare. I deconstructed Buffett's specious claim four years ago when he first made it. Apparently, it's time for an update.

His assertion is that he and the super-rich pay a lower tax *rate* than their "secretaries and receptionists." The key word here is "rate." Obviously, when considering the amount of total tax dollars collected, the rich pay an inordinate share – far more than their "fair share" – of the overall income tax burden. The top 1 percent pays 37 percent of all individual federal income taxes; the top 10 percent pays 70 percent; and the bottom 50 percent carries only 2 percent of the burden.

Buffett extracts a pound of lie from an ounce of truth while throwing in a heavy dose of half-truths and convenient omissions. While it's true that rich and not-so-rich investors pay lower tax rates on things like capital gains, dividends, and interest on municipal bonds than is paid on ordinary wage and salary income, there are perfectly good reasons for that.

Corporations that pay dividends to shareholders do so with after-tax dollars, having already paid a corporate income tax on their earnings. The lower tax rate that shareholders have paid in the past on dividend income when they file their individual tax returns serves to offset some – but not all – of this double taxation. (The lower tax rate on ordinary dividend income, unfortunately, is being eliminated.)

Likewise, the capital gains tax is also double taxation, as eloquently explained by economists Victor Canto and Harvey Hirschorn in more words than space allows here. Moreover, if a stock increases in value over the years, much of the gain is illusionary; eroded by inflation. The capital gains tax makes no allowance for this. A lower tax on capital gains is a productive incentive for people to defer current consumption and invest in the future, creating wealth for themselves and society.

But Buffett's worst manipulation is lumping together income taxes and payroll taxes in the comparison with his secretary. Payroll taxes are for specifically dedicated programs like Social Security and Medicare. Investment income isn't and shouldn't be subject to the payroll tax, and Buffett has far more investment income than his secretary.

Income taxes are sharply progressive, with almost 50 percent of Americans paying nothing at all. Conversely, a uniform Social Security tax rate (normally 6.2 percent each for employee and employer; although a 4.2 percent employee rate is temporarily in effect) is levied on an employee's salary, capped at an income limit of $110,000 in 2012 (increasing each year with inflation). So, obviously, a lower-salaried secretary would pay a greater *percentage* of her income in payroll taxes than a much higher-salaried boss whose income is well above $110,000. But, again, this is for good reason. Social Security *benefits* are similarly capped. From its inception, Social Security was described as a forced savings plan for your own retirement or disability. If the Social Security tax on individuals had no limit, it would be just another income transfer/welfare program, which is precisely what liberals want.

With no cap, the normal, combined employee/employer rate of 12.4 percent on a $1 million salary would result in a tax of $124,000 in 2012 instead of $13,652. That's an increase of about $110,000. On a $10 million salary, that would be a tax increase of about $1,226,000. And this would be on top of income taxes, which Democrats also want to increase. This is grand larceny.

Tax Users vs. Tax*Payers*
September 6, 1996

If one clear message emerged from the Democratic National Convention in Chicago last week, it was this one: We misunderstood Bill Clinton when he proclaimed in his State of the Union speech, earlier this year, that the "era of big government is over." What he meant was that the era of *admitting* he's for big government is over. Smaller government was the last thing the Chicago Democrats had in mind. Platitudes and promises flew fast and furiously, and the ones greeted with the loudest applause were those with a public treasury price tag.

After Clinton, the candidate, promised the end of welfare as we know it, Clinton, the president, vetoed two congressional bills that would have done just that. Only the expediencies of election-year politics and the advice of Dick Morris persuaded him to sign it the third time around. Although Democratic conventioneers in Chicago were initially horrified by the symbolism of this, their spirits were buoyed by a procession of speakers who assured them that Clinton fully intended to repeal any meaningful welfare reform as one of the first acts of his second term – especially if Democrats won back the Congress.

Senate Minority Leader Tom Daschle declared that Democrats believe everyone should have the "freedom" to receive health care, attend college and benefit from several other goodies he ticked off. Interesting choice of words and so typical of a Democrat. Of course people should have that "freedom," and they do. But what Daschle meant and what the delegates in the hall understood, was that everyone should be *entitled* to all those things at someone else's expense. Democrats are big on entitlements, which now consume more than half the federal budget. In his acceptance speech, Clinton promised that he will balance the budget (but not during his term in office) without touching entitlements.

One expects political conventions to be highly partisan and self-serving, but the Chicago Democrats went far enough to give demagoguery a bad name. This was the first public rehearsal – before a live, friendly audience – of the half-truths and outright lies that will be the theme of the campaign. Here are some of the lowlights:

Taxes, Spending and Supply-Side Economics

✓ *Bob Dole wants to cut taxes 15 percent; this will drive up the deficit.* Bob Dole wants to cut the marginal *rate* you pay on your income taxes by 15 percent. This will let you keep more of what you've earned and stimulate economic growth. Tax revenues, as a result, are projected to *increase,* not decline. This will not add to the deficit. If Democrats want to argue about the magnitude of the simulative effect of tax rate cuts on the economy, let them. But they shouldn't lie about what Dole actually says he wants to do.

✓ *Republicans want to slash spending on Medicare and devastate the program.* Republicans want to restrain the *increase* in Medicare *spending* to 7 percent-a-year in order to keep the program from going bankrupt. Democrats want to increase annual spending by 10 percent, sticking their heads in the bankruptcy sands. A 7 percent increase is not a cut. Nothing is being "slashed" or "devastated.

✓ *The Republican Congress shut down the federal government during its budget dispute with Clinton.* Congress presented the president with a federal budget as required by law. Clinton vetoed that budget, creating an impasse. It was Clinton who shut down the government with a stroke of his pen. In similar circumstances when confronted with a hostile congress, Presidents Reagan and Bush swallowed hard, compromised where they could, and accepted budgets they didn't like rather than petulantly shutting down the government.

✓ *Clinton has cut 217,000 government jobs.* Yes, but not welfare state bureaucrats, and not because of any Clinton successes. From 1992 to 1995, 182,000 of the jobs eliminated, 84 percent, were civilians in the Department of Defense, thanks to the end of the Cold War. The biggest chunk of nondefense jobs eliminated were in the Resolution Trust Corp., thanks to the end of the S&L crisis.

The list goes on – but my space does not. If you watched both conventions, the principal distinction should be clear: Democrats are the party of tax users; Republicans care more about taxpayers.

A Tax Cut for Tax*Payers*
January 31, 2003

It's true. Rich people will benefit from the Bush administration's proposed tax reforms. And that's reason enough for Democrats to oppose it.

It's irrelevant that everyone's taxes will be cut and that it's good economic policy. The first rule of the Politics of Envy is never to relent in beggaring thy neighbor as long as thy neighbor earns more than you do.

For those of you not blinded by liberal ideology, a new mathematical technique allows us to objectively analyze the numbers and draw some rational conclusions. The device is called "percentages." It enables one to make relative comparisons between greater and lesser magnitudes.

Under the Bush proposal – which increases the child tax credit, removes the marriage penalty, increases the standard deduction, and accelerates tax-rate reductions – a typical family of four earning $40,000 will have its income tax liability virtually eliminated, from $1,178 down to $45. That's a 96 percent reduction. A family with $200,000 of income will see its tax bill drop from about $35,000 to $32,000.

Although that's $3,000 in savings, it's only a 9 percent reduction. Incomes subject to higher tax bills will save more in absolute dollars but get less of a break as a percentage of their tax liability.

Democrats describe this as a tax plan that benefits *only* the rich. Of course, they're lying. (Incidentally, a family of four with $35,000 in income will get no tax cut this time around precisely because they don't pay any income taxes; the Bush tax cuts of 2001 already removed them from the tax rolls.)

Bush hopes to end the double taxation of dividends and reduce taxes on capital gains. Both of these measures would stimulate long-term capital formation and raise the market value of equities.

This is good supply-side economic policy in any circumstances.

Democrats prefer their traditional brand of snake oil: soak the rich income-transfers to provide short-term demand stimulus of a couple of hundred billion dollars. This would accomplish little in a $10 trillion economy.

Bush's plan calls for across-the-board cuts in all income categories. Democrats oppose income tax cuts for higher-income Americans when the economy is weak and also when the economy is strong.

In 1960, when John F. Kennedy was elected president, the top federal tax rate exceeded 90 percent. He managed to get it down to 70 percent. By 1986, Ronald Reagan had cut it to 28 percent. Under Bill Clinton, the effective rate crept up to more than 40 percent.

When you add state and city income taxes, payroll taxes, excise taxes, property taxes, death taxes, etc., the tax burden on successful Americans is now oppressive. The Democrats' remedy is to tax them some more.

Most Americans disagree. In a recent *Fox News* poll, almost eight out of 10 said no one should be forced to pay more than 30 percent of his income to the government.

What you tax you get less of; what you subsidize you get more of. If you encourage producers by lessening their tax burden, you get prosperity. If you subsidize looters by giving them other people's property, you get dependency and economic ruin.

Democracy taken to excess has been described as two wolves and a sheep voting over what's for dinner. That would be the death of capitalism, and that would suit Democratic socialists just fine.

How to Score: GOP Style
February 17, 1995

What you tax you get less of; what you subsidize you get more of. That's the credo of supply-side economics, a school of thought that believes a society increases its standard of living when it actually produces more. This is in contrast to the liberal Keynesian notion that you create more wealth by artificially stimulating demand. Supply-siders cling to the old-fashioned belief that production must precede consumption. Increase taxes on productive behavior, and you'll get less of it.

Subsidize non-work alternatives through ever more generous welfare programs and you'll get more of that kind of behavior. In short, incentives matter. And the carrot is frequently more effective than the stick.

This conflict in philosophies is what's at the core of the current debate over *static* vs. *dynamic* scoring in economic models. I know that sounds awfully technical, but it's not as arcane as you might think. And the outcome of this debate will surely affect how much of your paycheck you get to keep after taxes.

One of the enduring liberal myths of the Reagan era is that there were huge tax cuts. Wrong. There were tax *rate* cuts: the percentage of tax you paid on your income. But the amount of dollars collected increased dramatically. (The national debt grew over the period because the level of federal spending increased even more dramatically.) The argument advanced by the Reaganites was that tax rates were too high and that by decreasing those tax rates, the resulting boost in incentives would actually produce more income and greater revenues to the Treasury. This is known as a "dynamic" revenue projection, and that's exactly what happened in the '80s.

A "static" revenue projection is one that assumes incentives don't matter, that higher tax rates will always produce more revenues and lower tax rates will always produce less. To test this mentality, Sen. Bob Packwood, R-Ore., asked the Joint Committee on Taxation to project how much revenue would be raised by increasing the tax rate on incomes over $200,000 to 100 percent. The JCT ran this through their static econometric model and came up with the following results: Tax revenue would increase by $204 billion in the first year, and by $299 billion in the fourth year. In other words, if you confiscated all income earned over $200,000, people would keep on working or investing to earn more just so they could give it to the tax collector. This is static scoring.

Any time an economic theory runs counter to common sense, it's not a very good economic theory. When a department store wants to raise more revenue it doesn't increase its unit prices, it cuts them. This is called a sale. Lower prices cause more units to be sold, hence more revenues. This is dynamic scoring. Lower marginal income tax rates mean a greater after-tax return on work and investment, hence more work and investment, more output, and a higher overall standard of living. Throw in less government and you've got an even better formula.

In 1979 when the Steiger Amendment ushered in lower capital gains tax rates, the Treasury department's static model forecast a loss in revenues. We got higher revenues. In 1986, capital gains tax rates were increased. The Congressional Budget Office's static model predicted capital gains tax collections of $225 billion by 1989. We fell $75 billion short of that as the volume of transactions suffered. A recent increase in the luxury tax on yachts produced not more revenue, as projected in a static model, but a depression in the industry as unit sales plummeted. Static models, you see, suspend the law of supply and demand. Unfortunately, nobody told that to the law.

Congressional Democrats and the Clinton White House prefer static scoring because of its bias against tax rate cuts and for tax rate increases.

Laura D'Andrea Tyson, Clinton's chief economic adviser, professes fear that dynamic scoring will overestimate revenues and worsen the deficit.

She has no corresponding concern that static scoring overestimates revenues by blithely assuming that tax rate increases will always produce more. What happens when they produce less?

Now that Republicans control Congress, perhaps they can bring some common-sense and a more realistic view of human nature into the budget process.

Should Government Workers be Considered Taxpayers?
November 15, 2012

With all the tumult over public-sector labor unions launched by the Battle of Wisconsin, there seems to be some dispute over whether those who work for government are actually "taxpayers."

Although, superficially, it may appear that they are, for the most part, they are not. Yes, they pay property taxes on their homes, sales taxes when they buy something and have income taxes withheld from their paychecks. But the fact remains, the source of their wages, salaries and benefits are, ultimately, the taxes of those who work in the private sector. If a government worker defers consumption in order to invest some of his pay in the stock market, he'll pay taxes on what that investment yields; but, it should be noted, the source of that investment gain is also the private sector. If he invests in a tax-exempt municipal bond, he may not pay taxes on the interest he earns, but, once again, the interest on that bond is ultimately provided by private-sector taxpayers. All income and wealth in a free-enterprise market economy comes from the private sector.

This may be confusing in a paper money and credit economy. So think of it in the context of a barter economy. Those who produce goods and services in the private sector, like farmers, textile manufacturers or carpenters, could agree to provide food, clothing and shelter to government workers. In exchange for that, the government workers would provide police protection, put out their fires and teach their children.

This certainly doesn't mean that public-sector workers don't earn their pay or that their jobs aren't necessary. Soldiers in Iraq and Afghanistan, for example, work for our government while risking their lives in our defense. They earn every penny and then some. We also need police and firefighters, jobs that, practically speaking, are best left to the public sector. Elected officials are necessarily public employees. Most K-12 teachers work for local governments, although this doesn't have to be the case. Public education could still be funded with tax dollars but delivered in private schools selected by individual parents through a voucher or scholarship system.

Nonetheless, it should be clear that the ability of government workers to receive compensation for their services is limited to the output of those who work in the private sector. Government taxes those private-sector providers and gives a share of what they produce to civil servants. Using a business analogy, think of all the things government does and its payroll as overhead on society and its economy. Overhead is necessary but can't take too great a share of revenues. That's the problem with government finances in Wisconsin and other states buckling under excessive public-sector payroll and pension costs.

Unlike the federal government, states and municipalities can't run budget deficits and print money. Their spending must be limited to their revenues. When their revenues fall, their spending must follow suit. It's understandable that government workers want to protect their rice bowl. They bridle at furloughs and pay freezes. But private-sector workers have suffered far worse during this recession and its aftermath, with large-scale job losses and pay cuts.

There's an old story about a company struggling to survive during a down economic period like this one. The personnel manager comes to the CEO's office. "Boss," he says, "employee morale is down because of all the pay cuts and layoffs." "Then we'll just have to keep cutting pay and firing people until morale improves," replies the boss. If our economy were booming and public coffers were overflowing, it would be nice to spread the wealth with generous rewards for government workers. But it isn't and we can't. Angry demonstrations, sieges at the state Capitol or even strikes against the public won't change that.

Reality

III. Politics

"Politics" is defined as the activity associated with the governance of a country or other area. Of course, politics can be a complicated process, and the history of the world shows that the results can be widely varied. In any case, whoever controls the levers of a government largely determines the destiny and well-being of the governed.

In this sense, monarchs, dictators and democratically elected governors all have derived their power from a broad political process and have exerted their will for both good and evil down through the ages. Wars within and among tribes or nations are ongoing results of political conflict. Whether people are subjugated, enslaved or free is ultimately a question of politics. How much or how little government imposes itself on its citizenry, demands from them, or influences the quality of life that they can live.

In addition to the personal ambitions and desires of individual political leaders and governors, there are underlying philosophies, religions and ideologies which characterize their pursuit of political dominance. An understanding of these factors provides us with keys with which to examine and evaluate the modern political scene in America today.

A good start is to recognize what President Ronald Reagan saw when he observed that: "As government expands, liberty contracts." Any student of history is well aware that the more intrusive a government is in the lives of its people, the prospects for life, liberty and the pursuit of happiness are correspondingly diminished

Leon Trotsky once noted that, "You may not be interested in war but war is interested in you." By the same token, you may not be interested in politics but politics is interested in you. Whether that applies to how much you'll pay in federal income taxes, whether or not our nation will go to war or who will run your local school board – it will all be a function of politics, with or without your involvement. So, if public ignorance and apathy are among our biggest civic shortcomings, woe betide those who say, "I don't know and I don't care."

Reality

The Great Political Divide

The Fundamental Differences between Liberals and Conservatives
August 6, 1986

It hardly matters whether the debate concerns economic policy, social issues, defense or foreign affairs; it just seems that all too often the fundamental differences between liberals and conservatives are simply irreconcilable. I think that's because they are. The only valuable, productive disagreements are between those who fundamentally agree. How can we come to terms on the details if we can't accept each other's basic assumptions? Between those who fundamentally disagree, especially in politics, we have not discussion but rhetoric, debating games and grandstanding.

If you'd like to better understand the irreconcilable differences between liberals and conservatives in this country, I'd recommend James Burnham's classic book, *Suicide of the West*. First published in 1964, it's just as insightful, or more so, today. Burnham addresses the basic conflict in world view and the order of values between liberals and conservatives. As a matter of fact, you may want to take this test yourself. First, let's list and define the key values Burnham isolates, then we'll prioritize them.

Liberty - Defined as national independence and self-government; sovereignty.

Freedom - In the sense of freedom or liberties of the individual.

Justice - To mean distributive justice of a social welfare sort; economic and social "justice" inclined more toward equality of result than merely equality of opportunity.

Peace - The absence of large-scale warfare among major powers.

Burnham observes that most people believe in all four of these values to one extent or another. We are frequently, however, forced to choose between one or another of them or, at least, to place them in order of relative importance.

Would you, for example, jeopardize peace to maintain liberty, or sacrifice individual freedom to achieve justice?

So here's the tough part: Rank these four values in order of their importance according to your own social and economic view of the world. In Burnham's judgment, the rankings might be:

Liberal	Conservative	Libertarian
Peace	Liberty	Freedom
Justice	Freedom	Peace
Freedom	Peace	Liberty
Liberty	Justice	Justice

Today's liberals have elevated pacifism to a principal value; they remain committed to the welfare state; and they increasingly oppose nationalism in favor of internationalism. To liberals, tradition is an obstacle. Their philosophy is utopian. Human nature can be changed; man is perfectible; disarmament is achievable; war can be eliminated. (Woody Allen once prophesied: "The lion and the calf shall lie down together, but the calf won't get much sleep.")

The conservative's order of values reflects a traditional view of human nature and society. It recognizes that the world is often a harsh and competitive place, populated by imperfect – and imperfectible – beings; that there are limitations to what public or private institutions can do to ameliorate this condition. Conservatives believe that the American experiment in democratic capitalism has produced the greatest measure of political freedom and economic achievement the world has ever known, and that it is threatened by serious adversaries both within and without. Conservatives believe that change can be for the bad as well as the good.

Liberals may not like the Soviet version of communism in practice, but they do not share the conservative revulsion to the theory of communism. As Burnham notes, liberals are "infected" with the promise of communism. They share many ideals: peace, egalitarianism, secularism, collectivism, full employment, free social services. How can liberals oppose communism when they share so many principles? The Soviet constitution – if it weren't a fraud – sounds, to some people, better than ours.

Liberals' preferred enemy is always to the right: South Africa, South Korea, Chile — never to the left. Cuba, Nicaragua, even the Soviet Union can be apologized for. To be fair, conservatives also apologize for right-wing governments, but that alliance tends to be pragmatic, not ideological. Liberals are genuinely sympathetic to the ideology of the left; they respect the intentions of leftist regimes if not their results.

It may well seem to many of our native liberals that they have more in common philosophically with redeemable, "progressive" Nicaraguan or Russian communists than with hopelessly "reactionary" American conservatives. Don't look for much in the way of detente in the war of ideas on the home front.

Separating Liberals and Conservatives
March 31, 2000

Before someone tells me where he stands, it's usually instructive to know where he sits. Beliefs, values and philosophy, I find, are often more important criteria when assessing a candidate than his positions on particular issues. The details of the issues will change. When they do, individuals will be guided by their beliefs – if they have any.

Ideological labels are a sort of shorthand for gauging those beliefs. Labels have their limitations, to be sure, but they can also be fairly accurate reflections of past performance and good predictors of future behavior. I've observed that those who protest the loudest about being labeled often have the most to hide.

There are plenty of definitions going around. A liberal is one who will give you the shirt off of someone else's back. A conservative is someone who doesn't want anything done for the first time. Liberals don't care what you do as long as it's mandatory. Leonard Peikoff described liberalism as, "A cry from one heart to another, bypassing any intermediary, such as the brain."

In *Bonfire of the Vanities,* a novel that transports the reader through a horrific odyssey of New York's criminal justice system, Tom Wolfe defines a liberal as a conservative who's been arrested. Then there are neo-conservatives: former liberals who are now conservatives. And neo-liberals: former liberals who are still liberal. I like Irving Kristol's explanation: "A neo-conservative is a liberal who's been mugged by reality, a neo-liberal is a liberal who's been mugged by reality but has refused to press charges."

There is no one, perfect definition of liberal and conservative. Most thinking people have tendencies, but there's always room for exceptions. Although I regard myself as a conservative in the contemporary use of that term, I'm a liberal in the original sense – a classical liberal – in the tradition of Locke, Hume, Burke and Adam Smith. Back then, "liberal" connoted individual liberty. While his progressivism told a different story, Woodrow Wilson once observed that, "The history of liberalism is the history of man's efforts to restrain the growth of government." This was before Franklin D. Roosevelt and the New Deal.

In a letter to the editor, a proud, unabashed, self-avowed liberal sought to turn the tables on "right-wingers," as he labeled them, who would use the term "liberals" as a slur. He said he welcomed the label. Citing *Dictionary.com* as his definitive source, he instructed us ignorant right-wingers that a liberal is one who is broad-minded, not limited by traditional or authoritarian attitudes or dogmas, one who is free from bigotry, favoring new ideas for progress, tolerant of the ideas and behavior of others, etc. You get the idea.

Well isn't that special? While library bookcases are overflowing with volumes on this subject, our liberal friend confines his search for truth to an entry of a few dozen self-serving words in an online dictionary that treats the term behaviorally rather than as a political agenda. Dictionaries are wonderful tools, but they have their limitations. They're a starting point; not the oracle. Would he rely on *Dictionary.com* to explain the meaning of life? And I don't mean the meaning of "life." I mean the "meaning of life." Maybe he could also sum up the collected studies of philosophy, theology, mythology, metaphysics, history and science in a couple of sentences on that subject, too.

Another convenient cliché is that liberals are progressive and conservatives are against change. Really? This generalization has severe and disqualifying limitations. How is that conservatives are the ones that want to do away with the income tax, end the public school monopoly and privatize Social Security, while liberals staunchly defend the status quo in these areas?

Once upon a time, the status quo was government oppression in the form of monarchy and serfdom. Eighteenth century revolutionary thinkers like Burke, Hume, Montesquieu and Adam Smith advocated a break from that tradition asserting natural, God-given rights to individuals. In the form of political economy, this movement later became known as "classical liberalism," connoting individual liberty. It ultimately took the form of self-determination, private enterprise, property rights, free trade, limited government, self-reliance, individual rights and responsibilities, and an aversion to high taxes.

Over the years, the terminology has morphed, with big government leftists – true to their confiscatory instincts – even expropriating the term "liberal," which has lost its intrinsic meaning and is now simply a label identifying those on the left.

If the root of the word relates to individual freedom, it would hardly apply to the collective and coercive public policy agenda of liberalism today imposing quotas, politically correct behavior, regulations and taxes. Today's liberals have so sullied the term that even *they* have shied away from it, reverting to an oldie but a goodie from the lefty lexicon, "progressive."

Moving beyond epithets and simplistic dictionary definitions, the practical differences between contemporary conservatives and liberals are best observed by contrasting their values, beliefs and positions on fundamental and enduring public policy questions. Here are a few samples:

• Conservatives believe in individual freedom and responsibility. Liberals believe in sacrificing individual freedom for socially desirable outcomes. Liberals believe that one of government's primary roles is social engineering.

• Conservatives believe in limited government. Liberals believe in intrusive government when required to achieve societal needs. (Exception: social-issues conservatives advocate government intrusion on matters of abortion, drugs and pornography.)

• Conservatives believe in free markets. Liberals believe in government controls and central planning.

• Conservatives believe that some problems have no solution, that they can only be mitigated at best. Liberals believe that most every problem has a government solution.

• Conservatives are concerned about the production of wealth. Liberals are concerned about the redistribution of it.

• Conservatives believe in equality of opportunity. Liberals believe in equality of outcome.

• Conservatives believe that human nature is what makes us imperfectible. Liberals believe that human nature can be changed and perfected.

• Conservatives are nationalists. Liberals hope for world government.

• Conservatives believe in peace through strength. Liberals believe in peace through cooperation and good will.

And conservatives are not paranoids. I know I'm not. Even

though there's a worldwide plot by my enemies intended to make people believe that I am.

The Continuum from Left to Right
July 22, 2015

I've written this column several times over the years, to include topical figures of the day. I'm updating it here with contemporary names and a few historical ones as reference points.

The political center is valuable turf. Americans are leery of extremists. That's why politicians, interest groups and media types are so fond of mushy terms like "moderate." When we talk about liberal bias in the media, we're talking about a crowd that clusters around the left-center of the political spectrum. When media liberals protest that there are others farther to their left, they're correct, of course, but so what? Yes, the late Gus Hall, perennial head of the Communist Party USA, was to the left of *The New York Times* editorial board, but that doesn't make the *Times* middle-of-the road, much less conservative. Colorado is south of Wyoming but it's still considerably north of the equator.

Discerning consumers of news, opinion and political rhetoric filter what they read, see and hear. They're sensitive to the source. It's important to know where someone sits before he tells you where he stands. So here's a little drill, the point of which is to show gradations in ideological positioning among a sampling of prominent people, organizations and media along a continuum from left to right. Any such exercise is subjective, of course, and complicated when you lump together a hodgepodge of economic, defense, foreign policy, domestic and social issues to come up with a composite placement. (Incidentally, libertarianism defies placement on a left-right scale.) Consider this a starting point for discussion:

Far-Left - Communist Party USA, Socialist Workers Party, Green Party, National Lawyers Guild, *The Nation* magazine, *Mother Jones* magazine, Institute for Policy Studies, Media Matters for America, Code Pink, *MSNBC*, MoveOn.org, *Daily Kos*, Ed Schultz, Rachel Maddow, Noam Chomsky, George Soros, Bernie Sanders, Elizabeth Warren, Ralph Nader.

Left - *New York Times,* ACLU, National Education Association, Barack Obama, E.J. Dionne, Eugene Robinson, Paul Krugman, Thomas Friedman, Thom Hartmann, People for the American Way, Sierra Club, Environmental Defense Fund, Children's Defense Fund, League of Women Voters, National Organization for Women, Hillary Clinton (running for the Democratic Party nomination).

Left-Center - Hillary Clinton (as the Democratic Party nominee), *Time* Magazine, *The Washington Post, ABC, NBC, CBS, CNN, PBS, NPR*, Brookings Institution, Bill Clinton, Joe Lieberman, *Economist* magazine, *USA Today.*

Center - Other than Justicia, the blindfolded lady holding the scales of justice, I'm hard-pressed to place anyone or anything in the absolute center.

Right-Center - Mike Rosen, Ronald Reagan, *Wall Street Journal* (editorials)*, Weekly Standard, Fox News Channel*, Heritage Foundation, Hoover Institution, American Enterprise Institute, Federalist Society, Club for Growth, Peggy Noonan, George Will, Charles Krauthammer, Paul Ryan, Marco Rubio, Chris Christie, Scott Walker, Jeb Bush, Mitt Romney, Hugh Hewitt.

Right - *National Review* magazine, *American Spectator* magazine, *Human Events, Investor's Business Daily* (editorials)*, Newsmax, Conservative Review,* Ted Cruz, Mike Lee, Rick Santorum, Rush Limbaugh, Michael Savage, Grover Norquist, Tea Party, Eagle Forum, Phyllis Schlafly, Pat Buchanan, National Rifle Association.

Far-Right - Ku Klux Klan, Aryan Nation, John Birch Society, Militia Groups, Timothy McVeigh, Lyndon LaRouche, Liberty Lobby (now defunct), the late Fred Phelps of the Westboro Baptist Church.

Long Live the Differences
March 25, 2006

Some people believe that all social problems have solutions; other people believe that some problems cannot be solved, only mitigated, and that public policy is a matter of tradeoffs. People in the leftist camp tend to fall into the first category, those on the right, in the latter.

In the *Political Junkie Handbook*, Michael Crane offers a provocative listing of "100+ Differences Between the Left and Right." Here's a sampling with some of my own embellishments and additions:

Left: Human rights are more important than property rights. Right: Property rights are the foundation of all rights.

Left: Karl Marx. Right: Adam Smith.

Left: Humanity. Right: Individuality.

Left: Quotas. Right: Merit.

Left: A fair and living wage. Right: Wages must be based on productivity.

Left: Protectionism. Right: Free trade.

Left: Wage and price controls. Right: Supply and demand.

Left: Regulate. Right: Deregulate.

Left: Coercion. Right: Volunteerism.

Left: Idealism. Right: Common sense.

Left: Counterculture. Right: Judeo-Christian tradition.

Left: Feminize men/masculinize women. Right: Men and women are equals on opposite poles.

Left: Boys and girls are the same, except girls are better. Right: Respect the differences between the sexes.

Left: Herstory. Right: History.

Left: Nurture. Right: Nature.

Left: Mass transit. Right: Automobiles.

Left: Marijuana. Right: Cigars.

Left: Welfare. Right: Charity.

Left: Differently abled. Right: Handicapped.

Left: Visualize peace. Right: Peace through strength.

Left: Feelings. Right: Thoughts.

Left: Centralization and government planning. Right: Decentralization and free enterprise.

Left: Cooperation. Right: Competition.

Left: Alec Baldwin. Right: Charlton Heston.

Left: Alger Hiss. Right: Whittaker Chambers.

Left: John Maynard Keynes. Right: Frederich Hayek.

Left: John Kenneth Galbraith. Right: Milton Friedman.

Left: Jean Jacques Rousseau. Right: Edmund Burke.

Left: Gore Vidal. Right: William F. Buckley, Jr.

Left: Michael Moore. Right: George W. Bush.

Left: 2+2 = whatever. Right: 2+2 = 4.

Left: Public schools as laboratories for social engineering. Right: Basic and rigorous academics.

Left: Government school monopoly. Right: Choice and competition.

Left: Veggie soy burgers. Right: McDonald's.

Left: Granola. Right: Wheaties.

Left: Communes. Right: Gated communities.

Left: Mom & Pop's Organic Food Emporium. Right: Wal-Mart.

Left: Boulder. Right: Mayberry, RFD.

Left: Sandals. Right: Wingtips.

Left: Ward Churchill. Right: Bill Bennett.

Left: Hunter S. Thompson. Right: Thomas Wolfe.

Left: Demonstrators. Right: Cops.

Left: Pacifists. Right: Marines.

Left: Takers. Right: Doers.

Left: Tax receivers. Right: Taxpayers.

Left: There is too much inequality of wealth. Right: Free people are not equal; equal people are not free.

Left: Redistribute wealth. Right: Create wealth.

Left: Equality of outcome. Right: Equality of opportunity.

Left: Security seeking. Right: Risk taking.

Left: Labor unions. Right: Right to work.

Left: A rat is a pig is a dog is a boy. Right: Mankind is the pinnacle of creation.

Left: Environmental purity. Right: Environmental/commercial tradeoffs.

Left: Windmills. Right: Nuclear power plants.

Left: Bicycles. Right: SUVs.

Left: Volvo. Right: Lexus.

Left: Self-esteem is an entitlement. Right: Self-esteem is earned.

Left: Al Franken. Right: Rush Limbaugh.

Left: Capital punishment is uncivilized. Right: Murder is uncivilized.

Left: World government. Right: U.S. Constitution.

Left: Foreign aid. Right: Foreign investment.

As Ayn Rand once observed, if your differences appear to be irreconcilable, the first thing you should do is check your premises.

Which Dean was I with?
August 18, 2006

John Dean is the former White House legal counsel to President Richard Nixon who served as the chief prosecution witness during the Watergate investigation and trials. In exchange for his damning testimony, Dean scored a plea bargain that spared him doing hard time like some of the others caught up in the scandal.

Since then he's made a career out of speaking and writing bad things about Republicans and conservatives. Perhaps this is his way of doing penance, if not a condition of his plea bargain. On the heels of his last book, *Worse Than Watergate: The Secret Presidency of George W. Bush* (Secret? I thought it was in all the newspapers.), Dean's latest contribution is, *Conservatives Without Conscience*, a purported play on words of Barry Goldwater's 1960 book, *The Conscience of a Conservative*. Incredibly, Dean claims, "I still consider myself to be a 'Goldwater conservative' on many issues," as he proceeds to attack the GOP for moving radically right, as he sees it.

During a recent in-studio interview with Dean on my radio show, I took him through a number of Goldwater's positions from government spending to taxes, from Social Security to Vietnam. As a 1960s Goldwater conservative myself, I must say I don't recognize much of Goldwater in Dean. And I can assure you he certainly isn't a Ronald Reagan conservative.

His new book is heavy on criticism and psychoanalysis of conservatives by liberal academics, particularly social scientists. What a surprise: Left-wing college professors disapprove of conservative Republicans. He refers to one "researcher" who told him that, "Authoritarian conservatives are enemies of freedom, anti-democratic, anti-equality, highly prejudiced, mean-spirited, power hungry, Machiavellian and amoral." Whew, that's a mouthful! This, of course, is unbiased clinical research from an objective academic liberal.

Another of his expert witnesses is John T, Jost, a professor of psychobabble at New York University, who collaborated in a study, *Political Conservatism as Motivated Cognition*. Jost and company concluded that conservatives, "have a heightened psychological need to manage uncertainty and threat," and that psychological factors associated with conservatives include "fear, intolerance of ambiguity, need for certainty and structure in life, overreaction to threat, and a disposition to dominate others." Really?

Tendentious "studies" like this, conducted by liberals, tend to work backward from predetermined conclusions – in this case that conservatism is a psychosis. A similarly inclined *conservative* professor of psychology or social science – if there were any – could make much the same observation about liberals.

To begin with, liberals are hopeless utopians. Even worse, they're *coercive* utopians. They're the ones with "a disposition to dominate others." Isn't that what liberal nannyism is all about? They want to tell others what to eat and drink, not to smoke, whom to hire, whom not to offend, what kind of car to drive, etc. They want to tax your income and redistribute it to others while you're alive and tax your estate when you die. Talk about domination.

A need to manage uncertainty and threat, and create structure in life? What would you call liberal inventions like cradle-to-grave welfare, Social Security, academic tenure, labor unions and socialized medicine?

Overreaction to threats? Liberals would ban any substance at the drop of a rat. They're scared of guns, obesity, fast foods, popcorn, cell phones in cars. Talk about fear, Al Gore is positively phobic about his vision of an impending global warming holocaust. On the other hand, liberals habitually *under*react to tangible threats like the looming financial collapse of Social Security and Medicare when the baby boomers retire. They were blind to the threat of communism before and during the Cold War. They're in denial today about the global ambitions of Islamofascists, while the ACLU is paranoid about the "trashing of the Constitution" when essential and reasonable trade-offs are made between freedom and security to deter terrorist acts.

Fear? All people fear something. Conservatives and liberals simply fear and desire different things based on their ideology, their political agenda and their disparate notions of human nature, the role of government and the way the world works.

Dean laments the "incivility" of some conservatives, today, as if this were the exclusive province of the right. When I asked him about the incivility of people like Michael Moore, Cindy Sheehan, the MoveOn.org crowd and hysterical left-wing bloggers on the DailyKos, Dean ducked the question. And how is it that this self-described "Goldwater conservative" never finds occasion to criticize lefties and Democrats?

He said he was John Dean, but he sounded strangely like Howard Dean.

Ultimately, It's Left or Right
December 8, 2006

"Not *left* or *right*; *right* or *wrong*!" That's the current marketing slogan of a local talk radio station (not mine). It's a clever turn of a phrase and an interesting approach to establishing product differentiation from competing talk stations that promote the conventional split between liberals and conservatives. This imaging strategy is designed to convey the impression that the programmers, personalities and producers on that station somehow rise above the limitations of ideology and the pettiness of partisan politics.

In theory, this might attract listeners that supposedly want something different from the standard issues-oriented talk radio fare. In practice, that station is pretty much like any other of this genre and the hosts and topics split along the same liberal-conservative divides on political, social and economic matters.

But let's get back to that slogan: "Not left or right; right or wrong!" It's catchy, but does it hold up rationally? Right or wrong is highly subjective. Now, I'm not one of those abstract moral relativists who flatly declares that there are no rights or wrongs. Sometimes there are. But irreconcilable disagreements on public policy are often based on honestly conflicting differences of ideology, values, religious beliefs, notions of human nature, economic understanding, concepts of the role of government, and objectives, to name just a few variables. In those cases, right or wrong cannot be objectively determined. That becomes simply a matter of opinion. In the final analysis, it usually does come down to left or right.

Thomas Sowell, in his book, *A Conflict of Visions*, addresses the ideological origins of political struggles. He observes that competing notions of fundamental concepts like freedom, equality, justice and rights are dependent upon either a leftist's or rightist's beliefs about the nature of man.

Today's leftists – or liberals – are ideological descendants of the likes of William Godwin, Rousseau and Harold Laski, and have an "unconstrained," utopian view of man's perfectibility and the unlimited potential of government programs.

Rightists – or conservatives – have a "constrained," practical

104

view of man's imperfections and limitations, and the limitations of government. Adam Smith, Thomas Hobbes, Edmund Burke and Milton Friedman are in this camp.

The fundamental socialist notion that a man will work as hard and as creatively for the benefit of strangers as he would for himself and his family is a classic conflict between the unconstrained and constrained vision. Such community selflessness might work for a while on a homogeneous Israeli kibbutz, but not in a diverse society of 300 million people.

And make no mistake about it – contemporary liberalism is rooted in socialism, the Marxist Prime Directive: from each according to his ability, to each according to his need. The historic, literal definition of socialism: state ownership of the means of production, has evolved over the years. The model today – and the goal of American liberals – is a European-style democratic socialism. As Friedrich Hayek noted some 30 years ago: "Socialism has come to mean chiefly the extensive redistribution of incomes through taxation and institutions of the welfare state." The appearance of private ownership is maintained but it becomes increasingly an illusion as government dictates the terms of production through regulations, and reallocates the fruits of production through taxation and social spending.

It's currently fashionable among liberals, especially those of a more radically leftist variety, to shun the "liberal" moniker – which suffers from bad public relations these days – in favor of an oldie but goodie: "progressive." But little has changed from the Progressive Era of 100 years ago. It still means "progress" on the road to socialism.

The right believes in individual freedom and responsibility, property rights, free markets, limited government, nationalism, sovereignty, peace through strength, and traditional American values. The left believes in collectivism, entitlement, social engineering, multiculturalism, racial preferences, expansive government, central economic planning, peace through world government and post-modernism. Conservatives believe in equality of opportunity. Liberals believe in equality of outcome, the kind of leveling egalitarianism that punishes excellence through high taxes in order to subsidize mediocrity, misfortune, sloth and failure.

Capitalism works because it's consistent with human nature. Rewarding excellence breeds more of it. Socialism is doomed to fail because it misreads human nature and sends counterproductive economic signals, discouraging behavior that breeds prosperity and encouraging behavior that breeds poverty. Conservatives believe in voluntary economic exchanges. Liberals believe in mandates, controls and requirements that direct individuals to behave in a socially desirable manner – as determined, of course, by liberals.

Conservatives believe they are right, and liberals believe themselves to be right. That argument can't be won. Ultimately, it's not right or wrong; it's right or left.

Fascists Reside on the Left
September 8, 1995

In the last session of the Colorado Legislature, the Republican majority had the good sense to defeat, in committee, a so-called "single payer" health-care system championed by Democrats. This is the big-government approach to health care inspired by countries like Canada and Sweden which are farther along the road to socialism than we are. You may recall that we had this debate nationally, when Bill and Hillary's version of statist healthcare Utopia was rejected by the American public.

One of the opponents of the local version was Sen. Bob Schaffer, R-Fort Collins, who was kind enough to send me an exchange of correspondence on this topic between him and some activists from the Denver Gray Panthers, who were lobbying for the measure. The Gray Panthers are no better or worse than the horde of other special-interest groups lined up at the public trough. Like the rest of them, their credo is simply: "After me, you come first." In this case the "me" is older people.

The main source of the Panthers' anger at Senator Schaffer was his characterization of their health care model as socialist or fascist. One outraged respondent, a World War II veteran, protested that he, himself, had enlisted in his country's armed forces to fight fascism 50 years ago.

The Panthers' confusion no doubt stems from the use of the term "fascist" as a popular epithet for leftists to hurl at principled conservatives. Maybe this is a good time to set the record straight. The irony here is that Schaffer is using the term correctly. Government-controlled health care does smack of fascism.

Fascism, Nazism and communism are all variations of the politics of the left. Mussolini, Hitler and Stalin were cut from the same cloth. In constructing the Third Reich, Hitler borrowed from Mussolini's fascist model in Italy after World War I. But Hitler was a socialist. He was just a *nationalist* socialist (that's where the abbreviation "Nazi" comes from), as compared to Marx and Lenin who were international socialists. They were devoted to this ideology and wanted the whole world to adopt it. Hitler didn't give a damn about the welfare of the world, except that he wanted to dominate it.

Safire's Political Dictionary, identifying the root of the term "fascism," traces it to *fascio*, the Italian word for "bundle" or "group." Fascism is inherently collective. The McGraw-Hill *Dictionary of Modern Economics* offers this definition: "A totalitarian, collective system of government in which central control is exercised over all economic, political and social activities....It is based on an exaggerated nationalism which entirely eliminates individualism and regards the state as the highest expression of the will of the group.... Private ownership of production is maintained, but extreme restrictions are imposed on private economic freedoms. Decisions on production, investment, prices and wages are all subject to arbitrary government control."

This hardly sounds like the limited government, free market, individualist philosophy of conservatives like Milton Friedman, Ronald Reagan or Newt Gingrich. It sounds a lot more like the agenda of liberal Democrats, radical environmentalists and advocates for socialized medicine.

The essential difference between fascism and communism is that under communism the state officially owns the means of production, while under fascism, although the illusion of private ownership is maintained, the state effectively controls what you can do with your property or your income. This is what conservatives want less of in this country and it's precisely what liberals want more of.

Once you've established the principle that health care (or housing, or food stamps, or child care, or automobile insurance, or a job, or a guaranteed minimum income, etc.) is a right – or an *entitlement*, in contemporary political terminology – and that government has the responsibility of providing it at someone else's expense, then the only thing left to debate is the details. The devil may be in the details, but why unleash him in the first place?

It's the very premise of boundless government entitlements that's being challenged these days. What the national debate is all about right now is scaling back the reach of government, not expanding it. After all, we don't want fascism here. Do we?

Yes, They're Socialists
July 16, 2009

At a recent meeting of the Republican National Committee, a resolution was offered calling on Democrats to rename their party the "Democratic Socialist Party." Obviously, this was little more than a publicity stunt since Democrats aren't about to take any instructions from the GOP. But it raises a legitimate point. Why do liberal Democrats in this country bristle at the "S" word when their counterparts in Europe embrace it proudly?

The SPD is the oldest political party in post-World War II Germany. Its official name is the Social Democratic Party (Sozialdemokratische Partei Deutschlands). In France, President Francois Mitterand ruled from 1981-95 as head of the Socialist Party. The single most powerful interest group on the left, here and in Europe, is labor unions. So at least give the Brits credit for candor. They call their major left-wing party the Labour Party.

The Democratic Party in the U.S. is also the party of organized labor. It just doesn't call itself that. There's not much difference in ideology or agenda between German SPDs, French Socialists, British Labourites and American Democrats, only a question of degree and timing. The Democrats' aversion to calling themselves what they really are is simply a matter of practical political marketing.

Yes, President Barack Obama and the Democratic Party are socialists. And that's not name-calling. They're not communists. They don't advocate a constitutional, single-party dictatorship of the proletariat. But they do want to escalate our "progress" on the road to Euro-socialism. (That's what they mean when they call themselves "progressives," the fashionable term for left-liberals.)

Contemporary liberalism/progressivism is very much rooted in socialism. The Marxian Prime Directive remains: from each according to his ability; to each according to his need. The historical, textbook definition of socialism included state ownership of the means of production. These days, the rhetoric of American socialism has become more coy and euphemistic. You might call it "neo-socialism," wherein the appearance of private ownership is maintained but becomes an illusion as government dictates the terms of production through regulation and reallocates the fruits of production through taxation. As Friedrich Hayek noted more than 30 years ago, "Socialism has come to mean chiefly the extensive redistribution of incomes through taxation and institutions of the welfare state."

The takeover of General Motors and Chrysler leaves little of the illusion of private ownership, with the federal government firing and hiring chief executives, knee-capping holders of secured debt, dictating production and disproportionally reallocating shares of common stock to unions.

Cap and trade is the biggest government intrusion into private industry since the Great Depression. Legislators and government bureaucrats will set arbitrary standards for CO_2 emissions for industries and individual companies, imposing massive costs and energy inefficiencies throughout the economy while chasing the illusion of manmade global warming. The "greenest" thing about it will be the money that lines the pockets of lobbyists and the companies that receive favorable treatment, and the campaign war chests of politicians.

After a few local stops for appearance's sake, Obamacare will be an express to socialized medicine. The price tag will be wildly in excess of the Democrats' phony projections as were the original cost estimates of Medicare and Medicaid.

Never has our government spent money it doesn't have on this scale in peacetime. The massive increase in federal debt to fund these programs will soak up trillions in capital, crowding out financial resources that otherwise would be available to private enterprise. If all this isn't socialism, it's a good imitation.

The Myth of Big-Business Conservatives
July 7, 1995

Liberals have offered some lame excuses to rebut the charge that the major media are slanted in their direction. One of the lamest goes something like this: "How can the media be biased when its outlets are run by business people? Everyone knows business is conservative."

If by business people we mean *big-business* people, that brand of conservatism might include terms like: traditional, reluctant to change, and risk averse. They may also be conservative in dress and manner. The political definition of conservative, however, is another matter.

Conservatives believe in competition, free markets, deregulation, ending subsidies, scaling back government social spending, privatizing public education, term limits. They don't believe in socialized medicine of the Bill and Hillary variety. Some conservatives have a social agenda as well, including issues like homosexuality and abortion.

Most businesses, especially big corporations, wouldn't touch those last two issues with a 10-foot pole. On the others, they tend to be either silent or opposed to the conservative position. In the *Wall Street Journal* on March 13, Chrysler President Robert Lutz had this to say: "Large manufacturers need to remind Republican leadership that in the past, Republican positions and policies have been extremely damaging to big business. On trade and health care, the Democratic positions very often were more aligned to the interests of big business." This may be shortsighted, but it's what passes for conventional corporate wisdom.

You see, the bigger a corporation gets, the more it resembles government. It gets bureaucratic, political and stodgy. Top executives and middle managers become careerists; they protect their turf and their budgets; they don't like to take chances. What they like most is to get in league with government to protect themselves from competition.

Individual business people may be registered Republicans and ideologically conservative in their private lives, but they don't behave that way when acting corporately. Unfortunately, most business people, when in their pinstriped uniforms, are pacifists in the war of ideas – if not collaborators with the forces of big government.

"Pragmatic" corporate PACs are notorious donors to incumbent Democrats. Corporate charity is similarly pandering. In its 1994 study, "Patterns of Corporate Philanthropy," the Capital Research Center found that of the 36 nonprofit advocacy groups receiving $250,000 or more from corporations, 27 were liberal, and that for every $1 given to right-of-center public affairs groups, $3.42 was given to left-leaning organizations.

Corporate politics is a war of survival. A high public profile on controversial issues can expose you to criticism in the liberal media and boycotts from activists. Call it the Coors Syndrome if you like. In years past, Joe and Bill Coors were identified with a number of noble causes about which they felt strongly. It might have been good for the republic, but it made it tougher for the marketing people to sell beer. The company keeps a lower profile now. Other businesses have learned from the Coors experience. Ben and Jerry, of course, can use their ice cream revenues to support liberal causes with impunity. But that's different; in the media, liberal causes are OK.

Unmotivated to use nonmedia businesses as a vehicle to advance conservative ideas, business people are even less inclined to do so in media businesses. The days of the publisher/journalist writing his own editorials are over. Today's newspaper or TV executives are MBAs and marketing types. They're concerned about budgets, return on investment, market share, advertising revenues and Nielsen ratings, not editorial viewpoints. They care more about principal than principles. They'd just as soon leave the content end of the business to the "professionals" – as long as the bottom line holds. If you don't see yourself as a combatant in the war of ideas, why take on the entrenched liberal establishment in the newsroom or on the editorial page? Who needs the hassle?

CBS is a $4 billion business that racked up a 102 percent return on stockholders' equity in 1994, third-best in all the Fortune 500. It's filthy rich with business executives. If they're conservative, why don't they have a like-minded anchor? Why *do* they have liberals like Dan Rather and the whole crew at *60 Minutes*?

Politics Is Inherently Partisan

Majority-Party Politics
November 13, 1998

"Disaster." That's the word Democrats, and even some Republicans, have used to describe Republican fortunes in last week's election. The Democrats, of course, are cheerleading for their side. But discouraged Republicans are being too hard on themselves.

In Colorado, Republicans had a great year, holding their legislative majorities while electing a governor for the first time in a quarter century. In 14 contiguous states, from Nebraska to North Dakota, Republicans have all 14 governorships and dominate congressional delegations and state legislatures. Nationwide, there are still 31 Republican governors and 17 Democrats.

The GOP did lose a few state legislative bodies, but still control many more than it did in 1994, trailing the Democrats by only 53-45. In Congress, the GOP kept its 53-45 advantage in the Senate and, although losing five seats in the House, still remains the majority party. Given high Republican expectations, the 1998 election was a disappointment and a setback, but not a disaster. What happened to the Democrats in 1994, when they lost their congressional majorities and took a bath at the state level as well; *that* was a disaster.

If the GOP wishes to rebound in 2000, it needs to learn some hard lessons from this year's showing. The most important is party unity. After years in the minority-party wilderness, rank-and-file Republicans have to understand what it takes to be a majority party – which is where all the power is. That requires, first, an understanding of what party politics is. It's the art of the doable. I'm a Republican, not because the Republican philosophy and political agenda are a perfect fit with my own – no party could offer that – but because it's the best fit available. A majority party can't be all things to all people. The bigger the tent, the more compromises its occupants have to make. Ideological purity in politics is a self-indulgence enjoyed only by those with no realistic aspirations for affecting public policy or exercising power.

Bill Owens' razor-thin victory over Gail Schoettler is an object lesson. Owens is a mainstream conservative; Schoettler, a mainstream liberal. The choice was clear. Once nominated, the only intra-party opposition Owens encountered came from his right. Soon to be former state party Chairman Steve Curtis, with his own social-issues agenda, judged Owens to be insufficiently pure, and engaged in a preposterous demonstration of disloyalty when he told a talk show host that he wouldn't say whether he'd vote for Owens.

What did he hope to accomplish? If supporting Owens compromised Curtis' principles, he had no business being party chairman when the ultimate function of the job is to get Republicans elected. It's not as if Bill Owens was some kind of kook like David Duke or Geoffrey Fieger.

Then we had Tim Leonard, running as the candidate of the American Constitution Party, a single-issue anti-abortion faction. It wasn't enough for this crowd that Owens was pro-life and Schoettler was pro-choice. In their minds, Owens wasn't pro-life *enough*. In the end, the measure of Leonard's support was the mere 11,000 votes he got out of more than 1.3 million. But since Owens won by only 8,000, it was almost enough to cost him the election. When you consider that virtually all of Leonard's votes would have otherwise gone to Owens, you can see how self-destructive this kind of moral exhibitionism is. Had they denied Owens the election, the anti-abortionists would have been rewarded with a pro-abortion governor. This is political insanity.

Americans who are conservative on economic, domestic and defense issues and who also have a strong religious orientation are a vital part of the Republican Party. They're called the religious right, and represent perhaps 20 million votes. The GOP can't be a majority party without them. But the religious right must realize that there are limits to what the party can do to advance its agenda without driving unaffiliated swing voters away. This isn't Iran, where Islamic fundamentalists run the government. Mainstream American politics is secular. It comes down to a rational trade-off. The religious right doesn't have the votes to be a majority party on its own. They can make the GOP the majority party and exercise some influence from within, or splinter off and let the Democrats win by default, in which case they'll have no majority-party influence.

Republicans vs. Democrats on Matters of Principle
December 10, 2009

A conservative Republican National Committee member from Indiana, Jim Bopp, has drawn up a checklist of conservative principles for GOP candidates. He'll offer a resolution at the RNC's winter meeting proposing that candidates would have to agree to at least seven of the 10 points to qualify for party support and funding. Liberal pundits and Democratic activists have kindly offered unsolicited advice to Republicans that this is a bad idea. Coming from people who hope for nothing but Republican defeats at the polls, this advice is of questionable value. If liberals really thought this would be bad for the GOP, they'd stay mum.

Rather than an outright litmus test, the list is an affirmation of the general Republican vision, offering voters a real alternative to Democrats. I've gone through it point by point and can't imagine that even squishy Republicans would have much difficulty in scoring at least a seven. The list includes support for smaller government, lower deficits and lower taxes; market-based health care reforms instead of Obamacare; market-based energy policies instead of cap and tax; secret-ballot union elections for workers; legal immigration and assimilation; victory in Iraq and Afghanistan; nuclear-weapons containment of Iran and North Korea; self-determination of individual states on marriage laws; denial of taxpayer funding for abortions; and, protection for individual rights on gun ownership.

I fully understand there are congressional districts where no Republican, much less a rock-ribbed conservative, can hope to win (like Denver in Colorado's 1st Congressional District). But even in moderate-to-liberal congressional swing districts, where a moderate Republican has a shot, a Republican who scores six or lower is probably in the wrong party. While I recognize that in order to achieve a legislative majority the GOP must be necessarily hospitable to liberalish types like Maine senators Olympia Snowe and Susan Collins (what can you do – it's the Northeast), the line has to be drawn somewhere (e.g., Lowell Weicker in Connecticut).

I applaud the GOP for clearly telling voters where the party and its candidates sit on fundamental beliefs so that voters can better understand where the candidates stand on issues. Let me help Democrats do the same, with my checklist of their principles:

- The U.S. Constitution is too restrictive and amending it is too much trouble. We support judges who will re-interpret it according to their ideology and political preferences and legislate from the bench.

- Individual liberty and property rights must be subordinated to the collective welfare. Those who have "too much" must be leveled through high taxes; those who have less are "entitled" to their fair share of the income and wealth of others. From each according to *his* ability, to each according to *her* need.

- Private enterprise is obsessed with profits. Capitalism is synonymous with greed. Without labor unions, workers will be exploited, unjustly paid and unfairly treated. Only government bureaucrats can be trusted to regulate commerce, determine what will be produced, how it will be produced, at what price it will be sold and how heavily it will be taxed.

- Americans are too materialistic and wasteful of natural resources. Our lifestyle must be scaled back and our wealth more justly distributed to underprivileged nations.

- Life is fraught with risk. Americans must be protected from their own bad choices through regulations and from depredation through cradle-to-grave social programs.

- Guns are too dangerous and can be used to commit crimes. Americans cannot be trusted to own them.

- Patriotism is selfish and destructive. Nationalism is evil and leads to war. U.S. military spending must be cut and American sovereignty sacrificed to the greater good of the world community, as determined by a majority vote in the United Nations.

Most Democrats should have no trouble scoring a perfect 10.

The "Nonpartisan" Sham
October 20, 2006

I got an email recently from someone who asked if I could direct him to a Web site or some other source for objective, nonpartisan analysis of candidates and election issues. I told him no such oracle existed. "Nonpartisan" is surely the most overused and deceptive term in politics. It's supposed to indicate neutrality and independence from any particular political party. It might even suggest objectivity. But objectivity is an ideal, not a reality. We are, each of us, the product of our experiences, perceptions, values, beliefs and, yes, biases. None of us is capable of objectivity.

Some use the term "nonpartisan" as a cloaking device to disguise an agenda or ideology. I cringe when I hear politically committed think tanks described as "nonpartisan," They may not be *officially* linked to the Democratic or Republican Party, but that doesn't mean they aren't intellectually aligned with one or the other.

In Colorado, the Bell Policy Center may not be an official arm of the Democratic Party, but it's liberal through and through, and has a rooting interest in getting Democrats elected as the vehicle for converting its ideology into public policy. Similarly, the Independence Institute's conservative/libertarian agenda is geared toward the Republicans.

Nonpartisan, therefore, doesn't mean nonpolitical and it certainly doesn't mean non-ideological. Now, don't get me wrong, I like ideology. That term combines two of my favorite things: ideas and logic. I'm both ideological and partisan. I just don't like it when people or organizations are deceptive about such things.

Maybe you've heard a political ad running on the radio by AARP. It starts with what's supposed to be a clever attention grabber. Personally, I find it annoying and stupid. A chorus of voices admonishes you: "Don't vote. Don't vote." The punch line is that you're not supposed to vote *until* you've become sufficiently informed by going to the AARP Web site to be suitably indoctrinated with its "objective" assessment of the candidates and issues. AARP, of course, is officially "nonpartisan," but it's certainly not impartial. Its agenda is decidedly collectivist and liberal, and its political fortunes are invested with the Democratic

Party.

Another paragon of "nonpartisanship" is the Colorado Education Association, the state's largest teachers union. This is the local affiliate of the "nonpartisan" National Education Association, which each four years tops all other special-interest groups with the largest contingent of delegates to the Democratic National Convention. In its endorsements of Colorado congressional candidates this year, the CEA went seven-for-seven with Democrats. For the state legislature, 57 of 61 endorsements went to Democrats. The CEA's campaign contributions fit a similar pattern. Conveniently, they'll find a handful of squishy Republicans who oppose school choice, competition and vouchers. A token GOP endorsement here and there, a few crumbs to their campaign coffers and – presto! – the CEA is "nonpartisan."

Then, there's *The Denver Post*. Over the last couple of weeks we've been treated to the *Post's* bi-annual charade of legislative endorsements. The *Post* is also "nonpartisan." Now, there's little doubt from *Post* editorials and from the liberal spin in so many of its "news" stories that the journalists who work there favor Democrats and Democratic policies. But they have to play the game. A scorecard like the CEA's, with Democrats getting more than 90 percent of the endorsements, would be a bit obvious. There'd be little value, then, in a *Post* endorsement. So the *Post* spreads it around, making sure to endorse Republicans mainly in districts where a Republican victory is already assured.

Nonetheless, the *Post* favored Democrats in 31 of 53 contested races for the Colorado House, with 10 Democrats and two Republicans running unopposed. In the Senate, it was Democrats in 10 out of 16, with two other Democrats running unopposed. This would expand the Democratic majority in both bodies.

But the *Post* outdid itself in its endorsements for the U.S. House. In Congressional District 1, super-liberal Diana DeGette has no Republican opponent. If there were one, DeGette would surely have gotten the *Post's* endorsement. In the other six congressional races, the *Post* endorsed five Democrats. To avoid a GOP shutout, the *Post* had to come up with a token Republican. But Districts 3 and 7 are close contests, and in Districts 4 and 5, usually GOP strongholds, Democrats may actually have a chance this year. So the *Post*, incredibly took a few moments off from its ceaseless hammering of Tom Tancredo to actually endorse him in the 6th Congressional District. Why? Because they had to endorse at least one Republican and Tancredo is a lock for re-election. Now, I love Tom, and I endorse him without reservation. But the *Post* can't stand him. This is all so transparent. Have they no shame? Apparently not.

Populist Ploys All About Power
September 22, 2000

It's ironic that a man running for the most powerful political position in the world would adopt as a campaign theme: "I'm for the people, they're for the powerful." I'm talking about Al Gore, incidentally, not Ralph Nader. Nader's saying that, too, but Gore could get elected.

This is the anthem of class warfare that's been used with varying degrees of success by a succession of populists, progressives, communists, socialists, liberals and other sundry demagogues for about as long as there have been elections.

The political calculus is pretty simple. Demonize, say, the top 10 percent of the population as too rich and too powerful, and pander for the votes of the other 90 percent. (But be careful not to divulge that these days the lower boundary of the "too rich" top 10 percent includes families making $75,000 a year.) Attack overpaid CEOs; there are certainly fewer of them than "workers." Rail against oil companies and HMOs; it's a sure-fire political winner since everyone would like to pay less for gas and health care.

In order to sell this snake oil, you have to persuade the gullible and resentful that power is exercised only by the other side, which spends its money for evil purposes. When Clinton and Gore take money from the fat cats of the Hollywood left, that's good money, as are contributions from Bill Gates' competitors lobbying for a Justice Department assault on Microsoft. When labor unions spend tens of millions in soft money to run TV ads attacking Republicans, to Democrats that's in the public interest. When Republicans and their supporters defend themselves, that becomes a "special interest."

If corporate interests are all-powerful, why have they allowed corporate income taxes, price controls and so many regulations? If the rich rule, why do they pay an inordinate share of income taxes, while the bottom 50 percent pays almost nothing? Why are there death taxes?

The rich can't rule. Money doesn't vote, people do, and not nearly enough of them are rich. It's only because there are still enough non-rich voters who hope someday to become richer themselves that the socialists haven't yet taken over.

The power and political clout of the poor and middle-class can be measured in the hundreds of billions of dollars spent each year in a myriad of government public assistance and entitlement programs.

Businesses represent the producer interest in society. That's where all our wealth comes from. Government doesn't create wealth, it only consumes and reallocates it. It would be preposterous if business interests didn't have a place at the public-policy table. Who's going to run the auto industry, Ralph Nader?

Sure, business lobbies have influence. And so does the American Association of Retired People, the teachers unions, the AFL-CIO, government employee unions, trial lawyers, environmentalists, the ACLU, MADD, the NAACP, NOW, disabled activists, gays, religious groups and the poverty lobby, to name just a few. James Madison called this an offsetting "multiplicity of factions."

Power takes many forms. Influence is power. Leftists like Gore and Nader disparage private interests in a market economy while they relish the power their side wields in controlling the major sources of public influence in our society. The left presides and its agenda prevails in public education, academia, the major media, the arts and the entertainment industry. The left dominates the world of philanthropic foundations, underwriting all kinds of collectivist causes. You don't think all this is power?

No, Gore the Populist isn't against power; he's just against power exercised by the opposition. If elected, he and his coalition will have no qualms about using their power to control your life.

Will Gore's New Millennium resurrection of the politics of envy carry the day? It might. To paraphrase Abraham Lincoln, you can't fool all of the people all of the time, but you can fool enough of them to rule a large country.

Politics is not a Civil War
January 3, 1997

Winston Churchill once said of civil servants that "after a time, they tend to become no longer servants and no longer civil."

That uncivil remark would probably earn Sir Winston a rebuke, today, from something called the Penn Commission on Society, Culture and Community. The commission – a collection of academicians, journalists, politicians, authors and assorted social commentators – will meet twice a year over the next three years under the auspices of the University of Pennsylvania. Its target will be what it calls "an explosion of incivility" in the nation, and the world, for that matter. The project was stimulated by the mean level of discourse in recent political campaigns.

Well, I suppose it's something to do. I didn't notice any talk show hosts on the roster, but that's probably because the commission lumps all such characters together as part of the problem. I can't imagine that anything practical will come out of this process. What's more, I don't accept the underlying premise.

The nature of politics is no nastier than it's ever been, there's just more of it, and amplified with modern technology, more ways to communicate incivility. The biggest difference between today's brand of rancor and that of yesteryear is style. Shakespeare, for example, had a marvelous touch when it came to insults, which were often so refined they could be mistaken for compliments.

Even the politicians had more class. Benjamin Disraeli once said of Lord John Russell: "If a traveler were informed that such a man was leader of the House of Commons, he may well begin to comprehend how the Egyptians worshipped an insect."

When told by the Earl of Sandwich that he would die either of venereal disease or on the gallows, John Wilkes replied: "That depends, sir, on whether I embrace your mistress or your principles."

Supreme Court Justice Hugo Black, attending the funeral of a political rival, was asked by a late-arriver how far the service had gone: "They've just opened the defense," replied Black.

Teddy Roosevelt once described William McKinley as having the backbone of a chocolate éclair. Harold Ickes, Secretary of the Interior under FDR, declared that Sen. Huey Long suffered from "halitosis of the intellect."

Books have been written about searing insults hurled by and at Winston Churchill. One of his favorite targets was Lady Astor, the first woman to hold a seat in the British Parliament. When she told Churchill, "If I were your wife, I'd put poison in your coffee," he retorted, "If I were your husband, I'd drink it."

Scolding him at a cocktail reception one evening, she exclaimed, "You, sir, are drunk." Said Churchill, "You, madam, are ugly. In the morning, I'll be sober."

George Bernard Shaw, in a note offering him a pair of tickets to the opening night of Shaw's latest play, wrote: "Bring a friend – if you have one." To which Churchill, replied: "I cannot come on opening night but can come the second night – if there is one."

One apocryphal tale of insults with a homespun flavor involves a Florida populist attacking his highfalutin opponent with carefully chosen polysyllabic words for the benefit of a backwoods audience. Reminding his country constituents that he was one of them, educated at the state university, he went on to describe his opponent: "Florida wasn't good enough for him. He went north, to one of them Ivy League places. And do you know what he did when he got there? The very first day, right there on campus in front of God and, everybody, he matriculated. That's what he did, folks. Let him deny it. And ask him about his sister. Do you know where she chose to live? No, not here, but up there in that wicked New York. And do you know why? Let me tell you. Because that poor girl is a thespian. That's why."

Ah, those were the days. It's easy to be nasty and insulting. But being nasty and insulting with creativity and style – that's the trick. And that's what's missing today. The Penn Commission is on a mission to restore a lost virginity that we never had. Politics has historically been about as civil as the Civil War.

Tired, Bored, Polarized
June 10, 2011

I thought some recent emails from my radio listeners might serve as a thought-provoking springboard. One scolded me for being divisive and for polarizing the American political system. His desire was that "we could all come together under common sense, reason and reality." Another told me he was tired and bored of my explanations of why the left and the right disagree on many public policy issues.

I suggested they read Thomas Sowell's book, *A Conflict of Visions*. It explains the historic, irreconcilable philosophical differences and contrasting visions of human nature and the role of government in society between deep thinkers on the left and the right.

Our political system can certainly forge public-policy compromises that reasonable people can live with, at least temporarily. But often we don't "all come together" simply because we don't all agree or share the same values, goals or vision about the way the world works. Furthermore, not everyone is reasonable; we don't all agree on what constitutes common sense, reason and reality; and emotions often trump reason.

Polarization is nothing new in American society, and was here long before I came along. Although our founders recognized they couldn't "come together" under King George III, that sentiment wasn't shared by a good number of loyalists in the American colonies (see: Benedict Arnold). The Civil War also comes to mind as a somewhat divisive point in our history. And let's not forget the 1960s.

I must admit that there are outspoken people who disagree with me. As to the fellow who was tired and bored of the battle between leftists and rightists, that, of course, is his prerogative. I'm tired of demagoguery, intellectual laziness and ignorance, but I have no illusions that any of those things are going away. The irreconcilable argument between left and right goes back at least to Marx and Engels' publication of *The Communist Manifesto* more than 160 years ago – and won't be ended by anything short of the rapture.

If today's battle between left and right is particularly intense, it may be because the expansion of the welfare state, the left's model of political economy, has finally hit the wall. The evidence is inescapable, with huge budget deficits at all levels of government, unfunded liabilities for entitlement programs and government pensions in excess of $100 trillion, and stratospheric increases in the national debt. Current spending is unsustainable and future projections are far worse, with government spending as a share of GDP greatly exceeding the nation's tax capacity.

But the left is in denial, and digging in its heels. Pick any social spending program and they'll claim it's an "investment" that will save money in the long run. These so-called savings are breaking the bank. Unless we rein in government spending and borrowing, there won't be any fiscal long run. What liberals ignore are the consequences of each incremental increase in the borrowing and tax burden on the economy and on after-tax incentives for productive businesses, entrepreneurs and investors.

That doesn't deter left-wing economist Paul Krugman, an unrepentant Keynesian who learned nothing from FDR's failed economic programs. He wants to double down on Barack Obama's counterproductive stimulus binge, let the national debt be damned.

The compassion of leftist utopians and their obsession with what they call "social justice" have liberated them from the constraints of economic reality. Soaking the rich, or even drowning them, won't come close to filling the spending gap. And where do the golden eggs come from after you've killed the last goose? No matter, doctrinaire leftists are blinded by their ideology; a failed one at that which they'll defend to the death of our economy. This may be harrowing, but it certainly isn't boring.

Moderates Schmoderates

August 28, 2008

The Democrats' convention in Denver is over, concluding with rhetorical flourish by Barack Obama, the Pied Piper of Platitudes. And all will be sunshine, lollipops and rainbows in the land. Ideology and partisanship are out. Good government and moderation are in.

Nonsense. Obama is no "moderate." He's a partisan Democrat and a man of the left, which is exactly how he'd govern as president. In order to win, however, he well understands that he'll have to disguise his ideology and seduce a majority of swing-voting "moderates."

In the war of ideas, moderation is a cop-out. Moderation isn't a philosophy. It's the absence of a philosophy. Moderates don't innovate. At best, they can act as political brokers, attaching themselves to other people's ideas. C.S. Lewis once observed that, "You can't be a good egg all your life. Sooner or later you have to hatch or rot." Self-described moderates are pre-hatchlings who have not emerged and who might never emerge from their intellectual shell. An ideology is a consistent philosophical theory of the way the world works. George Will has defined it as the "politics of basic beliefs." It's something thinking grownups come to grips with at some point in their lives.

What's the foundational belief of moderates? Moderation for the sake of moderation? They believe in a little bit of everything – or, perhaps, nothing.

The term makes more sense as a modifier of something tangible than it does as an intrinsic belief. It's an adjective or an adverb. One may drink moderately or dress in moderation or be moderately well-off. As a matter of degree, there's a valid distinction between a moderate liberal and a radical left-winger. As a noun, a moderator is one who stands between two advocates in a debate. The debaters tell us what they believe in, the moderator is neutral. That's fine in a debate, but it's no way for a human being with the gift of reason to go through life.

G.K. Chesterton noted that, "The human brain is a machine for coming to conclusions." He described man as "An animal that makes dogmas. As he piles doctrine on doctrine and conclusion on conclusion in the formation of some tremendous scheme of philosophy and religion, he is, in the only legitimate sense of which the expression is capable, becoming more human...When he says that he has outgrown definitions, when he says that he disbelieves in finality, in his own imagination, he sits as God, holding no form of creed but contemplating all, then he is by that very process sinking slowly backwards into the vagueness of vagrant animals and the unconsciousness of the grass. Trees have no dogmas. Turnips are singularly broadminded."

When a voter or a politician calls himself a moderate, I'm unimpressed. The word has no meaning in the realm of ideas. It gives me no insight to one's mind or soul. It suggests, instead, a chameleon pretending to be all things to all people or an intellectually lazy lightweight who hasn't taken the trouble or lacks the capacity to form a personal philosophy.

I care less about a politician's specific stands on particular issues than I do about his values and basic beliefs. Once in office, the circumstances, details and issues will change. When they do, he'll be left to make decisions on the basis of his convictions. If he doesn't have any convictions, he'll base his decisions on other criteria – like a compulsion to get re-elected or loyalty to factional interests.

Edmund Burke told his constituents in Bristol, England, that on matters of great import he would vote his beliefs, not their dictates. If they disapproved of his beliefs, they should vote him out. In Parliament, he explained, he stood as their representative, not their delegate. It's a vital distinction. And it's the difference between a statesman and a politician.

"No Labels" Makes Little Difference in Debate
January 27, 2011

I didn't think much of the so-called "No Labels" movement when I first heard about it. I think even less of it after interviewing one of its spokesmen, Holly Page, on my radio show.

I hoped for a free-ranging discussion about the organization's vision and beliefs. What I got, instead, was an impenetrable, human press release. Page was like a broken record, stuck on a handful of slogans, platitudes and vagaries. Her resistance to answering any substantive questions could have withstood waterboarding.

No Labels presents itself as the voice of reason and moderation, above parties and ideology. For public consumption, it claims to have no foundational beliefs or philosophy, just a dedication to the process of civil discourse. It echoes Rodney King's profound question, "Why can't we all just get along?" Of course, we all could if we simply agreed about everything, which we don't, so we can't.

For all its professed moderation, No Labels doesn't hold back in demonizing others with gratuitous, inflammatory terms like "hyper-partisanship" and "ideological extremism." There are, no doubt, some who fit those descriptions, but what about those of us who are merely ideological and partisan? That is, we have positive ideas and productive associations with political parties. What's wrong with that? Abraham Lincoln was a Republican, and FDR was a Democrat. History has treated them respectfully.

No Labels likes to hang its hat on the word "centrist." And it is centrist. It's not radically left, like *MoveOn.org* or the *Daily Kos*. But it's certainly not right-center. It's left-center. Those labels do matter, and they're instructive. They tell us where people sit on the political and ideological spectrum, which helps us comprehend why they stand where they do. No Labels founders and key players like Holly Page are overwhelmingly Democrats whose resumes are heavy with Clinton connections.

"Not left. Not right. Forward," is the No Labels slogan, tailor-made for a T-shirt worn by callow, idealistic youngsters in a middle-school mini-government program. "Forward" connotes progress, which is a code word. No Labels, you see, is really progressive, the label liberals adopted when liberal went out of fashion. So the direction is, of course, (left) center, as we progress on the road to an American version of Euro-socialism.

Whoops, there are those labels again. But they do paint an accurate picture that saves a thousand words. Viva labels!

No Labels isn't really ideologically neutral. That will become apparent in the public policy positions it endorses. It's just another way of packaging basically liberal ideas for the benefit of the politically naïve. The two major parties aren't going away and one or the other will continue to dominate.

In my futile attempt to bring Page down to Earth, I asked about her beliefs on basic matters of public policy, from economics to defense to social issues. She clammed up, offering only the platitude, "What's best for America." Presumably, we all want that. But we don't all agree on what's best and how to get there. Her scripted comeback was to accuse me of putting my party above my country. That's a classic false dilemma.

Of course, I don't. Nor do Democrats. But I believe that as an instrument of public policy, Republican values, philosophy, agenda and prescriptions are generally the best course of action for America. Democrats prefer their party, as do members of any number of minor parties. We may agree on some things, but we'll always disagree on enough to make the political soil fertile for a multiplicity of parties in a free society.

No Labels asks us to "put our labels aside." What difference would it make? Dropping or changing a label won't change my beliefs, principles or vision, any more than the No Labels crowd has changed its. And none of this will bridge the political divide.

The Public Divide
April 25, 2013

"Congress has a very low approval rating. So what did we do? For the most part we voted them back into office. What a nation of idiots we are." That sanctimonious pretense of wisdom in a recent letter to the editor reflects a fundamental misunderstanding of the body politic and the dynamics of our two-party political system, about which many citizens, like that one, are clueless.

As to voting legislators back into office, if an incumbent isn't re-elected, some other Republican or Democrat will take his place and will just as reliably serve the party's electoral coalition. That's why when it comes to the power of legislative majorities, party trumps person.

"We" didn't vote anyone back into office. There is no collective "we" in elections. It's "you" and "I" and "they." Some people voted some of those members of Congress into office and other voters who strongly disagree with the first group voted some other members of Congress into office. And for every winner, there was a loser who still got plenty of votes.

Of the nation's 435 congressional districts, fewer than 50 are truly competitive. Each of the others is either a Democratic or Republican stronghold (like Denver for the Democrats or Colorado Springs for the Republicans). Over the last 50 years, the re-election rate for incumbents in the U.S. House has averaged 93 percent. It's slightly more competitive in the Senate because the vote is statewide, but incumbents still get re-elected at an average rate of 81 percent. Republican senators are safe in Oklahoma; Democrats in California.

It's true that polls show a dramatically low approval rating for Congress; only 9 percent in a recent survey conducted by Public Policy Polling, with Congress less popular than other choices in that poll, including cockroaches, root canals, traffic jams and colonoscopies. But what does that really mean?

Partisan Republicans and partisan Democrats aren't necessarily unhappy with legislators from their own party for whom they voted. It's the other party's legislators they disapprove of. So the disapproval of Democrats for Republicans and Republicans for Democrats is mathematically combined to produce the low approval rating for Congress as a whole.

Get it? If congressional Democrats were to magically roll over and adopt the Republican agenda, the overall approval level of Congress would soar as Republicans and Republican leaning independent voters suddenly tell pollsters they're delighted, while Democrats would still disapprove. Reverse the labels and get a similar result. For whatever that's worth.

Different people approve or disapprove of Congress for different reasons. Ironically, the most common criticism is about Congress's partisan inability to agree and come together on legislation in the "public interest." But most of the people who express that particular criticism don't agree with each other on just what the public interest is. This is demonstrated in today's great divide between Democrats and Republicans, liberals and conservatives, north and south, and flyover America vs. the left coast and Northeast.

The difference isn't merely partisan; it's philosophical. The congressional divide is a reflection of the sharp public divide. Whether you approve or disapprove of President Obama, he's certainly not a uniter. He hasn't bridged that philosophical divide; his agenda and political style have widened it. About half the country doesn't want to see our nation, as Obama puts it, "fundamentally transformed."

America finds itself – driven by history, demographics, the economy and foreign affairs – at an ideological crossroads. Democrats, led by the resurgent neo-progressive movement with its roots in late 19th century socialist populism, are intent on moving the country sharply left in the direction of greatly expanded government, social engineering and collectivism. Republicans are standing in their way, defending their vision of limited government, constitutionalism, individual liberty, private enterprise and traditional values. This ideological conflict defies compromise.

Reality

Party Trumps Person

Party Trumps Person
October 10, 2008

As Election Day approaches, it's time for my quadrennial column on party vs. person. A superficial cliché goes something like this: "I'm an independent thinker; I vote the person, not the party." This pronouncement is supposed to demonstrate open-mindedness and political sophistication on the part of the pronouncer. Hey, it's your vote; cast it any way you like – or not at all. But idealism and naiveté about the way our electoral process, government and politics work shouldn't be mistaken for wisdom.

For better or worse, we have a two-party system. Either a Republican, John McCain, or a Democrat, Barack Obama, is going to be our next president. No one else has a chance. Not Ralph Nader, not the Libertarian candidate, the Communist or the Green. Minor party candidates are sometimes spoilers – like Nader costing Gore the presidency in 2000 – but they don't win presidential elections. Ross Perot got 20 million popular votes in 1992, and exactly zero Electoral College votes.

In Europe's multiparty, parliamentary democracies, governing coalitions are formed after an election. In our constitutional republic, the coalitions are already in place. The Republican coalition is an alliance of conservatives, middle- and upper-income taxpayers (but not leftist Hollywood millionaires and George Soros), individualists who prefer limited government, those who are pro-market and pro-business, believers in American exceptionalism and a strong national defense, social issues conservatives and supporters of traditional American values. The Democrat coalition includes guilt-ridden liberals, collectivists, labor unions (especially the teachers unions), government workers, academics, plaintiffs-lawyers, lower- and middle-income net tax-*receivers*, identity-politics minorities, feminists, gays, enviros, nannyists and activists for assorted anti-gun, anti-capitalist, anti-business, anti-military, and world-government causes.

I say party trumps person because regardless of the individual occupying the White House, his party's coalition will be served. A

133

Democrat President, for example, whether liberal or moderate (conservative Democrats, if any still exist, can't survive the nominating process), can only operate within the political boundaries of his party's coalition. The party that wins the presidency will fill cabinet and sub-cabinet discretionary positions in the executive branch with members of its coalition. Likewise, the coalition will be the dominant source of nominees to the federal courts, ambassadorships, appointments to boards and commissions, and a host of plum jobs handed out to those with political IOUs to cash in.

It works the same way in the legislative branch. After the individual members of a new congress have been seated, a nose count is taken and the party with the most noses wins control of *all* committee and subcommittee chairmanships, the locus of legislative power. Let's say you're a registered Republican who prefers that party's philosophy of governance. And you're a fair-minded, well-intentioned person who happens to like a certain moderately conservative Democrat running for U.S. Senate. So, you decide to cross party lines and vote for him. As it turns out, he wins, giving Democrats a two-vote majority, 51-49. Congratulations! You just got Charles Schumer, Patrick Leahy, Diane Feinstein and Hillary Clinton as key committee chairs and a guarantee that your Republican legislative agenda will be stymied.

That's the way the process works. Does this mean that in our two-party system it comes down to choosing between the lesser of evils? Exactly! That's not to say that either party is really "evil," it's just an expression. If we had 300 million custom-tailored minor parties, everyone could find his perfect match. But that's not practical. You can be a purist and cast your vote symbolically with a fringe party, or be a player and settle for the least imperfect of the Republican or Democrat alternatives.

A vote for McCain is a vote for the party of constitutionalist judges, Adam Smith, the NRA, General Petraeus and Ronald Reagan. A vote for Obama is a vote for judicial activism, Karl Marx, the ACLU, the NEA, the AFL-CIO, the NAACP, Al Gore, Cindy Sheehan, Keith Olbermann and Rosie O'Donnell.

Roughly a third of Americans vote Republican, about a third Democrat; just under a third could be called swing voters, with the remainder falling into various fractional categories of extremists and single-issue voters. The swing voters decide elections. The trick for a candidate in a contested race is to attract enough of them to win. That's why major-party office-seekers tend to move toward the political center during election campaigns.

For better or worse, this is simply the way things work in a two-party system like ours. Third party candidates, with rare exceptions like Minnesota Gov. Jesse Ventura, are mostly a distraction. Although they seldom win, they can affect the outcome, helping or hurting either the Democrat or the Republican.

When I hear people say there's no difference between the two major parties, frankly I'm puzzled. Unless you're terribly uniformed or so far out on the radical fringes that left-center and right-center blend together; the differences in the two parties' philosophies and agendas are stark. Just a few examples:

• Taxes - Democrats want to soak the rich (and, inevitably, the middle-class). Republicans want across-the-board tax cuts.

• Government spending - Democrats always want to increase spending, especially for income-transfer "entitlements." Republicans want to reduce government's share of national income.

• Social Security - Democrats want to continue the Ponzi game until it collapses, then soak the rich. Republicans want to privatize it.

• Defense - Democrats want to continue to defund and emasculate the military. Republicans want to restore our capabilities and maintain a permanent, effective and credible fighting force.

• Health - Democrats want socialized medicine in stages. Republicans want to maintain private delivery of health care, funded with subsidies for the poor, and tax incentives, like self-directed medical savings accounts, for everyone else.

• Labor - Democrats are in the pocket of big labor unions. Republicans believe in free markets, competition and right-to-work protections.

• Education - Democrats believe public schools are laboratories for social engineering. As a wholly-owned subsidiary of the teachers unions, they're committed to spending more money and protecting the government monopoly on the delivery of education. Republicans believe in basic academics, rigorous standards, accountability, competition, choice and vouchers.

Reality

If you want to truly influence public policy, choose your lesser evil and get in the game. It's the only one in town.

Your vote; your choice.

Conservatives, Right-Wingers and Wackos
May 5, 1995

Liberals sometimes have a hard time making distinctions. That might explain why they rarely use the term "conservative" all by itself, without some modifier preceding it, like "ultra-," "flaming" or "hard-line." To them, mere conservatives apparently don't exist.

With the bombing of the Alfred P. Murrah Federal Building in Oklahoma City, the public is getting a closer look at extremists on what can, for a change, accurately be labeled as the far right. The last time we had a spate of terrorist bombings in this country in the late 1960s and early '70s, it was carried out by far-left extremists, railing against the Vietnam War, corporate America and the Establishment (remember that term?).

George McGovern and Eugene McCarthy – prominent liberals of that era – were no more responsible for the violence then than Newt Gingrich or Phil Gramm are today. That may be a fair, objective statement, but in politics perception is reality.

The Democrats have run out of ideas. Liberalism – big, expensive, intrusive, utopian government has been tried and failed. The only thing the Democrats have left is criticism of the Republican vision. Prior to the Oklahoma City bombing, liberals – in politics and the media – already were straining to demonize the "Contract With America" and those who advocated its principles. Epithets like "mean-spirited" and "cold-hearted" had become standard usage.

In the wake of Oklahoma City, desperate Democrats can be expected to up the ante. Their strategy now will be to link the GOP to right-wing extremists. Mainstream, responsible conservatives had better take heed and leave no doubt as to the gulf between their philosophy and the rantings of the wackos. The swing voters in the American political center, who changed the face of Congress in the last election, can be fickle. They may want a new direction for government but they don't want an armed revolution.

Downsizing government, repealing meddlesome regulations, reducing taxes, privatizing bureaucratic functions, reforming welfare, devolving political power from the feds to the states, limiting the terms of pork-barreling politicians: none of these policy proposals is mean or hateful. They're only different ways of governing. Conservatives have no cause to be defensive about ideas like this.

Right-wingers and wackos have a wholly different agenda. These are people mired in conspiracy theories and paranoia: The Council on Foreign Relations, the Trilateral Commission, the Bilderbergers, the Illuminati, the Federal Reserve, international bankers, the Queen of England (whom Lyndon LaRouche is convinced runs the world drug trade), Jews, Freemasons or the Pope. To conspiracy fanatics, some or all of these are regarded as sources of evil in this world.

I'm reminded of the story about the man who, brought before a judge on charges of being drunk and disorderly, asks for leniency, vowing to never do this again. The judge says: "I recognize you. This is the 83rd time you've been in my court for the same offense. How can you expect me to believe you?"

"Your honor," replies the man, "this is a very complicated world. There are no simple answers."

That's the beauty of conspiracy theories. They give simple, if convoluted, answers to complicated questions about how the world works – questions that may not otherwise have answers. The full scope and infinite intricacies of international economics are beyond the comprehension of any mortal – even my hero, Milton Friedman. The notion that a handful of people can "control" the world economy is preposterous. But to embittered, paranoid, delusional souls on the outskirts of society, ignorant, bigoted people who want to believe their plight in life is the fault of others (in the hate-group du jour), conspiracy theories are nothing short of a revelation.

These people are not conservatives, and the GOP should have no truck with them. There will be plenty of disaffected former Democrats to recruit in the future. We can do without society's malcontents.

There will be cases where good, solid conservative ideas such as limited government, individual rights and responsibilities, and the Second and Tenth Amendments also are embraced by extremists. In that event, I'd offer George Will's sage comment: "An idea is not responsible for the people who believe in it."

Libertarians are Not Party Animals
July 7, 2000

It was appropriate that the Libertarian Party held its national convention over the Independence Day weekend. No other ideologically-based organization in our country understands and appreciates better the philosophy on which our nation was founded. I revere many libertarian ideals brilliantly articulated by great thinkers like Ayn Rand, Ludwig von Mises and Murray Rothbard. But I'm not a capital "L" Libertarian, and never will be. The party itself is an oxymoron. As rugged individualists, libertarians are strangely out of character joining anything as communitarian as a political party.

The Libertarian Party is more like a discussion group. Libertarianism is a cause, a vision – and a worthy one – but it's not a practical political agenda. Libertarians perform a vital service by doing battle in the war of ideas. Their influence can tug the inevitable public policy compromises marginally in their direction. Ironically, some of my most critical mail comes from Libertarians, who accuse me of selling out my principles by being a partisan Republican. I'll admit to being practical when it comes to politics, but that doesn't necessarily make me unprincipled. Politics is the art of the doable. Libertarians understand the concept of division of labor. So I'll work for achievable outcomes, and Libertarians can stand firm as purist defenders of the ideal, the Jesuits, so to speak, of market economics and individual liberty.

In a recent letter to the editor, a Libertarian rebutted an Al Gore supporter who had criticized George W. Bush's "risky scheme" for partial privatization of Social Security. He then declared that he wouldn't be voting for Bush, either; opting, instead, for the Libertarian Party alternative. But this is self-indulgent, ideological exhibitionism. The Libertarian alternative – in essence, fend strictly for yourself – isn't on the menu. A little privatization is better than none at all. In the real world of public policy, this Libertarian can't have what he wants. It'll either be socialism-lite or socialism-heavy. I may not like either; but I'll work for the lesser of evils. You need only look to countries like France and Sweden to see how much farther we could travel on the road to socialism. If Libertarians aren't comfortable with George W Bush, imagine their discomfort if President Al Gore, a Democrat majority in Congress, and liberal Supreme Court came to power. Then again, if the real passion of Libertarians is simply to complain about impurity, they'd have plenty to complain about.

As I said, I like many libertarian ideas. On the other hand I find their notions on national defense, for example, to be at best delusional and at worst downright suicidal. For purely practical reasons, as a national political force, Libertarianism is a lost cause. Their prescriptions in key public policy areas like taxation and Social Security are simply unrealistic in a nation with democratic institutions. America was more libertarian when it was more of a republic. Libertarianism appeals mostly to rational, independent, self-reliant individuals. It's founded on an antipathy to coercion. But it will never appeal to the masses who perceive it as too tough for them, who don't believe they're up to the challenge. They want their safety net, the bigger and more comfortable the better – especially at someone else's expense.

In a sarcastic remark directed at effete, armchair revolutionaries of the left, Oscar Wilde once said, "The problem with socialism is that it takes too many evenings." Pure socialists and pure libertarians are utopians. As overt national political parties, their respective agendas will never attract very many voters. Although I'm sorry to observe that socialism is appealing to more Americans than is libertarianism. Libertarians surely must see the success socialists and near-socialists have had in forming an alliance with the Democratic Party. Republicans may fall short of rarified libertarian standards, but they do share an institutional belief in limited government. I hope "practical libertarian" isn't an oxymoron.

Your Vote Does Count
October 18, 2012

"Your Vote Doesn't Count" is the cover story of the November issue of *Reason* magazine. It attempted to sell that idea with an abstract philosophical argument, dressed up in statistical probability, about the infinitesimal odds against your single-vote determining the outcome of an election.

So what? That's irrelevant. To use a basketball analogy, your one-point free throw in the first quarter contributed to your team's victory even if it wasn't the game winner. In an election, all votes *do* count, and yours is aggregated with all the others that come before or after it. That's why political parties work so hard to get every single voter out on Election Day (in Chicago, even dead ones).

Reason magazine's motive for offering this specious argument is transparently self-serving. It's to encourage people to vote for Libertarian candidates, especially Gary Johnson, for president. The your-vote-doesn't-count ploy is intended to counter the plea to Republican-leaning libertarians not to "waste" their votes on Johnson (who can't possibly win) but who might divert enough votes from Romney to elect Obama.

For the unenlightened, *Reason* is the premier monthly publication of the libertarian movement, with a circulation of about 50,000. I'm a regular reader. I should note, however, that I am not a movement libertarian. Although I admire a number of libertarian thinkers and have been influenced over the years by many worthwhile libertarian ideas and principles, I simply can't go all the way to dogmatic, uncompromising libertarian positions on matters of public policy, especially in the realm of national security and foreign affairs.

Even on economic issues, rock-ribbed libertarians refuse to be constrained by political reality. They stand firm on absolutist positions that have narrow popular appeal. I lost my starry-eyed idealism about what's politically doable many years ago. The purist variety of libertarians would rather be right, as they see it, than elected. A statistical measure of that is the average popular vote won by Libertarian nominees for president in the 10 elections from 1972 to 2008: four-tenths of 1 percent. In practice, capital "L" libertarians (that's the political party as distinguished from the philosophy) compose a discussion group masquerading as a political party. The discussion is fun and intellectually self-satisfying, but when it comes to electoral politics in this country, Libertarians are a cult.

Personally, I wish the U.S. were more of a libertarian society than it is, but it isn't and won't ever be. Self-reliant rugged individualists these days are greatly outnumbered by the millions of Americans hooked on one kind of government dependency or another. However inelegantly he phrased it, Mitt Romney was spot on when he candidly noted that Obama can count on at least 47 percent of the vote in November. At best, libertarian ideas can have some influence on policies of the Republican Party, my chosen vehicle in the real world of politics.

There are only two possible outcomes in this election: either Barack Obama or Mitt Romney will be president of the United States in 2013. It won't be Gary Johnson, the Libertarian, or Roseanne Barr of the Green Party. The Greens' man in 2000, Ralph Nader, stole just enough votes from Al Gore to elect George W. Bush. That taught leftists who voted for Nader a lesson. Their votes did count – inadvertently, for Bush. Practical libertarians (that's not necessarily an oxymoron; I actually know some) should take note.

As Ayn Rand observed, "You can avoid reality, but you cannot avoid the consequences of avoiding reality." Yes, you can use your vote to make a "statement." But you won't be governed by a statement. You'll be governed by either Democrats or Republicans. You may see it as the lesser of evils, but there are distinct differences between the two parties, and that's your only realistic choice.

Tripped Up by Minor Parties
October 21, 2010

Ever since the Democrats and Republicans cemented their status as the two major parties 150 years ago, minor parties have come and gone, but not one of their presidential candidates has ever won an election. To be sure, they can have an impact on the outcome, but only as spoilers.

In 1912, former president Teddy Roosevelt came out of retirement, running as a Progressive. He took enough votes away from Republican William Taft to hand the election to Democrat Woodrow Wilson. More recently, in 1992, Ross Perot created the Reform Party, finishing a distant third with less than 20 percent of the vote, but taking enough votes away from George H.W. Bush to win it for Bill Clinton.

At the state and local level, there is the rare minor-party victory, like pro wrestler Jesse Ventura's election as governor of Minnesota in 1998, but he gave way after one term to a conventional Republican. Americans certainly have the right to run for office with whichever party they choose. Some are motivated by unshakable principles, others by ego or delusions of victory. But practical voters should seriously consider the consequences of casting a symbolic vote for someone who has no chance of winning. After all the votes are counted, they'll generally be governed by either a Republican or a Democrat.

The Colorado governor's race is a bizarre anomaly. A minor party candidate, Tom Tancredo, is in a close race with John Hickenlooper and far ahead of Dan Maes, the discredited Republican nominee. But Tancredo is actually a longtime Republican, a late entry using a minor party only as a convenient vehicle when the Maes campaign imploded.

A better example is the at-large (statewide) race for University of Colorado regent. Incumbent Republican Steve Bosley, a CU alumnus, has been the board's chairman. He is the former president of the Bank of Boulder and creator of the Bolder Boulder race. He's a solid conservative who's worked tirelessly to improve the financial condition and academic performance of the school. He's also committed to more philosophical diversity within the faculty in areas that lend themselves to political spin and brainwashing, like political science, history and sociology. Notoriously dominated by leftists, the rare conservative in these disciplines has been among an endangered species for years.

Bosley's opponent, Democrat Melissa Hart, is a liberal, Harvard Law graduate who clerked for ultra-liberal Supreme Court Justice John Paul Stevens. She defends the status quo with its under-representation of conservative professors. (If conservatives dominated the faculty, liberals would be screaming bloody murder.) As a CU faculty member, Hart can be expected to favor the interests of her colleagues over students and taxpayers on matters of tenure, compensation and teaching loads.

And here's the minor-party conundrum: In 2004, Republican Bosley barely won election by a margin of one-half of 1 percent because a Libertarian candidate with no chance of winning drew away 3.3 percent. In 2006, liberal Democrat Stephen Ludwig won the other at-large regent seat, beating a conservative Republican by four-tenths of 1 percent because a Libertarian and a right-wing minor party candidate combined to siphon off 7.4 percent between them. This year, votes cast for the Libertarian candidate with no chance to win could tip the race from Bosley to Hart.

There's currently an embattled 5-4 majority of Republicans on the Board of Regents. The left-wing Boulder Weekly, in its endorsement of Hart, declared, "It's time to put an end to the right-wing agendas that have silently plagued CU for years." One has to be pretty far left to imagine there's too much conservative influence at CU. Just ask a conservative CU student.

A vote for Bosley will keep the flickering flame of intellectual diversity alive. A vote for anyone else will fortify the existing liberal death grip.

The Tea Party and Coalition Politics
November 7, 2013

"What if you threw a party and no one came?" Here's a contemporary paraphrase of that old cliché: "What if you threw a Tea Party and less than a plurality came?"

The answer is that some other party garnering more votes would wind up governing. This is a political dilemma for Republicans that Democrats hope to exploit. Ideology is about ideas and politics is about winning elections. I'm concerned about both but understand the distinction between the two. If you don't first win the election you can't implement the policies that power your ideology.

Whether some people like it or not, including about a third of voters who are registered independents, we have essentially a two-party system in this country and that's not going to change anytime soon. At the local and national level you'll be governed by either Republicans or Democrats and the coalitions that coalesce around each of those major parties. I'm a partisan Republican because I prefer its agenda and coalition. And I'm a conservative because I favor limited government, private enterprise and individual liberty, along with a number of other values that distinguish me from liberals and Democrats.

After the failure of Republicans to defund Obamacare or win substantive concessions from majority Democrats in the U.S. Senate during the partial government shutdown, I've heard some disgruntled Tea Partyers frustrated with the philosophical imperfection of the GOP declare that they will overthrow its national "establishment" and reform the party in its own image. Failing that, they threaten to form their own party. Either path would be political suicide and guarantee a progressive Democrat lock on power.

Philosophically, I share most of the Tea Party's agenda and I applaud its passion. It's a vital part of the Republican coalition. But it's only part of that coalition, not a majority of it, and certainly well below a majority of the American public. That's too bad. I wish more Americans embraced the fundamental values of our nation's founders and their vision of political economy. But they don't. If they did, Barack

Obama wouldn't have been elected – twice. Tea Partyers imagine their movement has a greater following than, sadly, it actually does.

Breaking away from the GOP would permanently condemn the Tea Party to minor party status, the fate of Greens and Libertarians who can strut in their purity but never govern. As for the all-powerful national GOP establishment, there's no such thing. There are fifty different Republican parties among the states, each with its own demographics, culture, coalition and power centers. Some are in power and governing, others are in states where they never will. The control and influence of national GOP leadership is limited.

Tea Partyers are understandably angry with our country's direction under the leftist "progressivism" of Democrats and a president that wants to "fundamentally transform" America into something our founders wouldn't recognize. But anger, frustration and sincerity aren't sufficient to forge a winning political strategy. I'm angry and frustrated, too, but I'm constrained by political reality. Denying the present reality won't change it but it can lead one to hubris and self-destructive strategies.

In Obama's second term, an implosion of feckless Democrat policies from the economy to foreign affairs to the Obamacare debacle will create new realities and opportunities for the Republican coalition, attracting enough swing voters to forge an electoral majority. If the Tea Party wants to be part of a governing coalition, it needs to be a member of that imperfect team.

Electoral College Preserves Republic
October 20, 2000

The CU Buffs have about as much chance of going to a bowl game this year as the Electoral College does. At least EC has an excuse; it fields a team only once every four years, although it's probably true that not many Americans understand why. Let's have a go at it.

How can it be possible in a democracy like ours, some people ask, for a candidate who gets more popular votes in a national election to be denied the presidency? That question contains two fundamental fallacies. First, we are not a democracy and never have been. This is a constitutional republic. Second, contrary to a widely held misconception, we do not have a national election for president. We have 51 separate elections, one for each of the fifty states and the District of Columbia. Yes, we go through the exercise of tallying the popular vote, but that's just for curiosity's sake; it has no legal bearing on the election.

Article IV, Section 4 of the U.S. Constitution reads: "The United States shall guarantee to every State in the Union a republican form of government." The word "democracy" appears not a single time in the Constitution, Bill of Rights or Declaration of Independence. We pledge allegiance to the flag and to the *republic* for which it stands. This is not a trivial distinction. Supreme Court Chief Justice John Marshall proclaimed: "Between a balanced Republic and a Democracy, the difference is between order and chaos."

Voting is certainly a democratic institution, but the founders took great care to craft a system sensitive to the excesses of direct democracy. They gave us a Bill of Rights to protect individuals from the tyranny of the majority, along with representative government, federalism, the separation of powers, checks and balances, judicial review, the presidential veto, and the Electoral College, to name a few "anti-democratic" safeguards.

Votes in the Electoral College were apportioned in such a way as to guarantee that less-populous states maintained their influence. Initially the Electoral College was to be an elite, deliberative body with considerable discretion. Today, it's evolved into a procedural device that

147

serves to award a state's electoral votes on a winner-take-all basis to the candidate that wins a plurality of the popular vote. The Electoral College may no longer be the lofty assemblage that Alexander Hamilton originally envisioned in Federalist No. 68, but it still has solid justification. It forces candidates to address the concerns of voters in all of the states. It reinforces the principle that the nation is not just a collective, amorphous blob, but a confederation of individual states, each retaining some sovereign powers and certain unique qualities, values and agendas.

In Colorado, for example, we'll cast fewer than 2 million votes for president this year. If the nation elected presidents strictly through a direct, popular vote, why would either major party candidate in a close contest waste time and resources here to pick up a few thousand vote differential when close to 20 million votes are at stake in New York and California? The answer is, he wouldn't, if it weren't for the Electoral College, which now awards all eight of our state's electoral votes to the candidate with the greatest popular vote. That's worth a little attention. Without the Electoral College, presidential politics would move sharply to the left as candidates pandered to the political appetites of the large voting blocs in the Northeast and California. Perhaps that explains why elimination of the Electoral College has been a recurring pragmatic liberal cause.

You'll recall that while winning 20 million popular votes in 1992, Ross Perot didn't get close to winning a single electoral vote. Ironically, Ralph Nader could conceivably draw off enough Democratic votes in California this year to deny Al Gore a plurality, in which case Bush would get *all* 54 of that state's electoral votes. You gotta love a system like that.

Redistricting's False Premise
May 19, 2012

It's no surprise that the battle over congressional redistricting in Colorado is headed to the courts. That's exactly what majority Democrats in the state Senate have intended from the beginning. They pulled a similar act ten years ago, grid-locking the legislature and a GOP Governor, Bill Owens. Then, they got the plan they wanted blessed by a Democrat-friendly lower court judge, John Coughlin, and later sealed by the majority of liberal Democrats on the state Supreme Court, put there by the 24 consecutive-year reign of Democratic governors Dick Lamm and Roy Romer.

This time around, Democrats cynically opened with a redistricting plan blatantly contrived in their favor, knowing Republicans would counter with a plan favoring GOP interests. In a normal negotiation, that could lead to a compromise. But why compromise when you think you'll get a better deal in court? That's the Democrats' strategy, as they clearly demonstrated when they filibustered their own plan as the clock was running out on the 2011 legislative session.

The ploy Democrats are using to justify their statewide gerrymander is the holy grail of "competitiveness." This is the false premise that the public would be better served if all of the nation's 435 congressional districts were contrived so no party had an advantage of registered voters. This is 1) nonsense and 2) without Constitutional or judicial justification. By this reasoning, why not redraw the borders of the fifty states to make all Senate seats competitive? For example, we could combine Republican Utah with Democratic Hawaii. Would it be called Hutah or Uwaii?

Article I, Section 2 of the U.S. Constitution requires only that representation among the states be apportioned "according to their respective numbers." That means approximate population equality: one man, one vote. That's it. There's no mention of "competitiveness." If a district is naturally competitive, that's fine. But there's no Constitutional mandate or case law to justify gerrymandering competitiveness. Population equality comes first. Then considerations like county, municipal and natural geographic boundaries, community

149

integrity, compactness, contiguity and the absence of racial discrimination. This was definitively stated in Carstens v. Lamm, 1982, in which "competitiveness" was conspicuously absent among the considerations listed. In Thornburg v. Gingles, 1986, and several other cases, remedies for racial discrimination have been given special consideration such as the protection of "majority-minority" districts.

Colorado may be purple in the aggregate but that doesn't mean each individual congressional district must be artificially made purple. Communities of interest are wholly entitled to be represented by like-minded legislators. Liberal Democrats in Denver or Boulder should be free to elect liberal Democrats, just as voters in Colorado Springs or Douglas County should be able to elect their fellow conservatives. And fickle voters in Colorado's CD-3, as it's currently laid out, can go back and forth if they choose.

Under this guise of "competitiveness," Democrats seek to rearrange CD-2, their Boulder stronghold, dragging in voters from heavily-Republican Douglas County in CD-6. They claim this will make both districts more competitive. That's only half true. Their scheme is to steal Republican votes from CD-6 so that they're wasted in CD-2, putting CD-6 in play for Democrats while leaving enough registered Democrats in CD-2 to protect their guy, Jared Polis, who's rich enough to put millions into his own campaign.

Then there's the "Brandon-Mander," named for Democratic Senate President, Brandon Shaffer, who plans to run for the U.S. House against Republican Congressman Cory Gardner who unseated Democrat Betsy Markey in 2010. The Dems have re-mapped CD-4 to accommodate Shaffer's political ambitions.

There's an alternative to this political circus. The Colorado Constitution reserves the duty of redistricting to the legislature, not the courts. This is a bi-partisan opportunity for Governor Hickenlooper to call a special session, rein in his party's redistricting radicals and negotiate a fair compromise.

Media and the Perpetual Campaign for Political Power

Mainstream (Liberal) Media
January 16, 2009

In its Saturday opinion section, the *Rocky Mountain News* gives readers a chance to Talk Back to the Media. Under the headline "Mainstream media hardly monolithic," a liberal reader took issue with conservative columnist Charles Krauthammer's criticism of the "mainstream media" for shamelessly favoring Barack Obama during the presidential campaign. The reader disputed this and, implicitly, the notion that the mainstream media have a liberal bias.

He supported his argument by employing the fallacy of overstatement, fabricating a straw man, which he then proceeded to rip apart.

The key word he leveraged was monolithic. How can the mainstream media be accused of monolithically supporting Obama, he asked, when that bastion of the mainstream media, *The Washington Post*, at the same time runs Krauthammer's column? The answer, of course, is easy and obvious. The mainstream media are not monolithically liberal (and cheerleaders for Obama), they're just overwhelmingly liberal (and cheerleaders for Obama).

Just as Krauthammer's an outnumbered conservative on the editorial pages of *The Washington Post*, David Brooks is an out-numbered conservative (and a pretty wishy-washy conservative, at that) on the editorial pages of *The New York Times*. Token conservatives provide a semblance of "balance" at liberal publications, just as the conservative *Wall Street Journal* features a weekly opinion column by the unbearably liberal Thomas Franks.

To offer anecdotal evidence of a differing editorial opinion or two doesn't negate the preponderance of evidence on the other side. The *Rocky* leans right on its opinion pages in spite of the fact that it also runs liberal contributors like Paul Campos and the radically left-wing Amy Goodman.

Personally, I've never liked the term mainstream media to begin with. Rush Limbaugh calls it the "drive-by media," which rightly connotes superficiality, sensationalism and a herd mentality. Calling the liberal media the mainstream media gives the false impression that their bias is reflective of the mainstream of public opinion. It isn't. It's left of the public mainstream.

That the mass media are dominated by liberals is so obvious as to be beyond debate. This includes *NBC, CBS, ABC, CNN, MSNBC, PBS, National Public Radio, The New York Times, The Washington Post, Time, Newsweek, The Associated Press,* etc. The public is onto this, as measured by their declining level of trust in these so-called news sources.

You have to be pretty far left to honestly regard *The New York Times* as conservative, but, incredibly, there are such people, like the aforementioned socialist Amy Goodman of *Democracy Now.*

To their credit, some members in good standing of the liberal media had the integrity to acknowledge the liberal bias, such as Evan Thomas (grandson of Norman Thomas, six-time Socialist Party candidate for president). Said Evan, when he was *Newsweek*'s Washington bureau chief in 1996, "About 85 percent of the reporters who cover the White House vote Democratic .... Particularly at the networks, at the lower levels among the editors and so-called infrastructure, there is a liberal bias. There is a liberal bias at *Newsweek*, the magazine I work for. . . . (then *ABC* White House reporter, now *Fox News* anchor) Brit Hume's bosses are liberal, and they're always quietly denouncing him as a right-wing nut."

Conservative outposts like TV's *Fox News Channel* (with 2 million viewers compared with the liberal news networks' 25 million), *The Wall Street Journal*'s editorial pages, *National Review* magazine and much of talk radio certainly counteract some of this liberal dominance of the mass media, but that doesn't alter the reality of liberal dominance – to say nothing of liberal domination of public education, academe, the arts and the entertainment industry. Liberals who dispute this are either delusional or liars. If the shoe were on the other foot and conservatives reigned in these places, liberals would be screaming bloody murder.

Force Feeding the News
July 3, 1998

Television is to news as a bumper sticker is to Shakespeare. I remember hearing an analogy once that went something like that. Your typical nightly, 35-minute TV news broadcast is a headline service with pictures. Five minutes of police blotter reporting – fires, murders, car accidents, etc. – five minutes of weather, five minutes of sports, ten minutes of commercials, and maybe a minute or two for business, science, politics, and affairs of the world.

I don't intend this as a slam on TV news. It is what it is. It's a business. Commercial TV news programmers work backwards from what they think the largest audience wants to see. They don't call it the mass media for nothing. If *Jim Lehrer's NewsHour* – a quality, in-depth show –moved from *PBS* to *NBC* and had to rely on the ratings, it'd be off the air in a month. Why do you suppose *Nightline*, with Ted Koppel, is on at 10:35, while *Friends* airs during prime time? TV news isn't there primarily to dispense information or even to offer "infotainment." Like everything else on commercial TV and radio, it's there to sell advertising to a mass audience. That's the business.

I can live with that reality. While we might lament that citizens with a right and duty to vote aren't better informed, this is a consequence of a free society. By contrast, in the repressive days of the former Soviet Union, legend has it that there were only two television stations. On *Station 1*, the Communist government spewed its propagandistic in-depth "news"; if you tuned to *Station 2*, you saw a KGB man staring into the camera ordering you to turn back to *Station 1*. Would you like that better?

Fortunately, in our media-abundant society, there are plenty of places you can go if you crave something more: Cable TV, talk radio, *NPR*, *PBS*, newspapers, magazines, books, the Internet, you name it. If you're not well informed, you have no one to blame but yourself. As for the masses, we can't lead or drag them to water, much less make them drink.

But that was before Rocky Mountain Media Watch came along. Actually, this pretentious undertaking is little more than a one-man show run by a liberal scold named Paul Klite. It's advisory board includes such media giants as David Barsamian from something called "Alternative Radio;" two representatives from Fairness and Accuracy in Reporting (a fringe group so far left they think *National Public Radio* is too conservative); and someone from Greenpeace. You get a sense of where they're coming from.

Klite, who I've had on my radio show, rails against what he calls the "corporate media." This is a buzz word right out of the Ralph Nader school of public discourse. Lefties, you see, equate "corporate" with "bad." I see it as just a way of organizing a business, raising capital and paying taxes. As for "big corporations," what's the alternative? We already have big government and big labor. If you're going to live in a prosperous, mass-production industrial society you've got to have big businesses. Who else is going to make your cars, TVs, appliances, airplanes, groceries, etc.?

When Klite says "corporate," what he really means is "private" or "commercial." That's what offends him. When I pressed him, he conceded that that what he'd prefer is more government-funded media. That way, we'd get the kind of information we really need, rather than what we want. Klite and his ilk, of course, would be there to decide what we need, what's best for us, untainted by commercialism. Since he regards *NPR* and *PBS* as too conservative, too establishment, you can be assured his recipe for our news diet would be rich in socialism. How he intends to force us to watch is another question.

Incidentally, the FCC recently threw out Rocky Mountain Media Watch's complaint asking that the licenses of four Denver TV stations not be renewed because their news coverage was too violent and trivial. Despair not, Mr. Klite, our glorious market economy offers you another remedy: Buy a TV station and try it your way. You can even incorporate, if you like.

Networks' Bias Rather Obvious
September 1, 2000

It's my job as a political commentator to watch network TV coverage every four years of the Republican and Democratic national conventions. What's your excuse? If you were part of the dwindling population of network viewers, you were treated to the same old liberal bias from *ABC, NBC, CBS* and *CNN*. The only change this year is that they were even more blatant about it, even in the days leading up to the conventions. Here's one of the more egregious examples, as monitored and transcribed by the Media Research Center, a conservative media watchdog group.

Dan Rather on the August 7th *CBS Evening News*, introducing that night's story on the just-announced Gore-Lieberman ticket:

"Democratic presidential candidate Al Gore officially introduced his history-making running mate today, Sen. Joseph Lieberman of Connecticut. History-making because Lieberman is of Jewish heritage and faith. The two started running right away. In their first joint appearance they gave a preview of the Gore-Lieberman fight-back, comeback strategy. Their message: They represent the future, not the past, and they are the ticket of high moral standards most in tune with real mainstream America."

You'll notice this was all positive, not a disparaging word. Now, contrast that to Rather's introduction to the July 25th story on Bush-Cheney:

"The official announcement and first photo-op today of Republican George Bush and his running mate Richard Cheney. Democrats were quick to portray the ticket as quote 'two Texas oilmen' because Cheney was chief of a big Dallas-based oil supply conglomerate. They also blast Cheney's voting record in Congress as again quote 'outside the American mainstream' because of Cheney's votes against the Equal Rights Amendment, against a woman's right to choose abortion – against abortion, as Cheney prefers to put it – and Cheney's votes against gun control. Republicans see it all differently, most of them hailing Bush's choice and Cheney's experience."

Can you believe this editorial masquerading as a news, story?

155

How generous of Rather to devote, as an afterthought, an entire word, "experience," to represent the GOP's case. Of course that was preceded, by a litany of the other side's party-line objections. The Rather intro overflows with negative Democrat spin. Have these people no shame?

I can't read the minds of Rather, Peter Jennings and Tom Brokaw. I don't know if they and their reporters, producers and editors are consciously exercising bias or simply doing what comes naturally as liberals. But the product is the same. It's unprofessional, unethical, annoying and insulting.

Untrustworthy Media
January 7, 2005

Once upon a time, way back in 1987, Mike Wallace and Peter Jennings took part in a seminar filmed for *PBS* entitled "Ethics in America" where they were placed in a hypothetical setting accompanying an enemy patrol during a Vietnam-like war. What would you do, they were asked, if American soldiers were about to be ambushed by these enemy troops?

Wallace declared emphatically, and Jennings with some trepidation, that as "journalists" they would not interfere to save American lives but would simply report the event as it occurred; that their first duty was not to their country or countrymen but to the objective canons of their trade.

If this is journalism's version of Star Fleet's Prime Directive — never to interfere with the development of alien life and culture — Edward Lee Pitts of the *Chattanooga Times Free Press* must not have gotten the memo. He was the reporter who contrived to plant a question with an American GI about unarmored vehicles in Iraq. The question was designed to embarrass Defense Secretary Donald Rumsfeld at a recent town hall meeting with the troops.

If you read the transcript of Rummy's entire answer, it was at the same time sympathetic, concerned, frank, practical, constructive and well-received by the soldiers. The edited version, disseminated by most of the media, conveyed a distorted impression, reduced to a sound bite: "You go to war with the Army you have, not the Army you might want or wish to have at a later time." We've come to expect this from the liberal media.

Fortunately, the public is growing increasingly wise to them. A recent Gallup poll places TV and newspaper reporters near the bottom of the list when it comes to credibility, slightly higher than car salesmen, congressmen, business executives and lawyers but considerably below nurses, doctors, military officers, cops and clergy. Barely one-fifth of respondents rated reporters "high" or "very high" on honesty and ethical standards.

No, not every reporter in the major media is liberal. But most

157

are. No, they don't all *consciously* spin the news in a liberal direction. But some do, and many more spin it that way unconsciously.

(Note: The likes of Limbaugh, Coulter, Hannity, O'Reilly and Rosen aren't *reporters*; they're *commentators*. They are admittedly opinionated.)

Sanctimonious liberal reporters describe themselves merely as the messengers of news that's often discomfiting. But your letter carrier doesn't edit your mail. He doesn't decide what information you'll get, what you won't and how it will be presented. And, in his professional capacity, your letter carrier isn't a crusader for some causes and an opponent of others.

Carole Simpson is a former *ABC News* weekend anchor. You might remember her as the *immoderator*, shilling for Bill Clinton at the first presidential town hall debate in 1992. She's still on the network's payroll spreading the word – as interpreted by a black, liberal woman in the media – for *ABC News* at high schools across the country. At a Washington forum covered by *C-SPAN* earlier this year, she proudly exclaimed that she was "someone who got into journalism in the 1960s because we wanted to change America."

Aha! Her use of the word *we* suggests she wasn't alone in this goal. Now, Simpson and I would disagree about many of her visions for change. And that would be fine in politics or on the editorial page, but her admission to being an activist in the media should have disqualified her as a "reporter."

Ann McFeatters, a nationally syndicated liberal columnist, matter-of-factly asserted in a recent piece that the job of journalists (she didn't exempt reporters) is to "comfort the afflicted and afflict the comfortable."

But liberal reporters are commonly selective in the targets of their affliction and comfort. They comfort tax users while afflicting taxpayers. They comfort the public education establishment while afflicting those who fight for choice, competition and excellence. They cover for the comfortable leftists who dominate higher education while afflicting conservative gadflies like David Horowitz. They selectively comfort favored regulators, bureaucrats, enviros, labor unions, nannyists and rich propagandists – like Michael Moore – with whom they sympathize.

Liberals in the media, held hostage by their bleeding hearts, just don't know any better. They can embrace all manner of populist causes that make little sense to conservatives who temper their compassion with reason and real-world economic constraints.

If there were more conservatives in newsrooms, and if liberals would listen, some of this might sink in.

Whose Side are Journalists on?

November 9, 2001

Journalists come in many varieties. A few are actually conservative. Even fewer, these days, are veterans with a firsthand understanding of what it means to be a soldier. As an institution, however, the dominant journalistic culture is decidedly liberal. The much-touted notion of journalistic skepticism and suspicion is ideologically selective. Corporate CEOs (except Ben and Jerry) and generals are not to be trusted, but EPA bureaucrats and anti-war protesters are. Journalistic objectivity is largely a myth. We see the world through our own filters, the product of our individual perceptions, perspectives, and biases.

Ernie Pyle was a Pulitzer Prize-winning World War II combat correspondent who reported from a foxhole, under fire, shoulder-to-shoulder with American fighting men. I'd love to hear his opinion of some of the crap that passes for war journalism these days. Yes, it's relevant to report on civilian casualties and damage in Afghanistan, but it's been overhyped. In a story on the bombing of Taliban targets, civilian damage should be a footnote, not a headline and a lead, as has been the case in the filings of Associated Press reporter Kathy Gannon.

Then there's Loren Jenkins, senior foreign editor at *NPR*. He complains that the Pentagon has made his job harder by withholding information about secret troop movements. He says his job is to find out and report on where the troops are, to "smoke 'em out," as he puts it. Would Jenkins and his ilk have let the Nazis know about Allied troops staging in England for the invasion of Normandy? "Smoke 'em out?" Hell no! They're our troops – at war. Jenkins would endanger their lives and their mission. Tell us about it after the battle.

Generals are often criticized for "fighting the last war." The same can be said of some journalists. This is not Vietnam. The Pentagon is not the enemy. The international terrorists who attacked the United States are. Liberal media types are so paranoid about being used as a tool of the military or the administration that, instead, they allow themselves to be used as a tool of the Taliban. Their obsession with civilian damage in Afghanistan is a case in point. Wait 'til they have a daily U.S. body count to trumpet.

Two weeks ago, on *C-SPAN*, *ABC* president David Westin was talking to journalism students at Columbia University. Asked whether he thought the Pentagon was a "legitimate" terrorist target, Westin clumsily sidestepped the question, invoking some preposterous notion of journalistic neutrality. He claimed that American journalists shouldn't be taking a position on such things. A few days later, under pressure from higher-ups, he apologized and reversed himself.

This same claim of neutrality has been expressed by others who seem to regard themselves – in our hyphenated times – as journalist-Americans rather than American journalists. Tom Brokaw won't wear an American flag lapel pin because he's afraid it would imply his lockstep support of Bush's policies. Huh? The flag doesn't stand for George W. It stands for our country, a far broader concept than our government or any incumbent. I didn't blame the flag when Clinton was president. There's no need for this silly pretense. Reporters can still be honest while rooting for our side to win. Did American journalists feign neutrality in World War I or II?

American journalists are not citizens of the world; they're citizens of the United States. That's who issued their passports. Within our borders, they enjoy our rights and are protected by our Constitution. In places like Afghanistan, they exist precariously at the whim of tyrants like the Taliban. When push comes to shove, it'll be American servicemen and women who will protect their lives, their freedoms and their rights from foreign adversaries as well as protecting their families back home. We are under attack by forces who abhor our values, our beliefs and our freedoms. Should there be any doubt which side American journalists are on?

Liberal Media Muddles Middle
July 13, 2001

When I speak of the mainstream liberal media, for the most part I'm referring to the seven sisters: *CBS, NBC, ABC, The New York Times, The Washington Post, Time* and *Newsweek*. There are also *The Los Angeles Times, Associated Press, PBS, NPR*, and others where liberal bias is the order of the day. Yes, there are conservative outposts like the editorial pages of *The Wall Street Journal*, a handful of magazines like *National Review* and *The Weekly Standard*, along with a number of local and national talk-radio shows. But all of the latter are self-admitted venues of conservative opinion. The mainstream liberal media pretends to be objective and balanced. Hah!

Bernard Goldberg used to be a *CBS News* correspondent. In 1996 he did the unspeakable. While still at *CBS*, Goldberg wrote an opinion piece for *The Wall Street Journal* affirming *CBS'* liberal bias, citing a story by *CBS* reporter Eric Engberg as an egregious example. Engberg's editorial-masquerading-as-a-news-story attacked Steve Forbes' proposal for a flat tax. For his candor, Goldberg became an instant pariah at *CBS*, and neither Engberg nor Dan Rather has spoken to him since. Isn't it ironic that self-anointed media watchdogs who are so quick to criticize every other individual and institution in our society have no tolerance for criticism of themselves?

In a recent *C-SPAN* appearance recounting this episode, Goldberg related a pointed conversation he had with Rather in which Rather insisted that the editorial page of *The New York Times* was "middle of the road." Noting that it had endorsed every major liberal position of our time, Goldberg was flabbergasted that anyone could regard the *Times* as middle of the road. The explanation, of course, is that self-serving liberals, like Dan Rather, regard their obviously correct, liberal position as middle of the road. It's those radical right-wing conservatives who just don't get it.

I understand the tactical advantage of pre-empting the middle and branding your opponents as extremists. I'll concede that *The New York Times* is not far-left in the mode of publications like *The Nation* and *Mother Jones*, but just because there are those to your left doesn't make you centrist. There are publications to the right of the editorial page of *The Wall Street Journal* but that doesn't make the journal middle of the road, either. Editorially, the *Journal* is right-center just as the *Times* is left-center. And, in conventional usage, the term we use for left-center is liberal.

Here's a test. At the risk of some simplification in the name of brevity, I'll list the liberal position on a cross section of political issues: anti-tax cut, pro-redistribution of income, pro-gay, anti-Boy Scouts, pro-feminist, pro-government regulation, pro-environmentalist, pro-government social spending, pro-affirmative action, pro-abortion rights, pro-judicial activism, pro-social engineering, anti-gun, anti-defense spending, anti-missile defense system, pro-socialized medicine, anti-oil exploration, anti-free market, pro-price controls, anti-big business, anti-free trade, anti-globalization, anti-capital punishment, pro-campaign finance reform, pro-union, pro-more spending for public education, anti-voucher system for public education, anti-tobacco, anti-SUV, anti-cop, anti-CIA, pro-suing everything in sight, anti-tort reform. I could go on.

The New York Times, in particular, and the mainstream media, in general, are consistently on the "politically correct" side of all of these issues and many more like them. If this doesn't define liberal in practical, contemporary terms, then nothing does.

One last point. A popular canard on the socialist-left, these days, is to throw around the term "corporate media," as if to equate corporate with conservative. The companies that comprise the mainstream media are all big corporations, to be sure, but their news and editorial staffs are populated overwhelmingly by dyed-in-the wool liberals, groomed in liberal schools of journalism. And their information product demonstrably reflects the mindset of that dominant culture. When lefties curse "corporations," understand that what they really hate is private enterprise. What's their alternative to "corporate media," government media? Wouldn't that be wonderful?

The DLEMM: Leftstream Isn't Mainstream
July 22, 2010

Technically, "media" is a plural noun ("medium," the singular). In contemporary political usage, however, as in "liberal media," it can be a singular verb. So, you might say, "The liberal media *is* in love with Barack Obama." In that context, the liberal media is treated as kind of a commune, including:

ABC, NBC, CBS, CNN, MSNBC, PBS, NPR, New York Times, Washington Post, Time, Newsweek, Associated Press, etc. – you get the idea.

That this community of overwhelmingly like-minded fellow travelers routinely spins its output with a liberal bias is beyond dispute. Anyone who claims the news pages of *The New York Times* aren't biased to the left is either delusional or lying. When more radical leftists ("progressives") deny this liberal media bias, it's merely a semantic ploy. From their perch on the far left, conventional liberals are centrists or even conservative only because they're not left enough.

When conservatives speak of the "mainstream media" (MSM), it has a derogatory connotation. They're referring to the liberal media hive. While MSM rolls easily off the tongue, I've never been comfortable with the term. It inadvertently conveys the false and confusing impression that the liberal media reflects (note the singular noun) the views or values of the mainstream of American public opinion. It doesn't. It's not mainstream; it's leftstream. Rush Limbaugh calls it the "drive-by media." That's better. It suggests superficiality, sensationalism and a herd mentality.

I happen to prefer "dominant, liberal establishment mass-media" (DLEMM). It's not very catchy but it's more accurate and precise. All five words are necessary. "Mass media" refers to wide audience reach as compared to boutique media, low-circulation journals, academic publications, newsletters or blogs. "Establishment" means old media as opposed to new media – like talk radio, the Internet and Twitter.

While there are conservative outposts in the mass media (like the *Fox News Channel*), I say "dominant liberal" because liberal outlets dominate. *ABC, CBS* and *NBC* have a combined prime-time news audience of about 20 million viewers compared to 3 million for *Fox* — which intolerant liberals indignantly begrudge.

Recognizing and identifying the existence of the DLEMM isn't the same thing as branding it a conspiracy. It's not a conspiracy in the sense that this is some kind of secret society. It couldn't be more public and ubiquitous. And it's not as if its members formally conspire to do what they do. They don't have to. They're cut from the same cloth. Starting in college, journalism students are self-selected. The kids who sign up for this major tend to be liberal.

Their professors are overwhelmingly liberal. When they graduate and take their first job at a newspaper, magazine or broadcast station, they're greeted and acculturated by the generations of liberals who preceded them along the same path.

As Tom Bethell once analogized, geese don't "conspire" to fly south in a V-formation in the fall. It's not as if they meet in the back room of a bar in Montreal and concoct a secret plan. They don't have to. It's instinctive. But they, nonetheless, fly south in V-formation. You can photograph the migration.

Media liberals don't conspire to spin the news in a leftist direction. They don't have to. It comes naturally to them and it's also apparent. All the more so, now that there are conservative alternatives with which to compare.

Conservative talk radio and the Internet are increasingly diluting the power and influence of the DLEMM. The left hates this because it disturbs its monopoly, which it believes to be the natural order of things. It's not enough that leftist thought dominates K-12 education, higher education, Hollywood, entertainment and pop culture. It wants to preserve its domination of the media, too.

That's not a good thing for diverse and open debate in a free society.

Subsidizing Liberal Bias
July 1, 2005

Liberals are forever complaining that the Bush Administration "manages the news," spins it to fit its agenda. They have a point. But every administration does this. Of course, these same critics never complain that *National Public Radio* and the *Public Broadcasting System* indulge their own biases. Why? Because *NPR* and *PBS* manipulate their programming to fit the liberal agenda. That's the status quo that liberal cheerleaders for *NPR* and *PBS* enjoy and tenaciously defend.

We expect politicians, including presidents, to be biased advocates for their own agendas. Journalistic objectivity and balance at *NPR* and *PBS* is purely a pretense. Sure, public broadcasting offers some quality programming and more depth than most commercial TV and radio news, but it'd be nice to see quality and depth of a more balanced nature. In spite of rare, token conservative offerings, public broadcasting is overwhelmingly liberal. From Bill Moyers to *Frontline*, from Nina Totenberg to *All Things Considered*, *PBS* and *NPR* list decidedly to port.

Perhaps that explains why Republicans in Congress are always trying to cut *NPR* and *PBS* budgets while Democrats perpetually fight to protect them. Hard as it might be, imagine how Democrats would complain about *NPR* and *PBS* if their programming had a conservative bias. Kenneth Tomlinson, the Republican who now chairs the board for the *Corporation for Public Broadcasting*, is under attack from Democrats in Congress and liberals everywhere. Tomlinson's sin is that he's called for long-overdue balance at *PBS*. I wish him luck. He'll need it.

In a tortured defense of *NPR* and *PBS* taxpayer subsidies, Bob Smith — a liberal talk show host on WXXI-AM, the *NPR* affiliate in Rochester, N.Y. — made the following claim: "You may be interested in knowing that the indirect subsidy we all pay each year because the ad revenue paid to Rush Limbaugh's network and his major market affiliates is fully tax-deductible at the source, is far greater than the total national taxpayer contribution to *all* public radio and TV stations. Rush Limbaugh raises your taxes far more than *NPR* and *PBS*."

166

This is a priceless insight into the liberal mentality, speaking volumes about their collectivist instincts and disdain for private property. Allow me to dissect, reorder and correct this babble:

1. Businesses are forced by government to pay income taxes.

2. Income taxes are assessed on business income; that is, a business's revenues minus its expenses. That's why it's called an *income tax*, as opposed to a gross revenues tax. If a company's costs exceed its revenues, it has no profits and, hence, no income tax liability.

3. This nitwit's contention is that the deduction a company takes from its revenues to advertise on the Limbaugh show, a legitimate business expense, constitutes an "indirect subsidy" because it reduces the company's potential tax liability. This is as absurd as objecting to a business expensing the cost of its payroll, raw materials or utilities.

4. In essence, Smith is saying that a business should be grateful the government doesn't confiscate all its revenues. As he and his liberal ilk see it, government has first claim on everything you earn. Anything you're allowed to keep, then, is an "indirect subsidy," for which you should thank government for its generosity.

In the real world, as distinct from the liberal's socialist utopia, what you earn is yours, not the governments. *You* have first claim on it. When government allows you to keep a greater share of what you've earned – whether you're an individual or a business – it's not a subsidy. It was yours to begin with. Conversely, any tax dollars that go to *NPR* or *PBS* is a subsidy, since those dollars were first earned by someone else, then taxed and redistributed to the beneficiaries. The same applies to food stamps, welfare, housing subsidies, Medicaid or any other government "entitlement" program. No one has a *right* to any of these payments; they're all charity.

The prospect of an *after-tax* return on your labor and investment is what motivates rational human beings to devote their time and risk capital in productive enterprises. Increase the tax and lower the expectation of net income and you get less investment, labor and output. That's why a country can't tax itself rich. That's a concept that the left seems unable to grasp.

Liberal Talk Doesn't Sell
April 4, 2003

In politics, it's been said, perception is reality.

Consequently, those who create perceptions wield enormous influence in our open society. For decades, the left has dominated the principal avenues for forming public perception. That includes the major media, the entertainment industry, and education. Having enjoyed a near monopoly in those areas, it's understandable that the liberal establishment finds the conservative presence in talk radio so annoying.

It's positively outrageous that conservatives would presume to exert their own influence on public opinion.

The remedy is a projected $200 million venture to create an exclusively liberal talk-radio network, with ambitious plans to expand into television production. (I thought programs like *The West Wing* had already broken that ground). The seed money is being provided by Sheldon and Anita Drobney, a pair of Chicago high rollers who have been major campaign contributors to Bill Clinton and Al Gore. They haven't named it yet, so let's call it *LibNet*. As a conservative radio talk show host, I'm delighted by the prospect.

The prevailing myth in leftist circles is that talk radio is stacked against liberals. It's true that conservatives have the largest audiences and the greatest success, but it's not because liberals have not had their turn at the mike. Headliners like Mario Cuomo and populist left-winger Jim Hightower have tried and failed. On the other hand, some liberals have done well and established a following.

There's Ron Kuby in New York, Bernie Ward in San Francisco, Mike Malloy in Chicago, and Lionel in national syndication. In Denver, a variety of local stations have experimented with a stream of self-professed liberals, none of whom have ever delivered an audience. It's not my fault that people don't want to listen to them. Station owners and program directors aren't especially political. If they have a bias it's a commercial one: they demand audience ratings.

While commercial radio has to meet the market test, *National Public Radio* doesn't, and its contributors enthusiastically underwrite programming with a liberal spin. *Radio Pacifica* is even farther left.

Similarly, *LibNet* is a political crusade. Its fat cat bankrollers aren't dependent on ratings. They just want to get Democrats elected.

(This is one of those unintended consequences of campaign finance reform. If their contributions to candidates and parties are limited, well-heeled activists can influence the elections by buying the media instead.) Conversely, it's important to note that Rush Limbaugh, Michael Reagan, Sean Hannity and any number of local, conservative radio hosts don't owe their exposure and success to subsidies from political benefactors. They built their audiences from the ground up, in a highly competitive environment, one station at a time, the old-fashioned way – they earned it!

What I like most about *LibNet* is that it will be *officially* liberal. *NBC, CBS, ABC, Time, Newsweek, The New York Times*, etc., are all liberal, of course, but they don't publicly admit it. *LibNet*'s hosts and the spin they put on issues will sound like an echo of the rest of the liberal media hive. Perhaps naïve and impressionable consumers of the daily fare from Dan Rather, Peter Jennings and Tom Brokaw and company will now make the connection and come to realize how they've been manipulated. This will only add to the audience of the unliberal TV news alternative: the outstanding, rapidly growing *Fox News Channel*.

Good!

It's well-established that liberals don't care what you do as long as it's mandatory. So, when *LibNet* flops and its angels tire of hemorrhaging money, the natural liberal reaction will be to impose some kind of quota, excuse me, *affirmative action* plan on the media. Biased network TV anchors, of course, would be exempted, unless *Fox* someday surpasses *ABC, CBS, NBC, CNN* and *PBS* combined. But radio stations would be required by law to employ an equal number of liberal and conservative talk show hosts. When that doesn't produce the desired results, the only thing that could stop them from *forcing* audiences to listen to the liberal talk show hosts would be the Eighth Amendment's protection against cruel and unusual punishment.

Advocacy Corrupts Journalism
February 7, 2013

Once upon a time, the medium that disseminated news to the general public was known as "the press." These days, that term has been replaced by "media," to account for the expansion of news reporting beyond print to include radio, television and the Internet. While the reach of the media has expanded, public trust continues to decline.

Here's an example of why. Josh Elliot is an *ABC-TV* anchor who reads the news on *Good Morning America*. In that role, he's supposed to perform as a reporter, not a commentator. Elliot is a youngish anchor from a generation of media liberals who don't even pretend to conceal their bias.

In March of last year, Elliot appeared at a gala put on by the Gay & Lesbian Alliance Against Defamation (GLAAD) to accept an award for "Outstanding TV Journalism." He won it for his segment "Battle Against Bullying," which decried the treatment of a gay teenager that led to his suicide. The segment itself was a legitimate news story about an outrageous incident. What was inappropriate was Elliot's attitude and remarks while accepting the award.

He shamelessly propitiated the GLAAD audience, declaring, "I will never be in a braver room than this." Really? How about a hospital ward full of combat soldiers wounded in battle? Or first responders – cops, EMTs and firefighters – who had risked their lives in the wake of a catastrophic attack like 9/11?

Even more troubling was his affront to the ideal of objective journalism as he preened, "I'm proud to work at a place that believes in advocacy journalism." So, his bosses at *ABC News* encourage reporters to brazenly cross the line that separates even-handed reporting from commentary? Doesn't this compromise his and their credibility?

This is further compounded by the selectivity of issues worthy of advocacy as perceived by liberal journalists who dominate the mass media. Their approved list of favorite causes also includes gun control, abortion, racial preferences, global warming alarmism and tax increases on the rich, to name just a few. Conservative causes like limited government, individualism, property rights, a strong national defense, private enterprise and constitutional originalism don't qualify.

This notion of noble advocacy has its roots in an old bromide fashionable in college journalism classrooms and reinforced in liberal newsrooms, claiming that the role of journalists is to "comfort the afflicted and afflict the comfortable."

Ironically, that turn of a phrase was coined back in 1902 by Finley Peter Dunne, a political satirist who actually believed that journalists should do no such thing. He put those words in the mouth of a fictional, curmudgeonly Irishman he created, "Mr. Dooley," whose sarcastic rant (translated from the original Irish brogue) went something like this: "The newspaper does everything for us. It runs the police force and the banks, commands the militia, controls the legislature, baptizes the young, marries the foolish, comforts the afflicted and afflicts the comfortable, buries the dead, and roasts them afterward."

Through Mr. Dooley, Dunne was, in fact, damning the journalists of his day for their bias and presumptuous sanctimony in picking winners and losers, advancing their own pet causes and editorializing in the guise of reporting. It should be obvious that the comfortable don't necessarily deserve to be afflicted, and those who are self-destructively afflicted don't automatically deserve to be rewarded.

Journalists aren't philosopher-kings with superior credentials to judge morality, justice and public policy. They're just people with a pen (or a keyboard) and an opinion — overwhelmingly, a liberal one. And their cheerleading for President Obama these past four years has further eroded what little remained of their credibility. While they pretend to "speak truth to power," they shout at conservatives and fall mute to fellow liberals. Behind every double standard lies an unconfessed single one.

What is a Journalist Today?
March 7, 2013

My recent column on liberal bias in news reporting ("Advocacy Corrupts Journalism,") drew some puzzling responses. In it, I criticized Josh Elliott, network TV news anchor on *ABC's Good Morning America*, for exclaiming his pride in working at a place that believes in "advocacy journalism."

One detractor accused me of inconsistency, criticizing another journalist for bias when I am biased myself. He wondered whether the "non-advocacy of the media" I seek applies only to "them" but not to me. In a final salvo, he declaimed, "Who is Rosen to call the kettle black?"

Well, if I'm the pot in his metaphor – where "black" is a substitute for "opinionated" – the kettle and I are both black. But I'm allowed to be. In fact, my task is to write for the opinion pages of this newspaper. I'm not a reporter, an anchor or a moderator. People who fill those roles are obliged to be fair and balanced, and to keep their opinions to themselves. Reporters betray their charge and are no longer simply reporting when they wander – either inadvertently or intentionally – into advocacy of one viewpoint over another.

For example, a commonly used sly device of reporters who seek to disguise their advocacy is to selectively and one-sidedly quote others who mouth the so-called reporter's personal agenda.

I made that distinction in my column, but for those who missed it, I'll make it even clearer: I have a conservative bias. I admit it. I have a philosophy, a vision of the way the world works, of human nature and of the role of government in society. I believe everyone is biased, to one degree or another. Perfect objectivity is impossible. We're all the product of our DNA, experiences and outlook.

Any mature adult who is still a philosophical blank slate is either intellectually lazy or an idiot. But one can be biased and still be rational, factual, honest and ethical in the presentation of his opinion. It's the differences in our respective visions, premises and assumptions that lead us to different (and sometimes irreconcilable) conclusions.

Unlike reporters, the writers whose work you read on opinion pages are not bound to be neutral observers. More often (and

172

appropriately), we're advocates. And as an advocate on the right, I have no duty to make the left's case. On the contrary, I do what I can to preempt and rebut their arguments. Analogously, a prosecutor in a criminal trial has no obligation to make the defense's case, nor the defense to make the prosecution's.

As for my criticism of "another journalist," that implies I am one myself. I don't know and really don't care if I fit that definition. There's great confusion as to what makes one a journalist these days. Does the term only accurately apply to reporters?

For 30 years, I've written an op-ed newspaper column. But I'm not a reporter, so am I therefore not a journalist? How about an editorial page editor? He may hang out with the crowd at the press club, but he also writes opinions and he's not a reporter. Does that mean he's not a journalist even though he works for a journal? How about edgy magazine feature writers; are they journalists? For more than 30 years, I've hosted a radio talk show on which I do overt commentary. Does that make me less of a broadcast journalist than TV news anchors and reporters who do covert commentary, like those who routinely cheerlead for Barack Obama?

As traditional newspapers and magazines continue to wither in this hyper-electronic age, the media universe is teeming with bloggers, tweeters, Internet talkers and who knows what next. Should they be called neo-journalists? Perhaps the label has lost its meaning. As for me, I proudly do what I do and don't pretend to be what I'm not.

Lavender Journalism
March 21, 2013

On Tuesday March 12, the Colorado Senate passed a bill to legalize civil unions for gay couples. The following day, the *Denver Post* published a front-page color photo of House Speaker Mark Ferrandino and his partner, Greg Wertsch, celebrating this historic event in Ferrandino's office with a kiss, mano-a-mano.

The *Post* anticipated that the photo would stir up a controversy, which it did, punctuated by reader comments – pro and con – in print, on-line and over radio airwaves. Linda Shapely, the *Post's* director of newsroom operations, responded in a blog post with the details of how the decision to run the photo was made in the Tuesday afternoon news meeting. As justification, she explained that the *Post* has shown straight couples celebrating with a kiss on election night; and also described this as one of those special photo "moments" when a picture is worth a thousand words.

I'm reminded of two such iconic moments: the full-page *Life Magazine* photo of an American sailor kissing a nurse in Times Square on V-J Day in 1945; the other, the little girl running naked from an aerial, napalm attack during the Vietnam War in 1972. These were both spontaneous (and far more compelling) snapshots. The *Post's* photographer claims the "kissing moment" he captured was a spontaneous event. But Ferrandino and Wertsch knew their actions were being chronicled by a newspaper photographer. What's more, conveniently placed between the two in the foreground on Ferrendino's desk was a baby bottle for the couple's foster child with no child in sight. Color me skeptical.

While Shapley's account of the *Post's* decision-making process at that news meeting makes some arguable, if not wholly persuasive points, she leaves something out which may have gone unspoken but was likely a strong factor. In addition to the *Post's* forthright support for gay civil unions and same-sex marriage on its editorial pages, it has long advanced a thinly-veiled crusade for these causes on its news pages. I don't believe the *Post* published this photo in order to offend or sensationalize. After all, it's not the *National Enquirer*. The "kiss" photo was a not-so-subtle exercise in advocacy journalism. Normalize the act of two men kissing and you've taken the next step toward normalizing and legalizing same-sex marriage.

Kisses come in different varieties. There's a romantic kiss between a boy and a girl; familial kisses between relatives (a tie in a football game is like kissing your sister); a ceremonial kiss on both cheeks from a French general when receiving a medal for valor; or a Mafia death-kiss before a whacking. The *Post*'s publication of the staged Ferrendino-Welcher kiss was, at least in part, a political kiss reflecting the agenda of the paper's dominant liberal culture.

Sure, it made many heterosexuals uncomfortable, even those of us who support civil unions and don't care what people do in the privacy of their bedrooms. That doesn't make us "homophobes" (a loaded political term if ever there was one). It doesn't mean we don't like gays. But that kind of kiss gives some, probably most, heterosexuals the willies; just as some gays may be turned off by heterosexuals kissing.

There was a time when *Post* editors would never have featured this kind of photo on the front page. Times change. Attitudes toward homosexuality have certainly evolved but still divide along generational lines, as reflected in public opinion polls. Older folks grew up in an era where gays were mostly closeted and socially stigmatized. Younger people see gays commonly and favorably portrayed in movies, on TV, in social media and in their classrooms. As the next generation displaces the last, civil unions and same-sex marriages will likely become increasingly acceptable. The *Post* is doing its part to accelerate that process on its unobjective news pages. You might call it lavender journalism.

The Tea Partyers vs. "Progressive" Leftists and Statists
February 18, 2010

Over the years, I've observed *Washington Post* columnist E.J. Dionne move from respectably liberal to left-liberal to delusional-left. His journey might be explained, in part, by the procession of presidents and congresses.

In the 1990s, he was mostly approving of the policies of Bill Clinton that tugged Clinton gently to the left. When Republicans took control of Congress in 1995, his frustration began to rise. After the election of George W. Bush in 2000, Dionne was soon afflicted with Bush Derangement Syndrome. He became increasingly angry and irrational. Although he survived the disorder, he was permanently scarred.

His attitude and mental health seemed to temporarily improve with the election of Barack Obama and the expansion of Democratic control of Congress.

Then came the relapse. As Obama's popularity declined and his leftist agenda stalled, Dionne has become positively apoplectic. Bush Derangement Syndrome has metastasized into Tea Party Derangement Syndrome, which has become epidemic among lefties.

The symptoms were glaring in a recent column in which he explained that he and fellow progressives don't regard Obama as especially liberal and can't understand why he's incurred the wrath of Tea Partyers. Dionne claims that Obama's stimulus plan was "if anything, too small" and that Obamacare stops too far short of the leftist dream of single-payer (socialized) medicine.

If Obama's march toward an American version of Euro-socialism is behind schedule, it's not because of any lack or commitment on his part. Fortunately, he was elected president, not king. He can only sign or veto legislation, he can't impose it. Opposition from the Republicans and the odd Democrat doesn't make Obama any less liberal.

Dionne, refusing to recognize that the left has overreached, doesn't present it this way. This was supposed to be their moment. Frustrated by the delay, he rationalizes that Obama is too "middle-of-the-road." This theme has been echoed by others on the left like John Meachem, the editor of *Newsweek*, who proclaimed in a 2009 story that

"We Are All Socialists Now." Recently, Meachem went so far as to describe Obama – arguably the most left-wing president in our history – as "right-of-center." One has to be pretty far left to place Obama on the right.

Conveniently re-creating Obama as a non-ideological centrist, Dionne asserts that the real reason Tea Partyers oppose him is because they're racists and anti-statists. When it was radical leftists staging rallies against Bush and comparing him to Hitler, Dionne and his ilk told us "dissent is the highest form of patriotism" (falsely attributing a quote from Marxist historian Howard Zinn to Thomas Jefferson). Dissent from the right, however, cannot be principled, so it must be seditious and mean-spirited. There's no need to dignify Dionne's charges of racism with a response. But Dionne reveals his true nature when he advocates "statism."

Statism vests supremacy and economic control in a powerful central government. Whether it be state socialism or its cousin, state capitalism, statism is intrinsically collectivist, subjugating individual freedom to a presumptuous notion of the common welfare.

Dionne dismisses anti-statism by narrowly associating it with 18th-century anti-federalists who opposed the Constitution. In fact, most of our founders mistrusted a powerful central government, which is why the Constitution enumerated and restricted federal powers, safeguarded the independence of states, and reserved ultimate power to the people. "Progressive" leftists like Dionne are inherent statists with unbounded faith in the virtue and wisdom of elite bureaucrats who share their ideology to run our government, our economy and our lives.

This is the great divide between left and right in our country. The root of opposition from Tea Partyers and an increasing number of Americans to Obama, Pelosi, Reid and their statist agenda is increasingly reflected in the polls.

177

Reality

IV. Government

A "Government" is essentially the form or system of administering the designated operations of a nation, state or other subdivision of a territory. Through history, there have been many forms of government established to carry out the rules, policies and activities of these various entities as civilization has advanced in the many countries of the world. These myriad systems have ranged from absolute monarchies to dictatorships to democratic republics and everything in between.

Since its inception, with the Declaration of Independence from England in 1776, the United States of America subsequently adopted its Constitution in 1787 to establish a federal republic, consisting of a union of independent states. The nation's formative document was carefully drawn to define how the fledgling republic would be organized and governed. The Constitution enumerated the powers and limited the scope of both the federal government and the respective states as well as established a unique system of three co-equal branches of the federal government; Executive, Legislative and Judicial. Our system of electing representatives, as well as a Bill of Rights outlining fundamental and inviolable protections of its citizens from the intrusions of the government, were also included in the document that set forth the rules for governing the new nation.

The Preamble to the Constitution succinctly prioritized the important aims the newly established government was designed to accomplish on behalf of the people. Rather than paraphrasing it, here is exactly how it was written:

"We the People of the United States, in Order to form a more perfect Union, establish Justice, insure domestic Tranquility, provide for the common defence, promote the general Welfare, and secure the Blessings of Liberty to ourselves and our Posterity, do ordain and establish this Constitution for the United States of America."

It should be noted that the "general welfare" clause in the Preamble and in Article I, Section 8 has long been a point of contention, with leftists claiming it was an open-ended justification for expanding the welfare state. But as James Madison, the principal author of the Constitution, made clear in *Federalist No. 41*, it was not originally intended as a blank check to authorize the federal government to create programs or spend money on anything it likes to make people happy or provide public assistance through "welfare" programs as we define that term today. Congress's power to "lay and collect taxes" and other imposts was strictly limited to its specifically-enumerated powers immediately following the "general welfare" clause in Article I, Section 8 that were appropriate and which were delegated to the federal government rather than the states.

To the founders who created the Constitution, limited government, especially at the federal level, was a foundational necessity intrinsic to their overriding value of protecting individual liberty, just as it has been to conservatives ever since. By contrast, expanded government has been a fundamental goal to those on the left and today's "progressives." While government is an essential institution in any society, in the United States of America our society is greater than our government. It's essential to understand that government is not society but, rather, a subset of our society. Only under totalitarian governments is government the equivalent of society.

This section, entitled "Government," encompasses issues involving our common defense, welfare, social security, healthcare and education. Also, how the Constitution affects the lives of our citizens on an ongoing basis.

Providing for the Common Defense – War and Peace

Peace Through Strength: The Inescapable Lesson of History
October 31, 1984

Of all the plums regularly offered to voters in election campaigns, peace must surely be the most popular. Have you ever heard a candidate who said he was opposed to it? If only the desire for peace or a politician's promise were sufficient to achieve it.

Neville Chamberlain became prime minister of Great Britain in 1937, largely because of his sincere dedication to the cause of peace. His view of the world, however, was based on wishful thinking, not reality, and his countrymen and most of the rest of the world paid the terrible price of war for his folly. History repeats itself, and we observe during this election year the peace race and its empty promises in classic form. The Mondale/Ferraro ticket has been a willing vehicle for any number of groups and individuals, marching under the banner of peace, whose policy prescriptions in the real world would cost us all dearly.

Jonathan Schell, author of *Fate of the Earth*, the peace-at-any-price handbook, talks of reinventing politics, just as Marx spoke of reinventing human nature. Henry Kissinger, in *Years of Upheaval*, offers a sobering dose of reality and a glimpse at what Schell's world might look like: "If peace is equated simply with the absence of war, if the yearning for peace is not allied with a sense of justice, it can become an abject pacifism that turns the world over to the most ruthless."

Perhaps our problem is that there are those with differing definitions of justice and ruthlessness. One of the leaders of the post-World War II peace movement was British philosopher Bertrand Russell. Russell was the one who coined the expression "Better Red than Dead," surely one of history's most dishonest intellectual exercises. In logic that is known as a false dilemma, Red or Dead are not the only choices. You can have another: alive and free. The point is that one might have to risk his life to protect his freedom, (to resist redness) but

181

that doesn't mean he must *lose* it. Many who have died defending freedom were prepared to do so, so that others – families, countrymen, future generations – could enjoy its fruits.

On another score, Russell was guilty of ulterior motives. As a member of the Fabian Society – the late 19th century contribution of British intellectuals to the cause of socialism – socialism was not something repugnant to Russell, but a desirable outcome. Enlightened redness was his favorite shade.

Scratch a typical peace militant today and you will likely find, beneath the surface, an opponent of capitalism, an advocate of world government, a detractor of the U.S. role in the world – what U.N. Ambassador Jeanne Kirkpatrick refers to as the blame-America-first crowd. The global view held by many of these people requires that the U.S. be weakened as a world power.

So they bludgeon us with images of nuclear holocaust and human extinction. They tell us we are arrogant to resist Soviet aggression if it risks nuclear war. Our freedom is selfish indulgence. We owe it to the rest of the world to capitulate if the other side is sufficiently menacing. We are to be guided by fear, not principle. Survival is all that matters. Welcome to 1984's version of "Better Red than Dead." It's a base and defeatist vision of the human spirit and is as odious today as it was when Russell introduced it.

Fear paralyzes. But the paralysis would take place only in free societies, while the Soviet Union continued to enlarge its arsenal and extend its empire. Nuclear weapons are political weapons, designed for intimidation – the language of Soviet foreign policy. Soviet targeting of the cities of Europe with SS-20 missiles was an act of intimidation intended to achieve political objectives, not the least of which was the dismemberment of NATO. The Soviet Union, regardless of arms-control agreements to the contrary, will always press for nuclear superiority – not parity – as its main instrument of foreign policy.

I was part of a delegation a few years ago that met with Secretary-General Joseph Luns and other NATO officials in Brussels. A remark by the Turkish ambassador at one of those meetings has stuck in my mind ever since. Contrasting the objectives of the Soviets and the West, he said: "NATO and the U.S. desire peace without victory; the Soviet Union wants victory without war."

Historian Will Durant observed that "Peace is an unstable equilibrium, which can be preserved only by acknowledged supremacy or equal power." In 1928, 63 nations joined in the Kellogg-Briand Pact to disarm and outlaw war. The Germans, Italians and Japanese ignored the agreement. The balance of power shifted, and, in spite of a wealth of good intentions and hopes for peace, World War II, the most destructive in history, ensued.

Good intentions and hope aren't enough.

When dealing with ruthless aggressors like leaders of the Soviet Union, the concept of peace through strength – even an uneasy peace – is more than a Reagan campaign slogan. It's the inescapable lesson of history.

Plowshares Make Lousy Swords
April 17, 1992

It's really wonderful that little kids no longer have to go to bed each night in mortal fear that the United States and the Soviet Union were at the brink of nuclear war. (Although I doubt that very many actually did.) It's great that the Cold War is over. We can hope that a warm, mutually beneficial relationship between the U.S. and the UFFR (Union of Fewer and Fewer Republics) will follow for many years to come.

The *way* the Cold War ended, however, is more than incidental. It's been said that the West's goal in the post-World War II era was "peace without victory," while the Soviet Union's objective was "victory without war." The point being that we never sought to subjugate them. Whatever you want to call the outcome, our side won. Had theirs won, on its terms, the post-Cold War world would not have been a very pleasant place in which to live. As gracious victors, we are now planning to pummel the vanquished with billions of dollars in aid.

The symbolic ending of this 50-year conflict was the tearing down of the Berlin Wall. It was profoundly ironic that this act took place not during a state of war but during a state of relative peace, and that the instruments of the wall's demolition weren't high-tech weapons of mass destruction but hammers and bare hands.

It's also ironic that we can thank, for this outcome, our warriors not our pacifists. It was Western geopolitical and military resolve, not good will, that produced this result. Although the Cold War may have *ended* peacefully, it had no shortage of violent confrontations. The East and West Germans who had the pleasure of dismantling the Berlin Wall were standing on the shoulders of others who risked or gave their lives resisting communism in places like Korea, Vietnam, Angola, Afghanistan, Central America, Hungary, or Czechoslovakia.

When the Soviets finally threw in the ideological white (or, in this case, red) towel, it was because they had been worn down militarily, strategically, technologically, philosophically and – finally – economically. To be sure, their ideology was rotten to the core, but so it had been for 70 years. In the absence of Western resolve, that rotten ideology may well have dominated the world or destroyed it.

In the post-Cold War euphoria, some believe America need fear war no more. There are always some who believe that, and they're always wrong. They'll be wrong this time, too. Seventy-five years ago this week, we entered a "war to end all wars." Although we won it, it didn't.

Make note of that as we hear the siren song of disarmament from this generation's wishful thinkers. In the absence of a direct Soviet threat, it's not only reasonable but provident that we adjust our defense posture. In so doing, we can save billions of dollars. But significantly reducing military spending is one thing; eliminating it is quite another.

The world still abounds with would-be Hitlers – large and small. And when they're gone, others will come to take their places. As long as the U.S. remains the world's No. 1 economic power, we must remain its No. 1 military power. It cannot be otherwise.

Our current post-Cold War active duty force is about 2 million. We may cut that by as much as half. But we'll continue to require naval, air and ground forces that can move quickly and decisively around the globe. And that'll continue to cost money. Defense spending, today, is about $300 billion – 20 percent of the federal budget. Even a major reduction won't bring that amount under $200 billion, about 10 percent of future budgets. There's only so much you can save. To begin to fund their grandiose spending promises, Democrats in Congress or running for the presidency would have to eliminate all military spending, and then some.

Beating your swords into plowshares isn't a prudent defense policy, unless you believe the next war will be fought with plows.

As the World Turns, Friends Become Foes
October 19, 2001

I'll confess that I'm not objective when it comes to American interests in the world. I'm rooting for our side. By the same token, some of our own citizens who belong to the Blame America First (BAF) Club – you know who they are – aren't objective either. They're rooting for the other side, whoever is the other side at the moment. Their loyalty is not to the petty cause of U.S. nationalism but to the glorious vision of internationalism, world government and universal social justice (read: *socialism*).

It's not surprising, then, that as we mount our counterattack on international terrorism, our domestic BAF agitators have mounted their soapboxes to attack America for its past alliances. Of course, they're still whining about U.S. support for anti-Castro forces in Cuba, the Contras in Nicaragua, the oligarchy in El Salvador, and our opposition to the Allende regime in Chile. But that's a familiar theme. They will always take the side of Marxist movements: *pas d'ennemis à gauche*, no enemies on the left.

Conflicts and alliances in the Middle East, however, often transcend conventional left-right ideological battles. (American Jews, for example, are normally reliable liberal Democrats, hot on social spending, cool to the military. But when Israel's involved, they suddenly become hawks.)

BAFers decry U.S. apostasy. They remind us that his evilness, Osama bin Laden, was once a beneficiary of U.S. support when we armed the Mujahedeen in their fight against Soviet invaders. If that's not bad enough, once upon a time we supported Iraq – home of the dastardly Saddam Hussein – in its war against Iran, then led by the merciless Ayatollah Khomeini. Why are yesterday's allies today's villains and vice versa?

As British Prime Minister William Gladstone once explained: "Nations do not have permanent enemies, they do not have permanent friends, they only have permanent interests." Politics and war make strange bedfellows. That's why we joined forces with the Soviet Union in World War II, because Nazi Germany was the greater enemy. Then we fought the Soviets in a Cold War for 50 years. Now, ironically, we're allied with them against the Taliban in Afghanistan. Go figure.

We won our independence in a revolutionary war against Britain, battled the redcoats again in the War of 1812 (that's when they set fire to Washington), then fought by their side in two world wars. We fought the Germans in WWI, and both the Germans and Japanese in WWII. Now we're friends. We were allied with the Chinese in WWII against the Japanese, but then fought them in Korea a few years later and have been adversaries ever since. We've been, alternately, friends and enemies with Italy, Spain, France, Mexico, Cuba and almost everyone else in the world that matters, except maybe Switzerland.

Yes, our country has often acted on pragmatism in picking its allies, and sometimes made bad choices. Listen, there aren't a lot of Jeffersonian democrats out there. All too often we're faced with the lesser of evils. But let's tally up the debits and credits. Lefties would deduct a few hundred points for Noriega, Marcos, Batista and an assortment of minor-league, right-wing autocrats. Now offset that with the credit we get for turning the tide in WWI, saving the world from Imperial Japan and the Nazis in WWII, rebuilding Europe, and facing down the Soviets in the Cold War, just for openers. That's worth 10 million points for the good, netting the best score ever for a great power in world history.

We have cause to be proud.

Defending Defense, Part I
March 7, 2008

In his recent *Rocky Mountain News* column, "Our runaway military," (Feb. 13), Paul Campos continues his recurring theme against homeland security and national defense. He bemoans the magnitude of U.S. defense spending, exceeding as it does all other nations. But how could it reasonably be otherwise?

As the greatest economic power in a forever contentious and hazardous world, we must necessarily spend the most on national defense. Would he prefer a world where China had the most formidable military? It would be nice if more of our "allies" carried their fair share of the burden, but they don't. They help out some, but they're largely free riders devoting a relatively meager share of their gross domestic product to defense while America does most of the heavy lifting and sheds most of the blood.

Campos complains that, "More than half of the federal government's discretionary spending ($625 billion in 2007) is devoted to the armed forces. Notice how he inflates the defense share ("more than half," he asserts) by comparing it only to *discretionary* spending. But discretionary spending is only about a third of the budget, and ignores major spending in "mandatory" categories like Social Security, Medicare, Medicaid, and interest on the national debt. In fact, U.S. defense spending in FY 2007 was just 20 percent of *total* federal spending. This is the kind of shameless manipulation of the data you find on left-wing blogs, perhaps Campos' source.

And his spending number is also wrong. Defense outlays (dollars actually spent) in 2007 were $552 billion, not $625 billion, as Campos claims. That $625 billion was the amount of defense authorizations, some of which will be spent in future years. It's bad enough Campos doesn't understand the difference; it's even worse if he does.

Campos wants to scale back our "gargantuan armies" (and, presumably, our navies and air forces) as he puts it. But they're hardly gargantuan today. That's why we've had to call up reserve and National Guard units for service in Iraq. In 1945, during World War II, we had more than 12 million troops on active duty, and about 3 million during the Korean and Vietnam wars. From Cold War levels of more than 2 million, our active duty force was cut by more than a third by 2001 to less than 1.4 million.

U.S. defense spending as a share of GDP was 4 percent in 2007. By comparison, in the 1980s, during the Cold War, it was about 6 percent. During Vietnam, it was as high as 9.5 percent. In 1960 (after Korea and before Vietnam), when JFK was elected, it was 9.3 percent. And in 1943, World War II consumed 30 percent of our GDP. As a share of our budget, today's 20 percent spent on defense compares to 27 percent in 1989, 52 percent in 1960 and 70 percent in 1943. Now that was "gargantuan."

Campos also protests the "more than a quarter-million uniformed troops stationed outside the United States." But this, too, is a reduction in force. During the Cold War the U.S. had a garrison of more than 400,000 in Europe alone, mostly in Germany. This was a stabilizing influence that arguably prevented World War III by deterring Soviet aggression. U.S. troops in Korea have played a similar role for more than 50 years.

However expensive defense may be, it's a lot less expensive than war.

In his rant against our "runaway military," Campos went on to invoke the ghost of George Washington, cautioning against "foreign entanglements" and "standing armies." I suspect the general might have some different views today in the wake of Nazi Germany, the Soviet Union, nuclear weapons, intercontinental ballistic missiles and satellite warfare.

In his gratuitous parting shot, Campos cites Dwight Eisenhower's warning against the dangers of the "military-industrial complex." That'll require an entire column of context and explanation, which I'll address in part two, in this space, next time.

Defending Defense, Part II

March 14, 2008

In my last column, I rebutted some of the misleading quantitative factoids offered by fellow *Rocky Mountain News* columnist Paul Campos in his most recent polemic against U.S. defense policy. ("Our runaway military," Feb. 13). However, as promised, my response to his enlistment of General and President Eisenhower as an expert witness in his anti-military cause requires an entire column alone.

Campos recalled Ike's 1960 farewell address, carried on radio and television to the American people, in which the departing president and commander-in-chief uttered his since-famous warning, "In the councils of government, we must guard against the acquisition of unwarranted influence, whether sought or unsought, by the military-industrial complex."

Those are words to the wise from someone who understood both the virtues and vices of the military machine. The problem comes when those words are taken out of context as they have been for decades by leftists, pacifists and assorted anti-military types who latched on to the phrase "military-industrial complex" as a simplistic buzzword. That was most definitely not a call by Ike for unilateral disarmament. Here are some of the other things he said in that same speech, conveniently ignored by Campos and his ilk:

Referring to the threat of communism, Ike declared, "We face a hostile ideology, global in scope, atheistic in character, ruthless in purpose and insidious in method. Unhappily, the danger it poses promises to be of indefinite duration. To meet it successfully, there is called for, not so much the emotional and transitory sacrifices of crisis, but rather those which enable us to carry forward steadily, surely and without complaint the burdens of a prolonged and complex struggle – with liberty at stake. Only thus shall we remain, despite every provocation, on our chartered course toward permanent peace and betterment."

In a plea for what Ronald Reagan would later call, "peace through strength," Ike observed that, "A vital element in keeping the peace is our military establishment. Our arms must be mighty, ready for instant action, so that no potential aggressor may be tempted to risk their own destruction."

Confronting the realities of the post-World War II era, Ike explained that, "Our military organization today bears little relation to that known by any of my predecessors in peacetime, or indeed by the fighting men of World War II or Korea. Until the latest of our world conflicts, the United States had no armaments industry. American makers of plowshares could, with time and as required, make swords as well. But we can no longer risk emergency improvisations of national defense; we have been compelled to create a permanent armaments industry of vast proportions."

He went on to say that, "We recognize the imperative need for this development. Yet we must not fail to comprehend its grave implications." In the next sentence came his famous caution regarding the "military-industrial complex." Ike's thoughtful message deserves better than to be manipulated and exploited by those who mindlessly attack even reasonable expenditures on defense – those who resent the American military because it offends their utopian vision of the make-believe world in which they'd like to live.

The military-industrial complex may, indeed, warrant scrutiny. But it's sure nice to have when you need it. In another era, when the threat to our nation was impossible to deny, Franklin Roosevelt praised just such a team as the "arsenal of democracy."

In 1960, when Ike was president, defense spending consumed more than half the federal budget. Now, it accounts for but one-fifth. Over the same period, transfer payments and other "entitlements," as they're euphemistically termed, have moved in the opposite direction, from less than a quarter of the budget to more than half. There's another complex, today, that dwarfs the military-industrial one, and against which it competes for taxpayer dollars. We could call it the "welfare-state recipient-bureaucrat-politician complex." Democrats, educrats and media liberals are conspicuously silent about that one.

More of What Eisenhower Really Said

September 2, 2010

In a recent column I corrected a common misconception about President Dwight Eisenhower's reference to the military-industrial complex in his farewell radio address to the nation. Ike wasn't critical of it. He recognized the necessity of this combination, although he warned against the possibility of its undue influence.

Apparently reluctant to give up the illusion of Ike as a pacifist, anti-warriors regularly circulate another passage from an Eisenhower speech, also taken out of context, on peace with the Soviet Union:

"Every gun that is made, every warship launched, every rocket fired, signifies, in the final sense, a theft from those who hunger and are not fed, those who are cold and not clothed...The cost of one modern heavy bomber is this: a brick school in more than thirty cities...It is two fine, fully equipped hospitals...We pay for a single fighter plane with a half million bushels of wheat....We pay for a single destroyer with new homes that could have housed more than 8,000 people...This is not a way of life at all, in any true sense. Under the cloud of threatening war, it is humanity hanging from a cross of iron...Is there no other way the world may live?"

Sadly, I'm afraid the concise, realistic answer to that heartfelt rhetorical question is "no." Plowshares make lousy swords, and nations that beat their swords into plowshares will wind up pulling plows under the sword of nations that don't. The lesson of history is that no other world has ever existed, nor is it likely to. To be sure, the money we invest in our national defense could be applied to more productive and humanitarian purposes, just as we would rather do other things with the money we spend on police forces, fire departments, burglar alarms and locks on our doors. But reason and prudence dictate that security is a prerequisite for freedom and prosperity.

Eisenhower, of course, understood that. Ike was a warrior, not a pacifist. He was also a statesman and a diplomat. The above quote was conveniently lifted from Ike's "Chance for Peace Speech," delivered in the first few months of his presidency, in April 1953, shortly after the death of Joseph Stalin. In the transition following 30 years of Stalin's iron rule, Ike was extending an olive branch and seeking to dissuade the new Soviet leadership from accelerating the arms race.

But he was by no means proposing unilateral disarmament. In that same speech, Ike also said: "This new (Soviet) leadership confronts a free world aroused, as rarely in its history, by the will to stay free. This free world knows, out of bitter wisdom of experience, that vigilance and sacrifice are the price of liberty. It knows that the defense of Western Europe imperatively demands the unity of purpose and action made possible by the North Atlantic Treaty Organization, embracing a European Defense Community."

As history unfolded, post-Stalin expansionist Soviet leadership rejected Ike's invitation, brutally crushed freedom and independence movements in Iron Curtain countries in Eastern Europe, extended its global reach, created a massive worldwide espionage network and stepped up the arms race. Led by the United States, the West stood firm, especially under the presidency of Ronald Reagan, and eventually prevailed.

As we confront the current threat to our security, freedom and prosperity, some of our less resolute allies have lost sight of the price of liberty, which requires eternal vigilance, sacrifice and the unity of purpose and action Ike prescribed.

Richard Nixon once observed that the wishful notion of peace imagined by utopians is achieved in this world only at their typewriter and in the grave, echoing George Santayana's dictum, "only the dead have seen the end of war."

Defending Our National Defense
January 20, 2011

With more than $4 trillion in federal budget deficits over the last three years and more than $3 trillion projected over the next four, there's good reason for concern over runaway government spending.

Of the $3.8 trillion budget in 2011, about two-thirds is so-called "mandatory" spending. This includes a cornucopia of social "entitlement" programs on budgetary auto-pilot led by Social Security, Medicare and Medicaid, along with interest on the national debt. The rest of the budget is classified as "discretionary" spending, the largest component of which is the military.

Leftists always rail against military spending, and now is no exception. Yes, Defense Secretary Robert Gates has proposed modest defense cuts ($78 billion spread over five years), but he's doing so at the behest of his boss, President Obama. The notion that we can make any substantial steps toward budget balance at the expense of national defense is a delusion. The elephant in the room is social spending. Discretionary spending is just over a third of the budget, and defense spending is just over half of that, which puts the military's share of total federal spending at less than one-fifth. About 40 percent of that one-fifth is personnel expenses, and we're already undermanned.

Aging equipment, especially aircraft, needs to be modernized, and equipment damaged or destroyed in Iraq and Afghanistan needs to be replaced. The U.S. Navy is down to 287 ships, 45 percent fewer than the 529 it had in 1991. Even if you slashed the defense budget by $100 billion in one year – an outrageously irresponsible act in these perilous times – that would have cut 2010's $1.5 trillion deficit by only 6 percent.

Writing in *The Wall Street Journal*, Mark Helprin recalled that President Obama, in a speech at West Point last summer, cited our lagging economy as justification for sharp cuts in defense spending when he claimed, "At no time in human history has a nation of diminished economic vitality maintained its military and political primacy." Huh? How about the United States? Still struggling through the Great Depression, in World War II we ramped up defense spending to 40 percent of GDP and 85 percent of the budget by 1945 in order to save the world from Nazi Germany and Imperial Japan, emerging as a free and economically stronger nation.

For the benefit of those with no knowledge of history who claim our current level of defense spending is unsustainable, here are some benchmarks: In 1960, when John F. Kennedy was elected – after the Korean War and before Vietnam – defense spending was 52 percent of the budget and 9 percent of GDP. In the 1980s, Ronald Reagan's defense build-up, which ultimately defeated the Soviet Union in the Cold War, averaged 26 percent of the budget and 6 percent of GDP. Today, defense spending is 19 percent of the budget and 5 percent of GDP.

By contrast, social spending (what the Office of Management and Budget categorizes as "payments for individuals") was a mere 26 percent of the budget in 1960. By 1989, the year Reagan left office, it was 47 percent. Today, it's 64 percent and growing. In 1960, non-defense spending was 8 percent of GDP; today it's 20 percent. And that's only at the federal level, not including state and local spending for social programs and government employees. This, not defense spending, is what's driving the U.S. and the European socialist democracies (that spend a lot less on defense) toward bankruptcy.

Providing for the national defense is the single most essential responsibility of our federal government, without which we have nothing – no freedom, no treasure, no country. The only thing more expensive than war is losing one. Leon Trotsky got one thing right when he observed that, "You may not be interested in war, but war is interested in you."

Obama Perilously Degrading U.S. Military
January 16, 2014

In a recent *Denver Post* point-counterpoint about defense spending, the voice of the opposition was represented by Mark Weisbrot of the Center for Economic and Policy Research. You should know where someone sits to best evaluate where he stands. Weisbrot's CEPR isn't just a liberal think tank, like the respected Brookings Institute. It's far left, with a particular animus for the U.S. military. And Weisbrot, a self-declared socialist, was a cheerleader for Hugo Chavez in Venezuela. The way those of his mentality deal with national security threats is to pretend they don't exist.

In his call for deep cuts in defense spending, especially the U.S. Navy, Wesibrot equated current inflation-adjusted Pentagon spending with levels of the Vietnam War. That's a misleading comparison in relative terms. In 1968, during the height of the war, defense spending was 46 percent of the federal budget and 9 percent of GDP. Today it's only 18 percent of the budget and 4 percent of GDP. For an honest picture of our spending priorities, what the government terms "payments for individuals" – a cornucopia of entitlement, health and welfare programs – has grown from 28 percent of the budget in 1968 to 66 percent today. And it's the social spending side of the ledger, not defense, that's busting the budget and driving the deficits. If we had spent zero on defense in 2013, a suicidal alternative, we'd have still had a deficit of $300 billion.

Barack Obama's "fundamental transformation" of America includes irresponsibly undermining our military capabilities. His ten-year budget cuts defense to 13% of federal spending and less than 3% of GDP. Anti-military doves assert that the U.S. spends more on defense than the rest of the world combined. It's a worthless comparison. We have a highly-trained, well compensated all-volunteer force and legions of civilian DOD employees that account for the lion's share of defense spending. China's surging military buildup isn't burdened by comparable personnel costs. Their labor and North Korea's come cheap. If our allies would carry their fair share of the free world's military burden, we could spend less. Unfortunately, they don't, taking cover under our defense umbrella. That's good for them; bad for us. But shortchanging our military, as well, isn't a practical alternative. Leaving the free world vulnerable to its enemies isn't in our interest.

Here's former Secretary of Defense John Lehman's appraisal of our shrinking defense posture: "Instead of a 600-ship Navy, we now have a 280-ship Navy...Instead of Reagan's 20-division Army, we have only 10-division equivalents. The Air Force has fewer than half the number of fighters and bombers it had 30 years ago...Air Force fighter planes today average 28 years old." True, many individual Navy warships today have greater technological capabilities than in years past, but when it comes to simultaneous projections of force around the globe, they still can't be in two places at the same time.

According to Defense Secretary Chuck Hagel, reductions in troop strength threatened by the recent sequester threatened to slash the Army from 490,000 to as few as 380,000 and the Marine Corps from 202,000 to 150,000. To even consider such a move is insane. The U.S. military has a huge investment in the training of our high-tech, all-volunteer force. Retaining these experienced professionals is vital for military effectiveness. You can't simply flip a switch and instantly replace them when faced with a national security crisis.

Security is a prerequisite for freedom and prosperity. The federal government has no greater responsibility than to provide for the national defense, without which nothing else we do as a nation would be possible.

Pacifists Prefer Promises and Delusions to Real-World Policies
May 20, 1988

Peace is a popular buzzword today. In the abstract, it rolls easily off the tongue. As a practical matter, it's a lot more difficult to translate into foreign policy in the real world. But pacifists prefer promises and delusions to policies. We hear of a number of peace groups defined in terms of their membership: Physicians for Peace, Teachers for Peace, Clergy for Peace, Computer Programmers for Peace, ad nauseam. We should hear more of what may be the largest category of pacifists: Hypocrites for Peace.

Opponents of U.S. involvement in Southeast Asia cited their love of peace and concern for humanity. Once the movement succeeded in bringing about the U.S. withdrawal from South Vietnam and the simultaneous communist victory, it fell deafeningly silent about the carnage that followed. One peace activist, folk singer Joan Baez – to her credit – stood up to denounce the brutality of postwar communist regimes in Vietnam and Cambodia. Rather than being joined by a chorus of fellow activists, she wound up doing a solo. Where was the sympathy for the boat people? Where was the protest over the internment, abuse and murder of South Vietnamese in the Orwellian "re-education camps?" Where were the demonstrations expressing outrage over the extermination of 2 million Cambodians by the Khmer Rouge?

Why the apparent double standard? Perhaps it's best explained by a French expression that addresses the blind spot common among liberals (pacifists tend to be liberals) when it comes to the sins of communist governments: *Il n'y a pas d'ennemi à gauche* – there is no enemy to the left. Communism professes a utopian egalitarianism that has a romantic appeal to the liberal mentality in a way that capitalism doesn't. Leftist regimes, consequently, are given special dispensation. Since their intentions are laudable, liberals rationalize, perhaps the ends justify the means.

Today, for those ideologically romantic liberals and for pacifists who are simply foolish, there's a new cause: the communist Sandinistas in Nicaragua. And, once again, we are seeing history repeat itself. The beacon of current hopes is the peace plan devised, sincerely but naively, by Oscar Arias, president of Costa Rica. This will be cynically exploited by the Sandinistas as predictably as their supporters in this country will cover for them. Already the signs are unmistakable.

The Sandinistas promised to allow pluralism and free political participation. Instead, we've witnessed deceit and crackdowns. On May 4, 23 opposition leaders were arrested and held for several hours without charge for attempting to meet with construction workers on a hunger strike. Non-government radio broadcasting, including *Radio Catolica*, the voice of the Catholic Church, has been restricted or shut down. Jose Castillo Osejo, a prominent radio news director, was summoned to the home of Tomas Borge, the head of state security, and harangued and beaten for airing programs critical of the government.

The Sandinistas have denied *La Prensa*, the nation's leading independent newspaper, sufficient newsprint to publish. Human rights proposals by the Miskito Indians, long persecuted by the Sandinistas, have been rejected out of hand. The promised release of 10,000 political prisoners has not materialized. Soviet military supplies continue to pour in, the draft has been accelerated and attacks against contras – cease-fire violations – have been recorded in a number of areas including La Vigia, Nueva Segovia and Jinotega.

Where is the criticism from American liberals and pacifists? Where are the protests? Where is the pressure to keep the Sandinistas on the road to peace and freedom? Where are the TV news reports?

The Sandinistas' intentions are obvious. Time is on their side. They'll go through the motions of negotiations, giving little or nothing and rolling back everything in the end. Meanwhile, the contras, abandoned by an irresponsible Democratic majority in Congress, slowly twist in the wind. When the time is right, the Sandinistas – and their Soviet and Cuban handlers – will crush them and remove the last serious obstacle to imposition of a full-fledged communist state in Nicaragua.

The legacy of this scenario will be prolonged misery for the unfortunate people of Nicaragua – after all, who but leftist intellectuals find communism appealing? Rather than peace in the region, the Sandinistas will foment further turmoil and war, using Nicaragua as the base of their self-proclaimed "revolution without borders" in Central

America. As this all unfolds, and as their oppression becomes more brazen, you might find yourself wondering what in the world the Sandinistas would have to do to make their apologists in this country angry.

Pacifism a Threat to My Freedom
October 5, 2001

According to the *New York Times* estimate, "several thousand" demonstrators for peace showed up in Washington, D.C. over the weekend to protest a U.S. military response to the Sept. 11 attack on America. The number was impressive for its insignificance. In this nation of *280* million, the meager turnout was reassuring as a stark contrast to the overwhelming support declared by Americans for President Bush's call to arms in the war against international terrorism. Not all the demonstrators in Washington were pacifists. The usual brigade of anti-capitalists, racism-baiters and America-lasters were there as well, doing what they do for sport. But let's zero in on the pacifists.

As a theme, pacifism is a natural for leftists and liberals. It promises a superficially desirable outcome; never mind that its vision is unachievable. In this tolerant society we indulge conscientious objectors and exempt them from combat even when our nation, at war, is forced to conscript others to military service. But as theologian Michael Novak explains: "We sharply distinguish between pacifism as a personal commitment, implicating only a person who is not a public figure responsible for the lives of others, and pacifism as a public policy, compromising many who are not pacifists and endangering the very possibility of pacifism itself." George Orwell noted that: "To abjure violence is a luxury which a delicate few enjoy only because others stand ready to do violence in their behalf." So, U.S. Marines in World War II died on Iwo Jima so that pacifists could sing *Kumbaya* in safety.

More than 100 years ago, George Santayana expressed that "only the dead have seen the end of war." Sadly, there's no rational cause to alter that pronouncement. Terrible as it is, war is reality. But reason and reality have never deterred pacifists. Winston Churchill once observed that "the only thing worse than war is losing one." Chinese philosopher-general Sun Tzu, two millennia earlier, instructed us that the object of war is peace – on the victor's terms. Peace is not an outcome or an objective. It's just a state or condition, and a temporary one at that. A quarter-century ago, historian Will Durant calculated that the world had known the absence of war in only 268 of the last

3,421 years. That ratio has declined even further since. Moreover, peace, in and of itself, is an insufficient condition. A goldfish in a bowl knows peace. Defeated and enslaved peoples may know peace. Americans, going back to the birth as a nation in the cauldron of the Revolutionary War, *desire* peace but *require* freedom and justice. We do not worship peace at any price.

Henry Kissinger put it profoundly and succinctly: "If peace is equated simply with the absence of war, if the yearning for peace is not allied with a sense of justice, it can become an abject pacifism that turns the world over to the most ruthless." On Sept. 11, we saw the brand of ruthlessness of which our attackers are capable. Only witless pacifists would turn the other cheek and rely on the good faith and mercy of such demons.

Unlike the repressive homelands of the terrorists that attack us, and the medieval, theocratic police state envisioned by the likes of Osama bin Laden, we are a pluralistic society. We protect the right of pacifists and other anti-war militants to assemble and advance their cause. But, I don't respect such people and I don't shrink from exposing their ideas as destructive and suicidal. Pacifists are my enemy because wittingly or not, they serve the purposes of my enemy and jeopardize my freedom. I believe in deterrence and peace through strength. I believe in punishing those who attack us as retributive justice and as a lesson to others. And I take to heart the advice of the Roman strategist Vegetius, that he who desires peace should prepare for war.

Maniacs Mean Business
August 25, 2006

Paul Campos is a leftist law professor at the University of Colorado-Boulder who appears on the opinion pages of the *Rocky Mountain News*. In a recent column attacking Sen. Joe Lieberman, Campos pooh-poohed the threat of Islamofascism, even scoffing at the very term. He branded as "transparently hysterical nonsense" a perfectly reasonable statement by Lieberman comparing this threat and the evil underlying it to Nazi Germany and the former Soviet Union. That puts Campos in the same bed of irrational denial with the likes of Michael Moore, who in October 2003 declared: "There is no terrorist threat in this country. This is a lie. This is the biggest lie we've been told." Good company, Paul.

Campos dismisses Osama bin Laden as little more than "a guy hiding in a cave somewhere armed with an AK-47 and a tape recorder, who commands the uncertain allegiance of a few thousand equally poorly armed fanatics." And he shrugs off the 3,000 killed on 9/11 and others who have died at the hands of Islamofascist assassins by noting that "more Americans drown in bathtubs every year than are killed by terrorists." His tortured point seems to be that by implementing heightened domestic security measures and launching counterattacks on al Qaeda and others abroad, we've stooped to the "politics of cowardice," as he puts it, thereby empowering bin Laden and his minions. Did I mention that Campos is a college professor at CU-Boulder? This, as George Orwell once put it, "is nonsense so great, only an intellectual could believe it."

Campos offers only condescending criticism and armchair bravado. What's his alternative? Do nothing and wait "courageously" for the next hit? Turn the other cheek?

Yes, the cost in lives to Americans has been relatively low by historical standards – so far. But the economic cost has been massive. As an open society protective of individual rights and due process (up to a point), we're especially vulnerable. Related defense and homeland security spending and the public and private cost of remedies and precautions since 9/11 has amounted to hundreds of billions. While necessary, these are unproductive overhead expenses. When you consider the economic opportunity costs and the cloud of risk that hangs over our society and financial markets, the price tag runs into trillions. But what choice do we have? This is a matter of national survival. World War II was expensive, too.

Terrorism is just a tactic. Islamofascism is a movement, a cause, and it's no illusion; it's all too real. Stephen Schwartz, one of the first Westerners to use the term, describes it as the "use of the faith of Islam as a cover for totalitarian ideology." He notes that fascism, by definition, goes far beyond the realm of conventional political differences, in that it is unrestrained by public civility or the law. It's wholly intolerant, militant, ruthless and aggressive. In the Islamofascist form it's messianic and theocratic. There can be no separation between church and state. This perverse version of Islam brooks no dissent. Nonbelievers and apostates must either convert or be executed.

Campos argues that Hitler and Stalin had more forces and ran up far bigger numbers of victims during their reigns. True, but they started small, too. The Cold War lasted half a century; the Islamofascist war against modernity and the "infidels" (us) could last much longer. The death toll? The tactics of asymmetrical warfare combined with modern technology provide ample opportunities to wreak mass destruction on open societies.

Just wait 'til the mullahs and ayatollahs in Iran get nukes. The leaders of the Soviet Union were rational. That's why the doctrine of Mutual Assured Destruction was effective in deterring a nuclear exchange between the two superpowers. Hell, Soviet communists weren't looking for salvation in the hereafter. They were Marxian dialectical materialists and atheists! They wanted power and perks in this life. Now, we're dealing with suicidal, religious zealots lusting for death and a martyr's rewards – 72 virgins and more – in a heavenly paradise.

Bernard Lewis, professor emeritus at Princeton, and author of "The Crisis of Islam," offers this passage from the Ayatollah Khomeini, quoted in an 11th grade Iranian schoolbook: "I am decisively announcing to the whole world that if the world-devourers [i.e., the infidel powers] wish to stand against our religion, we will stand against their whole world and will not cease until the annihilation of all of them. Either we all become free, or we will go to the greater freedom which is martyrdom. Either we shake one another's hands in joy at the victory of Islam in the world, or all of us will turn to eternal life and martyrdom. In both cases, victory and success are ours."

These maniacs mean business, Paul. Your bathtub is, at worst, a passive threat. It doesn't want to kill you.

Korean Commandos Crush Mock Terrorists in Practice Incident
September 24, 1986

Nobody's come up with a sure fire technique for preventing terrorism or dealing with terrorists, and nobody's likely to. Negotiations with terrorists in the midst of their act is sometimes effective in limiting the number of casualties – at that place and time.

The problem with this approach is that it gives terrorists exactly what they want: legitimacy, publicity and a market for striking their bargain. What's more, it encourages future acts of terrorism. A swift and sure military response to terrorism may (and sometimes may not) place at greater risk the safety of innocent civilians caught in the middle, but can, arguably, reduce casualties in the long run by deterring future acts.

I had the chance to observe a pretty impressive demonstration of the decisive military response during a recent visit to South Korea. While on a tour of the magnificent new 1988 Olympic facilities in Seoul – which will also be used for this year's Asian Games – I was treated to an exercise in anti-terrorist operations being conducted for the benefit of government representatives and officials of the Asian Games.

The exercise was a simulation of a terrorist hostage-taking. The scene was the Asian Games Village, a complex of sleek, all new, 15-story, high-rise apartment buildings.

Mock terrorists, including two dummies (mannequins, that is) stationed on the 10th-floor terrace of one of the apartments, were holding several foreign hostages at gunpoint, demanding that the government meet their political demands and provide them safe conduct. It was eerily reminiscent of Munich in 1972.

Suddenly, from behind one of the other buildings, up darted a troop-carrying Army helicopter, which had approached the village at ground level, concealed by the buildings from the view of the terrorists. The helicopter shot to the top of the building occupied by the terrorists. As it hovered 50 feet above the roof, ropes flew out from its cabin, followed in an instant by six South Korean Army special-warfare commandos. Dressed in black from hooded head to foot, they were an imposing sight. Ninjas came at once to mind.

They were on the roof in a second. And then, following their ropes, they were, in the blink of an eye, five stories down the side of the building, poised to attack.

These black phantoms use their ropes the way a spider uses a silk salient from its bowels. They literally fly. At the speed of a body falling from the roof, they descend using three different techniques: Feet first, head first, and if you can believe it, *perpendicular* to the building, actually *running* down its face.

Before the terrorists can react, explosive projectiles blow out the windows. The commandos are, in one motion, inside the apartment, accompanied by staccato blasts of automatic weapons. The next sight you see is that of the two terrorist dummies ejected like popcorn from the terrace, hurtling 10 stories to the ground below, without a rope. I wasn't looking at my watch, but the whole thing couldn't have taken much more than a minute. Wow!

I assume we have a similar elite strike team, although one was something less than encouraged by the performance of our "Delta Force" in the ill-fated attempt to rescue our embassy hostages in Iran. I know I've seen Rambo do this kind of thing in the movies, but there we have stunt men, special effects and the opportunity for multiple takes and editing. The Korean commandos did it in one take – and without a net. One of the prerogatives of an Olympic host nation is to introduce a sport of its own choosing as a competitive event in that year's games. If the Koreans select anti-terrorist acrobatics, they're a shoe-in for the gold.

I might add that this anti-terrorist demonstration was not secret. Accounts of it and photographs appeared the next day in the Seoul newspapers. To whatever extent terrorists are rational, they seek to exploit weakness. The South Koreans projected an image, and a capability, of grim resoluteness. The reputation of ROK Tiger troops as fierce combatants alongside U.S. forces in Vietnam is well established and well deserved. A clear message to would-be terrorists is that there are no easy pickins at the Asian Games or the 1988 Olympics in Seoul. In some quarters, that's known as deterrence.

Reality

The State of Welfare, Social Security and Health Care

Stimulating the Welfare State
February 6, 2009

Here's the opening paragraph from a *New York Times* story by reporter Robert Pear (please note that it is a news story in the oh-so liberal *New York Times*): "The stimulus bill working its way through Congress is not just a package of spending increases and tax cuts to jolt the nation out of recession. For Democrats, it is also a tool for rewriting the social contract with the poor, the uninsured and the unemployed, in ways that they have long yearned to do."

Reinforcing that assessment is this quote from White House Chief of Staff Rahm Emanuel: "Never let a serious crisis go to waste. What I mean by that is it's an opportunity to do things you couldn't do before."

It would be bad enough if HR 1, The American Recovery and Reinvestment Act of 2009 – a gargantuan $900 billion so-called economic stimulus bill – were merely an overblown accumulation of largely misdirected, politically motivated or wasteful government spending. Examples in the bill abound, like $50 million for the National Endowment for the Arts, $4 million for ACORN or $75 million to discourage cigarette smoking. But those items are nickels and dimes. Calling it "pork-laden" is too kind.

When *The Wall Street Journal* correctly noted that only 12 percent of this spending can honestly be regarded as growth stimulus, it didn't mean that the rest was pork, the traditional definition of which is wasteful spending on local projects (like former Alaska Sen. Ted Stevens' infamous Bridge to Nowhere). To be sure, that kind of pork will be passed around liberally from HR 1's pool of funds going to states and cities. No, it's worse than that.

Jim Manzi calls it "The European Social Welfare-State Bill." While it's framed as an emergency stimulus bill, only 15 percent will be spent in 2009 and almost half is scheduled for 2011 and beyond. As revealed in the above quotes from Pear and Emanuel, the bill's grander, ulterior motive is to expand or create government social programs that will long survive the current economic downturn and be set in political concrete. This is the Democrats' "new" New Deal.

Once established, government "entitlement" programs – largely transfers of income from net taxpayers to net tax receivers – are almost impossible to roll back, much less repeal. As the legions of voters dependent on or addicted to such programs increase, the Democrats distributing these goodies plan to perpetuate their reign.

I'll concede that this isn't motivated solely by political opportunism, although that's the overriding factor for a good many career politicians. For those more ideologically disposed, it's simply the irreconcilable difference between the leftist vision of a government-run collectivist utopia versus the rightist vision of limited government, private property, and individual rights, responsibilities and rewards.

In the current era of Euro-socialism, while leftist and (so-called) conservative governments have come and gone, the welfare state has survived and flourished politically. (Margaret Thatcher's UK government in the 1980s was an all-too-brief truly conservative interlude.) Unfortunately, whether in Europe or the United States, this game can only go on so long. At some point the diminishing fraction of net taxpayers is overwhelmed by the ever-increasing majority of net tax receivers. And that's when a welfare state implodes under its own unproductive weight.

For a preview of coming attractions, see the *2008 Financial Report of the U.S. Government,* an official publication that recalculates the officially stated $10 trillion national debt to account for the unfunded liabilities of Social Security, Medicare, Medicaid and other entitlement programs (which President Barack Obama and congressional Democrats plan to expand). The restated debt figure becomes $56 trillion, which will worsen dramatically as our population continues to age and entitlement spending consumes more than two-thirds of the federal budget by 2030. There's no way tax collections (even on the rich) can keep up. I'll be watching anxiously to see if Obama and the Democratic majority in Congress will challenge this ghost of Christmas future.

Welfare is When You Didn't Earn It
April 20, 2001

"Why When Government Give (sic) Rich Money it's Called a tax break but when they give poor Money It's called Welfare?"

Those were the words scribbled on a poster held by a young woman at a political rally last week at the state Capitol. Alongside her for the photo-op was Congresswoman Diana DeGette, D-Colorado, beaming her approval. The scene was captured in a newspaper photograph publicizing the event. The caption beneath the photo described the protesters as a coalition of labor, family, education and environmental groups that "claims the rich would benefit more than the poor under President Bush's budget, which cuts some funding for health and education."

Where does one begin to rebut this silliness? Of course, funding for health and education is most decidedly *not* being cut. In fact, Bush proposes to double the budget of the Department of Education over the next five years. Health, Medicare and Medicaid spending would all grow significantly. For the umpteenth time, it is simply not honest to describe an increase in spending for a government program as a "cut" simply because there are those who would increase that spending even more. The notion that this budget would "benefit" the rich more than the poor is preposterous. Out of the $2 trillion that would be spent in the next fiscal year, $320 billion goes for our collective national defense, and three quarters of the rest is devoted to income transfer programs to individuals, very few of whom are rich individuals.

Yes, the Bush budget calls for modest cuts in income tax rates which, I'm sorry to note, are phased in very slowly over far too many years. But even here, the greatest percentage cuts go to those with the lowest incomes. Obviously, the *dollar* amounts are greater for those with higher incomes precisely because they pay many more dollars in taxes. The top 10 percent of income earners (those making more than $80,000 a year), now pay two-thirds of all income taxes. The budget surplus we currently enjoy is thanks primarily to them. Why should they be excluded from their fair share of the tax cut? Because, in the tortured reasoning and emotional outpourings of those who would soak the rich at every turn, the money earned by successful Americans belongs first to the government. The "rich" should be thankful they're allowed to keep any at all. This is the socialist, entitlement mentality run amok.

Let's return to the question posed by the sign-carrying protester posing for the photo-op. Here's your answer: 1) If Congress passes the Bush tax-rate cut, the government will not be "giving" rich people a dime. It was their money to begin with; they earned it. Taxing someone at a marginal rate of 36 percent instead of 40 percent is not a gift. As William F. Buckley once put it, when someone stops blowing cigar smoke in your face, he's not giving you clean air. It was clean before he polluted it. 2) If the government gives poor people money, it's money that someone else earned. It's called welfare because it's a gift – charity – supposedly based on dire need. Poor people with no taxable income do not have a valid claim on income-tax relief precisely because they don't pay income taxes.

The Earned Income Tax Credit (EITC) is a $32 billion-a-year program for the *working* poor designed to wean them from welfare by rewarding enterprise. It's a mixture of charity and tax refund, depending on the economic standing of the recipient. To be eligible for the EITC, one must work. Holding a protest sign doesn't qualify.

If Rep. DeGette doesn't understand all this, she's a ditz. If she does, and she's exploiting the ignorance of others for political gain, that makes her a demagogue. Neither case is particularly flattering. I can't think of another option. Can you?

Budget Cuts Inevitable for Seniors
December 16, 1994

If you make $25,000 a year and spend $30,000, borrowing the rest on your Visa card, your cost of living isn't what you earned, ($25,000), it's what you spent ($30,000). You can't get away with that for long unless, like the *government*, you have the power to print money.

By the same token, the cost of government isn't what the Treasury takes in taxes, it's what the government spends. Right now, the federal government is taxing us to the tune of about 19 percent of our national income. But it's spending about 22 percent of that national income, $1.5 trillion, and that's the *direct* cost of government. The 3 percent difference, constituting the annual deficit, is borrowed.

The *indirect* cost of government is anybody's guess. Perhaps another trillion dollars or more in burdensome regulations, mandates, environmental controls, endangered species protections, bureaucratic overhead, excessive safety precautions, quotas in hiring and contracts, the Americans with Disabilities Act, miscellaneous inefficiencies, tax disincentives, subsidized sloth, you name it. And keep in mind, we're just talking here about the *federal* government.

Instead of raising the excess of what it spends over what it taxes by borrowing, the feds could hold a garage sale, conduct a lottery, write bad checks or steal the money from the Japanese, but the direct cost of government would still be what the feds spend – $1.5 trillion. The bottom line is, we just can't afford it. When we habitually run a federal budget deficit and fund it by borrowing money, the legacy of that irresponsible behavior is our accumulating national debt, now approaching $5 trillion. Its annual cost (the interest on that debt) is currently in excess of $200 billion, or 14 percent of the entire budget all by itself.

What this borrowing has paid for, in essence, is an artificial elevation in the standard of living of current generations of Americans at the expense of their children and grandchildren. They'll be the ones saddled with the responsibility of future principle and interest, while deriving little of the benefits of the spending spree that created it.

When the bill comes due it will either be paid or repudiated. If it's repudiated, economic markets will collapse as individual bondholders, mutual funds, banks, insurance companies, pension funds and a host of others holding government securities get stuck. If they choose to reduce the national debt, future Americans will have to lower their standard of living, in essence making sacrifices for the profligacy of the past. That is, they'll have to go through a period where they allow themselves to be taxed at levels that actually *exceed* government spending (with the resulting surpluses being used to reduce the debt).

Based on the experience of the past 40 years, we're already at our practical tax capacity. Budget discipline will have to come on the spending side, the cause of recent deficits. Under current policy, in 25 years, more than half the federal budget will be spent just on tending to the needs of senior citizens of the baby boom generation. So much for the long-term viability of Social Security.

Already, the largest area of government spending is on programs for older Americans, principally Social Security, Medicare, Medicaid and federal retirement. This is only going to get worse. The position of many of today's senior organizations, like the AARP, which claim to speak for them, seems to be: "We're 'entitled' to everything we get. If you want to balance the budget, do it at someone else's expense or wait until we're dead." If it's obvious that future generations of seniors are going to have to be among those making sacrifices, what's the justification for not starting now?

If the Republican majority in Congress is serious about balancing the budget, this is what they're up against. And they won't get any help from Bill Clinton.

Good luck!

Spread the Joy of Taxation
June 1, 2001

No, the tax bill passed by Congress last week isn't "massive" and it won't bust the budget. In fact, the tax reductions are too small and the rate cuts are deferred too far into the future. Federal tax collections are projected at $30 trillion over the next 11 years. With the passage of this tax reform bill, the feds will have to get by on a mere $29 trillion. This modest reduction in tax increases amounts to about 3 percent of total collections. Instead of a $6 trillion stimulus, taxpayers may only be overcharged $5 trillion, which leaves plenty for Social Security-related debt reduction.

As for individual income tax rates, just the lowest tax bracket will be cut immediately, from 15 percent to 10 percent. Bush asked that the highest marginal rate be reduced from 39.6 percent to 33 percent. Congress wouldn't give him that, and dropped the rate in stages only to 35 percent, stretched out all the way to 2006. It remains to be seen whether future Congresses will even allow that to happen.

There is absolutely no question that this plan disproportionately benefits lower-income Americans. With child-care credits and marriage-penalty adjustments, a family of four with $50,000 in annual income will ultimately see its income tax bill cut in half. Families earning under $35,000 would get a 100 percent reduction, paying nothing at all. In their shameful attempts to obscure this with demagogic rants, Democrats cry that more relief, in *absolute dollars,* goes to upper-income taxpayers. Of course it does, simply because the well-to-do pay much more in taxes. In 1998, the top 5 percent paid $414 billion, more than 50 percent of all individual income taxes collected. The bottom 50 percent paid only $33 billion, just 4 percent of the total bill. A tax cut that doesn't return dollars to people in proportion to who paid them is an income redistribution scheme in disguise.

And that gets us to the heart of the debate on taxation, and the long-term strategy of the Democratic Party. It's not just about fueling the ever-expanding government; it's also very much about income redistribution. The progressive income tax itself was designed as the fiscal centerpiece of the socialist vision: "from each according to his

215

ability, to each according to his need." This is the lifeblood of the Democrats' agenda.

And the income tax is their principal leveling tool. Seventy million Americans of voting age now pay nothing in income taxes. The new tax bill increases that number and sharply reduces the tax rates of those who pay very little. Consequently, fewer Americans will feel the pain of income taxation, making it easier for Democrats to add to their coalition of tax users anxious to increase the burden of taxpayers. This is not healthy for our republic.

Social Security is the next battleground. Bush wants to put the program on a sound financial footing, fully vesting individuals and enabling them to earn much higher market rates on their investments. Democrats would continue the current Ponzi scheme, funded by ever more progressive (there they go again) taxes. They complain that because Social Security taxes are capped at an income limit (that increases each year), lower-income people pay a greater percentage of their income than do upper-income people. This is true, but for a perfectly good reason. Social Security *benefits* are similarly capped. In 2001, about $10,000 of Social Security tax is paid on income up to $80,400. If there were no cap, an income of $1 million would produce a Social Security tax bill of $124,000; on $10 million, it would be $1.2 million, with, of course, no commensurate increase in benefits for the individual. This would be grand larceny.

Social Security was created and justified as a forced savings plan for your own retirement or disability. If the tax were unlimited, this would become just another income-transfer/welfare program, which is precisely what the Democrats want.

Social Security's Insolvency
April 14, 2011

Winston Churchill's famous description of the Soviet Union – "It's a riddle wrapped in a mystery inside an enigma" – also applies to our federal budget.

Take Social Security – while you still can. Jack Lew, President Obama's budget director, has proclaimed the program solvent with its trust fund in the black until 2037. Nonsense. The "trust fund" is essentially a bookkeeping entry.

Since 1937, when Social Security receipts from payroll taxes began pouring into the Treasury Department's coffers, all the money has been spent on everything the federal government provides, from guns to butter. Left in its place were IOUs, non-negotiable Treasury bonds, backed by the full faith and credit of the United States – for whatever that may soon be worth. These IOUs are counted as part of the $14 trillion gross federal debt.

Ironically, the annual surplus of Social Security receipts over payouts has made each year's overall federal deficit look smaller. But keep in mind, that money wasn't saved, it was spent. From a cash flow perspective, Social Security has always been a pay-as-you-go system, an intergenerational transfer of income.

In its official fiscal year 2000 budget, the Clinton administration told it like it is, explaining that government trust funds aren't "real economic assets" but merely "claims on the Treasury that, when redeemed, will have to be financed by raising taxes, borrowing from the public or reducing benefits or other expenditures. The existence of large trust fund balances, therefore, does not, by itself, have any impact on the government's ability to pay benefits."

The Social Security Administration used to put out a little booklet called *Your Social Security*. In the 1977 edition, it was explained this way: "The basic idea of social security is a simple one: During working years employees, their employers, and self-employed people pay social security contributions which are pooled into special trust funds. When earnings stop or are reduced because the worker retires,

217

becomes disabled, or dies, monthly cash benefits are paid to replace part of the earnings the family has lost."

The 1985 edition let the cat out of the bag. Compare the subtle wording changes:

"The basic idea of Social Security is simple: During working years, employees, their employers, and self-employed people pay Social Security taxes." Notice that the word "contributions" became "taxes" and "trust funds" is deleted.

The booklet goes on: "This money is used only to pay benefits and to pay administrative costs of the program. Then, when today's workers' earnings stop or are reduced because of retirement, death or disability, benefits will be paid to them from taxes paid by people in covered work and self-employment at that time." Aha! Now it's an intergenerational transfer of income.

Another myth is that Social Security doesn't contribute to the deficit. Of course it does. Once again, this is bookkeeping sleight-of-hand. Social Security taxes suck up a large share of our nation's finite tax capacity. Social Security spending accounts for one-fifth of the federal budget. Federal receipts from all sources are fungible (they lose their unique identity once delivered to the Treasury) and every dollar spent on anything is part of total spending. When the total exceeds revenues, we have a deficit.

But what of the reported $60 billion surplus in this year's Social Security account? Another bookkeeping illusion. It includes $116 billion of interest on the so-called trust fund, a $2.5 trillion pile of phantom Treasury IOUs. Since the feds are already running a $1.6 trillion deficit this year, they don't have that $116 billion, so they'll just add a few more IOUs to the stack.

Subtract that funny-money interest payment, and Social Security would show a $56 billion deficit in 2011, to say nothing of its long-term unfunded liability, variously estimated at between $18 trillion and $100 trillion.

This is solvency?

No "Crisis" of Uninsured
January 12, 2007

If your goal is to lay a political foundation for socialized medicine in this country, what better way to do it than to create the public impression that we have a vast army of people – even better, children – who are permanently unable to obtain health insurance. Depending on who's throwing around the sensationalized figures, that army numbers from 46 million to 59 million. In fact, that army is AWOL; it doesn't exist in anywhere near those numbers. The National Center for Policy Analysis and Dr. David Gratzer, in his new book, *The Cure*, effectively debunk these myths.

The ploy is to pretend that a rotating aggregate or a snapshot is the same thing as a permanent population. Fifty-nine million is the aggregate number of those who at *some* time during the year, even if for only one day, were without health insurance. This is a meaningless statistic.

Forty-six million is the snapshot figure, the average number who have no insurance on a given day. To see how misleading this can be, consider this: At any time perhaps 50 million Americans have a head cold. And during the course of a year, probably 300 million Americans will have a cold at one time or another. This is hardly the same thing as saying that 300 million Americans have a permanent head cold.

The uninsured can include those between jobs or students just out of school. The census bureau estimates the average family that loses its health insurance will be reinsured within 5½ months; 75 percent within one year. The Congressional Budget Office estimates that between 21 million and 31 million Americans may be uninsured for the entire year, including about 12 million foreign-born residents, many of whom are here illegally.

The largest group, 42 percent, of longer-term uninsured, about 19 million, are between the ages of 18 and 34. Most are healthy and could afford health insurance but choose to gamble, opting to run the risk of going uninsured rather than forgoing current consumption. This is motivated in part by the ease of acquiring government-regulated health insurance *after* becoming ill or obtaining free treatment at a hospital if unable to pay.

While the number of those without health insurance has grown by 3 million between 1996-2003, that's primarily because the nation's population has grown, much of it from illegal immigration. In fact, the percentage of those without insurance, 15.6 percent, is unchanged over the period. And it's not poor people who are adding to the ranks of the uninsured. Thanks to the expansion of means-tested Medicaid programs and State Children's Health Insurance Programs (SCHIP), the number of uninsured in households with annual incomes under $25,000 actually decreased by 21 percent between 1996-2005. At the same time, there are 117 percent more people without insurance among households with incomes over $75,000.

Let's look at the portion of the glass that's full, not just the empty part. According to the Census Bureau, more than 247 million Americans had either private insurance or were enrolled in a government health insurance program in 2005. That's almost 85 percent of the population. As many as 14 million of the uninsured are adults and children who are already eligible for existing government programs but have failed to enroll.

The serious problems are confined to about 10 million to 15 million who can't afford insurance but who make too much to qualify for Medicaid, and another 2 million to 3 million who are uninsurable because of specific diseases. But these problems are manageable. We already subsidize health insurance for those who can't afford it. So we can do a little more of that and provide special coverage for pre-existing conditions.

Yes, health insurance is expensive because health care is expensive, especially in the United States where we have an abundance of quality physicians, state-of-the-art equipment, extraordinary techniques and a smorgasbord of miracle drugs. Unlike the socialized systems in Canada and Europe, Americans can actually access these services in a timely fashion without having to wait for months or years.

Our health care costs are compounded by a plague of plaintiff's attorneys, nuisance malpractice suits, the drawn-out Food and Drug Administration approval process for new drugs, government regulations mandating excessive coverage, and medical consumers who have been conditioned to be insensitive to prices because of third-party payers and government subsidies.

Major reforms should include consumer tax deductions for catastrophic coverage and the expansion of tax-deferred Medical Savings Accounts for routine treatment.

We have health insurance problems, to be sure, but no "crisis," and no justification for converting the world's highest quality health-care system into another plodding government bureaucracy.

There's No Such Thing as a "Right" to Health Care
August 13, 2009

No, 47 million Americans are not permanently unable to obtain health insurance. This oft-cited, sensationalized statistic is a snapshot at any point in time, something akin to saying 50 million Americans may have a head cold at any point in time but soon get over it.

The Census Bureau reports that in 2007, more than 250 million Americans (85 percent of the population) had either private insurance or were enrolled in a government health program such as Medicare, Medicaid or SCHIP. The uninsured include those between jobs, students just out of school and millions more foreign-born, many of whom are here illegally. The average family that loses its health insurance is reinsured within six months; 75 percent are reinsured within one year. The largest group of longer-term uninsured is younger people who are healthy and can afford insurance but choose to gamble.

The serious problems are confined to about 15 million people, less than 5 percent of the population, who can't afford insurance or are uninsurable because of pre-existing conditions. These problems are manageable within our existing health care system rather than spending trillions on Obamacare to create a bureaucratic nightmare.

Health care is not a fundamental "right" in our society. The unalienable rights cited in the Declaration of Independence are life, liberty and the "pursuit" (not the delivery) of happiness. The Preamble to the Constitution speaks of "promoting" the general welfare, not *providing* it.

The Bill of Rights delineates a series of fundamental rights that individuals possess, by nature, and that government shall not infringe. Free health care is not one of them. If it were, it could only be delivered to one person by forcing another to provide it. And that would be a violation of the provider's individual rights. When you exercise your right of free speech, religious worship or assembly, it imposes no obligation on anyone else.

If someone is indigent, we don't let him die on the sidewalk outside a hospital. We treat that person, as we should. We'll even send an ambulance to get him. But whether the money to pay for this comes from taxpayers, private benefactors or by shifting the cost to other patients, it's still charity. Health care isn't a right. Neither are food stamps, housing subsidies or welfare. They're all charity. When the government refers to these benefits as "entitlements," it's because the recipients are granted them by statute, not as rights.

Food, clothing, shelter and health care are essential to maintain life, but individual Americans enjoy different levels in the quality of all those things in our market economy based on their ability to purchase them. This strikes some people as unfair, by the socialist definition of the term. Is it fair that people with more money can afford better homes, better cars, buy more expensive clothes and eat at more expensive restaurants? Is it fair that a rich man can afford the best lawyers in the country while an indigent defendant gets only a court-appointed public defender?

Of course it is, because individuals have earned those benefits, and because there is no practical alternative. Distributing homes, cars, lawyers or health care via a random lottery isn't practical; it's socialism. And socialism is doomed to failure because it lacks incentives and rewards for individual productivity and excellence. In the absence of that, it ultimately collapses when it runs out of the means to spend other people's money.

The same reasoning applies to health care. "Universal care," as President Barack Obama envisions it, would throw everyone in the same pit. We'd all become charity cases. Demand for medical care would soar, and supply would unavoidably be rationed. We'd sacrifice the world's highest quality health care system for the great majority of Americans to a socialist model that would improve the lot of a few at the expense of the many. Very bad idea.

Reality

Educational Reform Against the Monolithic Establishment

Education Friends, Foes
December 9, 2005

"Mike Rosen is no friend of public education." This assertion was passed on to me by an ally, a lonely free spirit within the public education establishment. It wasn't his view, mind you; it was the opinion of one of his colleagues.

Au contraire, Pierre. That indictment couldn't be further from the truth. Who could possibly be opposed to an educated public? It's the pathway to success in our society. I'm very much a friend of rigorous programs to create an educated public. And I'm also committed to our traditional approach of *funding* universal education publicly, with tax dollars. I don't, however, believe that the best way to productively educate the public is the way we do it now, through a government monopoly on the *delivery* of taxpayer-funded education.

Choice, variety and competition have been the bedrock of our free society and the formula for success in most every other field. Why should education be any different? There's certainly no shortage of competition in higher education, and that's delivered in large part by private institutions.

The fundamental problem with public education today is systemic. Public school districts have increasingly become politicized, corpulent bureaucracies in tow to their most influential constituent group: teachers unions.

The unions have inordinate influence in recruiting and electing like-minded candidates for school boards. Although individual teachers may be dedicated to the welfare of their students, the first priority and the *raison d'être* of the teachers unions – like any trade union – is the welfare of their rank and file. They negotiate tenaciously for expensive benefits packages, pension plans and restrictive work rules. Trade unions abhor competition among their members, and the teachers unions are no different.

225

That's why they resist compensation policies that reward individual performance or salary differentials for teaching specialties that are in higher demand or shorter supply. The unions prefer rigid pay grids based solely on seniority and post-graduate college credits. These "friends" of the public education status quo are, rather, foes of a better-educated public.

The education establishment is a closed loop. Teachers' colleges serve as the pipeline for labor and the wellspring of bad ideas for curricula and educational philosophy. From "look-say" reading to "new math," one failed experiment builds on another, impervious to complaints from parents. American students lose ground each year to the youth of other countries in math and science. Finite time and educational resources are redirected away from basic academics to social engineering. Young minds are molded to conform to the trendy liberal agenda, including diversity, self-esteem, multiculturalism, environmentalism, situational ethics, sexual reorientation, political correctness, etc. Little boys are to be refashioned to fit the feminist vision.

Teaching methods are dumbed down to accommodate the alleged short attention spans of the MTV generation. (Absurd. Instead, educators should be cultivating longer attention spans in students. The real world doesn't reward short attention spans.) Homework is de-emphasized because students don't want to spend time doing it and teachers don't want to spend time grading it. (So they do "homework" during class time!) Schoolyard games are redesigned to eliminate competition, scorekeeping or "violence" (like dodgeball.) Letter grades are disparaged (too judgmental and damaging to self-esteem.)

Is it any wonder that unionized teachers who themselves fear competition are loath to sing its praises to their students?

Dissenting parents are overwhelmed by the establishment. The power of the unions and the politicians aligned with them, combined with the apathy and naiveté of too many parents, make for an intractable status quo.

I have long despaired of substantive reform from within. What's needed is a virtual revolution in public education. The best way to break the stranglehold of the public education establishment and the vested interests is to empower students and parents as true *customers* rather than captive wards of the state. And the way to do that is through vouchers providing portable funding comparable to the current per capita cost of education in a government school.

The voucher would be redeemable at the school of one's choice — public or private. That way, the funding would follow the student. Over time, as more private schools come on line to meet the demand of newly-empowered lower- and middle-income parents (upper-income parents have always had the financial means to opt out of government schools), choices would abound. The power of this marketplace would be unleashed to give educational consumers what they want while forcing government schools to meet the test of competition by improving their product and responsiveness.

Nobel laureate economist Milton Friedman has advocated this proposal for many years, during which time public education has only gotten worse. It's an idea whose time is coming simply because there is no workable alternative.

Getting Too Involved in Schools
May 19, 1995

The bureaucrats who run the public schools repeatedly tell us they want more parental involvement. What they mean is that they want parental involvement on their terms. They want boosters, cheerleaders and lobbyists for higher school taxes. They want bake sales and raffles. They want the kind of PTA types who have a terminal case of Chronic Adult Teacher's Pet Syndrome (My acronym for which is CATPS). They want parents who are compliant with the tenets of the liberal, collectivist, educratic ideology. What they don't want are independent-minded parents with an "attitude" or parents with their own crazy notions of how their kids should be educated.

Anyone who doubts this need only observe how educrats react to charter schools. They hate them. Look at the latest incident in Denver involving P.S. 1. This is to be an experimental school for students in grades 6 through 10, affiliated with the Tattered Cover Book Store, that would concentrate on writing and "the use of the city as a classroom" (whatever that means). Personally, it doesn't sound like my cup of tea. My preference for a charter school would have a classically "boring" curriculum, with intensive concentration on basic academics, no social engineering, no touchy-feely stuff, a lot of homework and tests, and one that uses the classroom as a classroom.

But I'll support P.S. 1. on principle. It would open in August with 120 eager students housed in what used to be a warehouse next to the Tattered Cover's new downtown store on Wynkoop. You can be sure the parents of these students would be deeply involved in their kids' education. This is a self-selected group of people who cared enough to create their own school. They have a great personal stake in it and in their children's' success. Isn't that what the educrats say they want more of?

Apparently not in this case. You see, P.S. 1 is the wrong kind of school. The parents who think this is best for their kids are wrong. The DPS board, being infallible, knows this. In fact, just about all charter schools are the wrong kind of school. That's why school boards almost always oppose them. Anticipating this, the legislature empowered the

State Board of Education to overrule the boards and grant charters when they deemed them worthwhile. This has happened in a few instances, including, just recently, P.S. 1 in Denver. Unimpressed, however, with the state board's ruling, DPS member Lynn Coleman declared, defiantly: "We don't have the funds. I'm not giving them the money. I could care less what the state board said." Now, that's arrogance on stilts.

P.S. 1 parents are Denver and Colorado taxpayers. That's where the money comes from. It's not Lynn Coleman's money and it's not DPS's money. DPS doesn't generate money, it only spends it. This is a question of reallocation: money that would have been spent on these kids and the teachers who would have taught them in other DPS schools can be spent on them at P.S. 1 instead. When more charter schools are created, other DPS schools can be closed. Some charter schools might even take over existing DPS buildings.

If the educrats had any vision or a real sensitivity to the growing dissatisfaction of parents, they'd have created charter schools themselves, rather than having them forced down their throats by the legislature. Maybe a variety of creative charter schools with different approaches to educating kids would stem the current exodus from DPS, especially among higher-achieving students.

The public schools are fighting a losing battle because their philosophy of education is based upon a false premise. They believe there's one, centralized way to educate students. The National Education Association and ivory tower academicians in teaching colleges pump out one lame idea after another based on this faulty notion.

But there is no consensus among parents – the true customers of public education – and who's to say there should be? Why force everyone into the same mold? Give parents and students a choice, and let them pick out the kinds of schools they want. That's what charters and vouchers are all about. If it's any consolation to educrats, some might even select their model.

The debate isn't just about quality, responsive education. It's about power. The teachers union and the educrats are desperate to protect their monopoly, and they want the power to shape young minds. This is not power they'll surrender without a fight.

Dumb and Happy
November 7, 1997

One of the greatest virtues of a competitive market economy is diversification. Information about consumer preferences pours in from all directions. Different people and different companies react differently to it. We don't put all our eggs in one basket. Some succeed, some fail. The market rewards and penalizes accordingly. Ultimately, consumers determine the winners and losers.

Contrast this environment with public education, and you get a sense of why our schools are in such a sorry state. Highly centralized public education, the current model, is for the most part a monopoly. Decisions are driven not by consumer desires in the marketplace, but by boards and committees rooted in politics. Here, we do put all, or at least most, of our eggs in one basket.

Individual schools and philosophies are not allowed to succeed at the expense of others that would be allowed to fail. The assumption upon which all this is based is a consensus in society on how and what kids should be taught. And therein lies the fatal flaw. There is no consensus, and shouldn't be. Nonetheless, a prevailing orthodoxy dominates public education. It comes from educrats, the same people who gave you new math, open classrooms, multiculturalism, self-esteem and social engineering. These are also the people who don't like multiplication tables, discipline, knowledge-based history, homework and letter grades.

Alfie Kohn is one New Age educator who decries competition. He believes that "people actually do inferior work when enticed with grades, money or other incentives." One of his guides for teachers offers the following danger signs to watch for when seeking to create a "learner-centered" classroom environment:

- ✓ Desks in rows or chairs all facing forward.
- ✓ Lists of rules created by an adult.
- ✓ Star chart or other evidence that students are rewarded or ranked.
- ✓ Frequent periods of silence and/or teacher's voice the loudest or most often heard.

✓ Emphasis on facts and right answers.
✓ Students race to be first to answer teacher's "Who can tell me?" queries.
✓ Awards, trophies and prizes displayed, suggesting emphasis on triumph rather than community.

Personally, I like all of those things, but what do I know? Conventional wisdom among educrats is that the MTV generation has a short attention span, so you accommodate it by teaching in small bites and making it "fun." My approach would be the opposite. A short attention span is a bad thing to have, so rather than accommodate it, you help the kids cultivate a longer one. Education, like work, can't always be fun. A little more rigor in school is good preparation for life.

Another educrat is Steven Leinwand, a member of Bill Clinton's committee poised to write the questions for the proposed new national math exam. Leinwand thinks it's "downright dangerous" to teach students things like "six times seven is 42, put down two and carry the four." He sees this as elitist and discriminatory, since not all kids can master these procedures. I see, so if Johnny can't count, Billy shouldn't learn to, either, in deference to Johnny's self-esteem? Leinwand's solution is to arm student test-takers with calculators, lest the national exam reveal that they can't add, subtract, multiply or divide.

I don't mind the idea of standardized tests, but I don't like Clinton's heavy-handed federal government version of it. Among other things, I don't trust his brand of educator, like Leinwand or Kohn, to write the questions. To such people, public education has become social indoctrination according to their ideological model. I reiterate, there is no consensus. If this is the way they and others want to educate their kids, they're welcome to it. I, and others, might want something different. The public policy solution to that fundamental disagreement is also the market solution: charter schools and – even better – vouchers redeemable at the school of your choice, public or private. It's an idea whose time is rapidly coming, thanks in no small part to the educrats who have wrecked the public schools.

Reforming Schools like Pulling Teeth

June 9, 2000

Making the rounds in educratic circles is an allegory comparing dentistry to teaching. It's called *The Best Dentist*, and is the brainchild of John S. Taylor, superintendent of schools in Lancaster County, S.C. Because it reinforces their biases and tells them what they want to hear, this tract has been warmly embraced by the public school establishment and some of their apologists in the media.

The tortured premise of this self-serving exercise in illogic is that it's unfair to hold a dentist accountable for the bad habits, deprived living environments or physical defects of his patients. It means to parody reform efforts, like the one launched by Gov. Bill Owens in Colorado, to grade the performance of individual schools through the use of, among other things, standardized testing of students.

The allegory seeks to ridicule a supposed new state program that would measure the effectiveness of dentists by counting the number of cavities that patients have at age 10, 14 and 18, averaging the results, and then rating individual dentists accordingly. Isn't it obvious, we're led to conclude, that dentists with rich, healthy patients would be rated more highly than dentists with poor, unhealthy ones?

Yes, it is. And if that were the only consideration in the appraisal of dentists (or schools and teachers), a program like this would, indeed, be ridiculous. But, of course, it isn't. If the educrats who are touting this silly little fable don't see its glaring weaknesses, then the public schools are in even worse hands than we thought.

Test scores are just one component of a school's grade in Colorado. We had to start someplace in making an honest assessment of the status quo, but the initial scores are also recognized as a starting point, a benchmark. It's expected that schools in poorer neighborhoods will have lower scores. In subsequent years, those that show improvement will be acknowledged and rewarded. Parents will seek them out, and they'll serve as models for other schools.

Yes, there are variables beyond the control of teachers, like IQ, family income and parental involvement. And, yes, kids in affluent areas come with built-in advantages. But these are givens and can be

232

accounted for. Just because you can't control some things doesn't mean you can't control anything.

The point is that teachers aren't commodities, just as dentists aren't. Some are very good, some are mediocre and some are very bad. A great dentist can work wonders on even the worst mouth, and a lousy one can visit malpractice on even the best.

University of Tennessee researcher Dr. William Sanders, creator of the Tennessee Value-Added Assessment System, has found that individual teacher quality is the single most important factor in educating students, up to 20 times more important than class size. Disadvantaged kids are hardly hopeless. Innovative schools and better teachers have done wonders with them, as amply demonstrated in lower-income neighborhoods as diverse as the South Bronx, Chicago, Houston and Pueblo, Colo.

Just as you can audit a dentist's work by taking photos and X-rays of a patient, before and after, you can audit a teacher's work by pre-testing and post-testing individual students. While an incompetent dentist will soon lose his customers and ultimately his job, inept teachers are protected by tenure and their union. Unlike dentists, they have a captive audience and a government-protected monopoly. If you drop your dentist, you don't have to keep paying him. If you move your child to a private school and pay the supplemental tuition, you're still taxed to keep the government-school teacher on the job.

We need accountability, not excuses. We need to empower parents with choice and treat them as customers, not captives. We need to replace the outmoded labor union approach to compensation and job protection with market rewards and penalties. Identify the best teachers and pay them more; fire the worst ones. I'll give you a more apt dental analogy: Budging educrats toward meaningful reform is like pulling teeth.

Teaching Teachers about Pay
March 11, 2010

A familiar complaint from teachers and their unions is that their compensation isn't fair or right, and that others whose work is far less "important" are paid more.

Their favorite target is professional athletes. What kind of perverse society, they ask, would pay a semi-literate football player $10 million and a teacher only $30,000? The short answer is: one with a market economy, where the forces of supply and demand make these determinations.

The alternative is to place this power in the hands of a federal compensation commissar, supported by an immense bureaucracy, that would rate every job in our economy based on its relative "importance" and dictate its statutory pay rate. They tried this unsuccessfully in the former Soviet Union.

Look at it this way: Water is essential to maintain life. By contrast, diamonds are mostly a decorative affectation. But water is abundant and diamonds are rare. That's why diamonds cost more than water, one's personal values notwithstanding. And that's the way the world works. "Importance" is a subjective judgment but, in any case, not the definitive criterion. Religion is important, but lawyers and real estate agents are better paid than priests or nuns.

For the record, schoolteachers typically make a lot more than $30,000 a year. In Jefferson County, our state's largest public school district, the 2009-10 salary schedule starts at $33,616 for a rookie and tops out at more than $81,000. A mid-career teacher with a master's degree gets about $70,000 in salary along with tenured job security, a gold-plated pension plan and generous fringes that add another 25 percent. Since JeffCo teachers work less than nine months a year (187 days), that's an annualized total compensation package of more than $115,000.

Including higher education, there are more than 7 million teachers in the U.S., and a waiting list of people who aspire to these positions. There are tens of millions of Americans who have the ability to perform these jobs. The market-clearing price equilibrates supply and demand. Schools must pay that price to attract and retain employees. If there were a shortage of qualified teachers, schools and taxpayers would have to pay more. There isn't, so they don't.

By comparison, on the entire planet there are just over 1,000 individuals who can make the cut in the National Football League. And only a handful of them have the even rarer ability to quarterback a team at the highest level. That's why they're paid so much. Similarly, rock idols, movie stars, Howard Stern, Bill Gates, J.K. Rowling, Katie Couric and Rush Limbaugh make megabucks, while the president of the United States – with arguably the most "important" job in the world – is paid a mere $400,000. Teachers shouldn't take this personally; it's only economics.

Professional sports teams pay their players as much as they do because they expect them to generate revenues in excess of their compensation. Their budgets are constrained by what their customers are willing to spend. By the same token, the budgets of school districts are constrained by what the taxpayers are willing to pay.

While individual athletes may pull down some spectacular salaries, there aren't very many of them. The combined payrolls of all professional sports teams are a fraction of what the nation's 7 million teachers cost. Suppose we paid teachers – all of them – the same as a Major League Baseball utility infielder with a .270 batting average. The going price for that job is about $2 million. Let's see, $2 million times 7 million comes to a tidy $14 trillion. That's the equivalent of our nation's entire annual gross domestic product. And why stop at teachers? Cops, firefighters and social workers are important, too.

Don't tell the Obama administration about this. They'd pile it on the national deficit and call it economic stimulus.

Voucher War Not Yet Over
July 5, 2002

While last week's landmark Supreme Court decision in the Cleveland voucher case, Zelman v. Simmons-Harris, is encouraging for those who champion competition, choice and excellence in education, it's premature to pop the champagne corks.

This was just one battle in a protracted war for the hearts and minds of our children.

It's good that the court ruled that tax dollars already budgeted for educating kids don't necessarily have to be spent at government schools, but may be directed by parents to the private school of their choice, even if that private school has a religious orientation. This was obvious to any rational and fair-minded student of the Constitution. As long as no particular religion is favored by government over any others, and as long as parents are making the choice, there's nothing wrong in this policy that would violate the Establishment Clause of the First Amendment, which simply requires religious neutrality, not aversion.

It's bad and foreboding, however, that the court's decision was 5-4.

The dissenting justices displayed their overweening commitment to judicial activism and the liberal Democratic agenda. All it would take to reverse this decision in the future is the addition of one more liberal on the bench, displacing a conservative.

In fact, the constitutional challenge to the Cleveland voucher program wasn't motivated by concerns about religious freedom. That was just the latest pretext of the teachers unions who bankrolled the lawsuits.

This is all about the educrats' desperate campaign to kill the school choice movement in its crib. At the basest level, it's old-fashioned labor-union hardball, protecting their narrow self-interest from competition. As a political and ideological issue, it's about the power to indoctrinate impressionable young minds. Liberal educrats currently control public education. It's their agenda that prevails. They see the public schools as a great laboratory for social engineering. They are determined to mold the next generation in their "progressive" image.

You can understand why they fight tenaciously to maintain that power.

If the status quo were conservative control of public education, liberals would be screaming for educational choice.

I know there are individual, talented, dedicated teachers with no agenda other than to teach science or shop as best they can. Hell, there are even a few conservative Republican teachers. I'm not talking about them. My fight is with the unionists and ideologues that drive educratic policy and curricula. The liberal vision is egalitarian in the worst sense of that term: leveling students; hobbling the brightest to move at the pace of the herd. Their goal is to create little socialists. They value delusional "self-esteem" over rigorous academic standards, and multiculturalism over assimilation. They rue nationalism and individual competition. They don't like guns or the military. They want to remake boys in the feminist image.

I'd prefer a school for my kids where the values I hold dear would be featured. I'd like to groom little capitalists; add to the stock of entrepreneurs, not social workers; real estate developers, not greenies; Marines, not pacifists. I *want* them to absorb the wisdom in the classics penned by dead, white, European males before they're bombarded by the ravings of live, lesbian, university feminists. I'd like them to be held to high standards, with lots of homework, letter grades and none of that touchy-feely stuff.

But that's just me, and one size doesn't fit all. There's no consensus among parents about the best way to educate children, and there shouldn't be. I just want to make my choice for my kids, and I'm willing to let you choose for yours. In Cleveland, the public school monopolists were determined to force poor, minority parents to return their kids to failing government schools. I say, let a thousand flowers bloom and let alternative approaches compete in an educational marketplace. That's what vouchers and choice are all about. And that's just what educrats fear.

Public School Bondage
March 16, 2007

The state of Utah has just passed a landmark educational voucher program under which every family, depending on its income, will be reimbursed between $500 and $3,000 per child for annual tuition paid to the private school of their choice.

This will now give parents of modest means options that the well-to-do have long enjoyed. Their school-age children will no longer be a captive audience. Parents will be empowered as educational *consumers*, giving them choices and leverage consumers enjoy in all other spheres of our market economy. They'll be free to choose the educational model they believe best fits the unique needs of their children, and will be freed from the bureaucracy and politics of government education.

Predictably, the educratic establishment is in full counterattack. The Utah teachers union has launched a campaign to repeal the new law. If that fails, they'll try their luck in court. Their resistance is bred of desperation.

First, the union's survival is at stake. Under a voucher system, education is still publicly financed through taxpayer dollars. That doesn't change. But what does is the union's monopoly to *deliver* publicly funded education exclusively in government schools. Under a voucher system, competition would bloom.

Second, there's the ideological opposition to competition and free choice in education. The educratic establishment – from administrators, to the teachers colleges that staff the schools, to the unions that run them and the school boards they elect – is liberal to its core.

They covet their power to set the agenda, dictate subject matter and educational techniques, influence impressionable young minds and mold the next generation of liberal activists. They've turned their government schools into laboratories for social engineering, downgrading basic academics and old-fashioned notions of American exceptionalism, patriotism and individualism in favor of collectivism, political correctness, diversity, multiculturalism, environmentalism, feminism and delusional self-esteem. They have a death grip on these schools that they're loath to release.

As the United States falls further behind other nations in the math and science proficiency of students, and as the customer service rep on the other end of your telephone – somewhere in India – speaks better English than millions of American high school graduates, it's increasingly obvious that something's terribly wrong with public education in this country.

Yet educrats circle their wagons around the status quo. Tanya Clay House of the ultra-liberal People for the American Way recently declared, "We've never seen a shred of credible evidence that shows school vouchers actually help students learn. While all public schools must demonstrate success under No Child Left Behind, private schools are not held to the same level of accountability for their performance."

Nonsense. Private schools are held to account in the most effective way possible – they're accountable to their customers who are free to take their business elsewhere if they're not satisfied. All the evidence you need for vouchers is that parents who have used them to escape the government school monopoly fight to keep them.

Then, Clay House added this gem, "Every child deserves an excellent education, not just those admitted to a private school." I wonder if she realizes how self-contradictory that statement is. She's acknowledging that private schools provide educational excellence and that kids who are stuck in government schools are denied that! Does she suppose that wealthy parents who pay a premium to send their kids to private schools (without "a shred of evidence that they help students learn") are stupid?

Celebrating passage of the Utah voucher law, Andrew Coulsen of the *American Spectator* wrote, "Salt Lake City's legislation could very well become the domino that tips all other states into the camp of educational freedom." Wouldn't it be great if Colorado had the wisdom and courage to be next?

Vouching for School Choice
November 18, 2010, December 16, 2010

As a 2008 payoff to the national teachers unions. congressional Democrats killed a local school voucher program in Washington, D.C. in spite of its popularity among low-income black parents, presumably a Democrat core constituency, perhaps because teachers unions are more powerful and generous campaign contributors.

Now, vouchers may be making a comeback in D.C. But this time "D.C." stands for Douglas County, Colorado, a conservative stronghold in the state that actually has a slate of Republicans governing its school board, a rare occurrence in the politics of public education. And that explains why this district is considering a school voucher plan that would give parents the ability to choose private education alternatives in the county. Parents could select a school and a program that best suits their children's needs and interests. The presence of that choice would spur public schools to elevate the quality and variety of their product in a more competitive environment.

In 2003, the liberal majority on the Colorado Supreme Court, in a 4-3 vote, struck down a state voucher law for low-income students, claiming it undermined the control of local school boards. Since this DougCo plan is the brainchild of a local board, the liberal Supremes would have to contrive a different excuse to kill it.

Hoping to strangle any voucher program in its crib, the usual suspects, teachers unions and fellow-travelling parents in their tow, have wheeled out their shopworn, well-rehearsed arguments in opposition. Allow me to rebut some of them:

"This will drain money from public schools." No, it won't. Under the DougCo plan, only 75 percent of per-pupil state funding would follow the student to a private school. The remainder stays with the public schools. Fewer school students would require fewer teachers, fewer buildings, fewer buses and lower expenses, so the district's public schools would actually have more money: the 25 percent they get for the kids they don't have to teach.

"Money would be diverted to religious schools." So what? Taxpayer dollars already can be used for college tuition at religious

240

schools. You can use the G.I. Bill to go to Notre Dame or Yeshiva University. The U.S. Supreme Court has ruled that the Establishment Clause of the Constitution is offended only if government favors or discriminates against a particular religion. In a voucher program, the parents are making that choice. Might I disagree with some religious teaching? Perhaps, but I can live with that. I disagree now with a lot of what's taught in secular public schools.

"There currently aren't enough non-religious private schools available." Market demand stimulated by vouchers will attract new schools to fill the void. Popular charter schools have long waiting lists. Some may go private and expand.

"Private schools aren't any better than public schools and parents might make bad choices." I'll leave that judgment to individual parents. We call that "freedom" in our society. It works quite well in every other area. If you like your current public school, stay there. Why deny that choice to others?

"How would transportation be provided?" Motivated parents and private schools will figure that out. This is less of challenge than coming west in covered wagons.

"Vouchers are for bad school districts. Douglas County is a great one." No it isn't. It's simply above average – and the average isn't very good as measured by the performance of American students compared to their international counterparts. The level of academic rigor at even the best U.S. public schools is inferior to elite foreign competition. The academic performance of students in Douglas County is more a function of the socio-economic status and education of their parents than the quality of the schools. Students come home with good grades and parents imagine they're being well-educated.

Vouchers will give parents a greater opportunity to seek out private schools with truly rigorous academic programs. Heightened competition from those schools will force public schools to offer a better product to keep other parents from joining the exodus.

"This is a subsidy for wealthy parents whose children already attend private schools." There are plenty of non-wealthy parents who sacrifice to send their kids to private schools who will benefit from vouchers. Those parents and "wealthy" ones alike have been subsidizing public school districts for years with their taxes while relieving those districts of the cost burden of educating their kids. The more important point is that with or without vouchers, wealthy parents can afford to send their kids to private schools. Vouchers will allow many more parents who can't afford private schools to elect that option. Means-testing vouchers to disqualify wealthy parents still wouldn't soften opposition for those who are ideologically opposed to school choice.

"Studies show that private schools and charter schools don't produce any better academic results than public schools." If that's the case, those wealthy parents must be foolish to send their kids to expensive private schools. There are dueling studies about private/charter school vs. public school performance. The public school establishment, teachers unions and teachers colleges – all in bed together protecting their rice bowl – commission tendentious studies to downgrade the competition. Take them through that filter. Voucher advocates have their own studies with opposite conclusions. In the final analysis, with a voucher option, parents will decide for themselves.

In addition to academic rigor and performance, parents may make their selections on the basis of a school's values, pedagogical philosophy, curriculum and textbooks. If you think phonics is a better way to teach reading than "look-say," pick a school that offers that along with old-fashioned letter grades and more homework. Maybe you prefer an emphasis on traditional cognitive education (what you know) to trendy affective education (how you feel). Parents more interested in basic academics than liberal indoctrination, social engineering and multiculturalism can seek out a school more consonant with their goals for their children. Private schools are less likely to be burdened by the self-serving agenda of a teachers union.

"Some private (and charter) schools fail." As well they should. And some companies go out of business. That's what happens when consumers have choice and an enterprise doesn't perform to their satisfaction. Successful private and charter schools have long waiting lists. The public-school monopoly treats parents as captives, not customers. That's why too many failing and underperforming public schools that should go out of business continue to squander public resources and disserve students, parents and taxpayers.

Politics, bureaucracy, a one-size-fits-all mentality and the heavy hand of government have created our public school quagmire. Finally, vouchers offer a market alternative.

National Endowment for Vouchers
February 3, 2011

What do Warren Buffett, Bill Gates and Mark Zuckerberg have in common? Of course, they're all billionaires. Buffett made his money through shrewd investing, Gates as the Microsoft pioneer and Zuckerberg in social networking with Facebook. But I'm referring to their philanthropic pursuits.

The combined wealth of Buffett and Gates exceeds $100 billion. The youthful Zuckerberg is a relative piker at just a billion or two, but his heart is in the right place. All three have dedicated a portion of their considerable resources to improving the quality of public education in America. To be sure, this is a worthy goal.

Buffett is partnering with Gates through the Gates Foundation, which has already shoveled about $4 billion in recent years into public education. Zuckerberg has pledged $100 million to reform one of the country's worst public school districts, in Newark, N.J.

I'd give all three an "A" for effort and good intentions – but an "F" for process and effectiveness. Isn't it ironic that while they've made all their fortunes in the private enterprise system – that cauldron of choice, competition, innovation and achievement – their vehicle for education reform is exclusively in a government monopoly?

Gates apparently knows better. Attending the 2010 Aspen Ideas Festival, he heard Joel Klein, a friend of Gates and the former chancellor of New York City's Department of Education, declare, "The (public) school system is built on the three pillars of mediocrity: lockstep pay, lifetime tenure and seniority." Gates reinforced this, noting that this seniority system and the huge sums committed to pensions for retired teachers, what he termed an "accounting fraud," will force as many as 100,000 younger, more motivated teachers out of their jobs in the next couple of years.

A trio of documentaries released in the last year has caught the public's attention, especially minority parents in poor-performing schools. *The Cartel, The Lottery* and *Waiting for Superman* all had similar themes, exposing the political stranglehold of the teachers unions on public schools and the resulting mindless bureaucracy, waste,

244

fraud and malfeasance. Just read the voluminous work rules in a typical school district's collective-bargaining contract.

Parents of grade-school kids don't have time to wait for the illusory promise of public school reform. They desperately want better alternatives now. Last week in Ohio, an African-American mom was jailed for lying about her address in a desperate attempt to get her daughters into a better school in another district.

So here's my proposal to Buffett, Gates, Zuckerberg and other well-heeled philanthropists: Break the mold! Stop throwing good money after bad at the failing government-school establishment. It already has a powerful political constituency and hundreds of billions in taxpayer funding. Follow the lead of the late J. Patrick Rooney, chairman of the Golden Rule Insurance Company, the man who pioneered medical savings accounts. In the name of parental choice, he created a private-school voucher program for low-income Indianapolis families in 1991 that inspired similar efforts across the country, now serving more than 50,000 students.

Buffett has pledged to give 99 percent of his $47 billion net worth to charity and proposes that Gates and other billionaires do likewise. Great! Why not endow $100 billion for a national voucher plan? At 8 percent per annum on that principal (what the teachers' PERA pension fund assumes), it would generate $8 billion a year to fund a $4,000 (about half of what it costs to educate a Colorado public school student) voucher for each of 2 million students to attend the private school of their choice.

This would do more than just improve academic performance. It also would offer philosophical diversity to counter the public schools' liberal indoctrination of impressionable young minds. You'd think successful capitalists might want to defend and encourage capitalism.

Tyranny of the Tenured Left
September 13, 2002

As the late philosopher Richard Weaver profoundly observed more than a half-century ago in his book of the same name, *Ideas Have Consequences*. And where better to hash out those competing ideas than in the halls of higher education? If only that were so. Sadly, it's not. One enduring legacy of the turbulent '60s and '70s is the radicalization of America's colleges and universities. With a few notable exceptions, the tenured left is firmly in control and has manipulated the purpose of intellectual discourse in higher education from that of a free exchange of ideas to one of ideological activism.

Their mission is to indoctrinate impressionable, idealistic young minds and to enlist academe in a crusade to transform society in their leftist image. Political correctness – of the collectivist, feminist, post-modernist, oppressed peoples, enviros, anti-capitalist, one-world, etc. variety – reigns supreme. Thoughts or expressions that might give offense to even the most hyper-sensitive disciple of the official dogma will not be tolerated.

I'm speaking primarily about the arts and sciences: history, sociology, political science, economics, psychology, women's studies, etc. These are fields that lend themselves more to political biases and value judgments. Engineering, physics, mathematics, accounting and the like are another matter. Professors in those departments tend to be technicians rather than *sandalistas*.

Anecdotal accounts of classroom proselytizing by leftist instructors on college campuses are abundant. Just ask any politically aware, non-Marxist student who's willing to be candid. If you seek more formal evidence, then get your hands on the September 2002 issue of *The American Enterprise* magazine. There you'll find a study of 21 colleges and universities, prestigious places like Harvard, Stanford, the University of California at Berkeley, Penn State and even the University of Colorado at Boulder. Researchers tabulated – it's public record – the party registrations of arts and science faculty members and divided them into parties of the right (e.g., Republican, Libertarian) and of the left (e.g., Democrat, Green, Socialist Workers). The results are staggering but not surprising. At Cornell it was 166 faculty members of the left to six on the right.

Harvard was 50-2, Brown 54-3, the University of California at Santa Barbara 72-1 Syracuse 50-2, UCLA 141-9, and at CU-Boulder it was 116-5 – duh!

Party registration might not be entirely conclusive, but it's a good clue. A more precise sense of political ideology could be derived by reading the publications of these faculty members. I'd love to see such a study, and I have no doubt it would produce similar results. Isn't it ironic that the same institutions that obsess over "diversity" as it pertains to race, gender, sexual orientation and culture offer little diversity when it comes to philosophical and political beliefs? It's probably true that academia attracts more lefties than righties. Conservatives might be more inclined to gravitate toward more practical careers in the private sector. But there are many more conservative intellectuals who aspire to cushy professorships than is reflected by their representation on college faculties.

Yes, the ugly truth is that in their ivory-tower sanctuary, the tenured left discriminates against conservatives. When it comes to filling faculty positions, they favor their own, and conservative thinkers aren't generally welcome. The offshoot is that students are denied a well-rounded education. And the problem is compounded in state-run schools, where taxpayers in the political mainstream, ironically, wind up bankrolling a political culture that trashes the values they hold dear in classrooms filled by the children they've raised on those values.

The solution is obvious. Since the left is so fond of affirmative action programs and quotas, let's apply that remedy in the name of philosophical diversity, and launch a hiring campaign for conservative faculty members – not based on arbitrary classifications like race and sex but on the merit of ideas. I have no illusions that reigning faculty leftists will voluntarily loosen their grip. It's up to college administrators, trustees, regents or legislators to force the issue. Based on their duplicity or timidity in the past, I'm not optimistic.

Diversity in War of Ideas
September 19, 2003

We must be on to something. They're circling the wagons.

The Academic Bill of Rights, a plan to restore a semblance of ideological balance to the humanities faculties of state colleges, has the left up in arms. Virtually every liberal columnist and editorial cartoonist in town has attacked it, and the leftist higher education establishment is positively apoplectic. "McCarthyism!" they cry. How ironic. That's a more accurate description of the *current state* of affairs, where a de facto blacklist bars anything more than a token sampling of conservative professors to the club.

We're not talking about engineering, physics and mathematics. Those are hard sciences, not particularly vulnerable to political spin. The problem is in the liberal arts and humanities: economics, history, sociology, literature, psychology, women's studies, political science, etc. These are disciplines steeped in ideological subjectivity and political agendas. And it's where the war of ideas is fought to influence impressionable young minds.

The problem is that conservative viewpoints are grossly underrepresented among faculty members in this venue. And the leftists who dominate in these departments include too many proselytizers for their various causes who can't be trusted to fairly present differing viewpoints. You see them at anti-war "teach-ins." The solution is to provide more competition in the war of ideas by recruiting conservatives who can speak with the same conviction for the things in which they believe.

Students are entitled to a more balanced presentation, as are the taxpayers who subsidize their education and the payroll of faculty members. The people, not the professors and administrators, own the schools. This is a legitimate public policy issue. The left doesn't see a problem, no doubt because they're in control and like it that way. But listen to these same lefties complain about the imbalance of conservatives in talk radio. They're only for competition on someone else's turf.

This isn't about hiring Republicans, per se. No party litmus test has been proposed. The near exclusion of Republicans in humanities faculties is just a symptom, a clue. Party registration is a matter of public record and easily obtained to document the hiring bias. In the final analysis, department heads can thoughtfully consider an academic's papers and publications to determine his or her orientation. If you already have a stable of Marxian theorists on your economics staff, then hire a free-market champion of Ludwig von Mises or Milton Friedman. In history and political science we could hear a little less of the anti-American diatribes of Noam Chomsky disciples and a little more from those who prefer Will and Ariel Durant or Paul Johnson.

Leftist defenders of the status quo, which favors them, smirk that conservatives are suddenly advocating "quotas." Their reasoning is twisted. I have no objection to quotas when they're relevant and justified. Businesses frequently pay commissions only after sales people have exceeded their monthly quota. That's fine. On the other hand, I'm opposed to quotas based on race, gender or ethnicity in college admissions if they discriminate against more qualified individuals. Women and Jewish and Asian students are over-represented as a share of the population on college campuses. So what, as long as they've earned their way in? If the Denver Broncos have too many defensive players on their roster, they recruit offensive players. If colleges have an unfair imbalance of liberal faculty members, they should recruit more conservatives. Call it a quota or anything else you like. It just makes sense.

It's the liberals who are inconsistent. Their selective support of quotas isn't based on relevancy or individual rights, but on social engineering, job security and protection of their power to indoctrinate students. Whatever happened to their commitment to "diversity" where it really matters: in the realm of ideas?

Another specious argument is that conservative applicants aren't available because they're all getting rich in the private sector.

Nonsense. There are only so many senior executive jobs to go around.

Being an elite member of the professoriate is a cushy job and lifestyle. It pays in the six figures, with great hours, and offers grad student assistants to teach your classes while you write books, give paid outside lectures, and enjoy sabbaticals, generous fringe benefits, tenure and a fantastic retirement package. Yes, the field probably attracts marginally more liberals than conservatives, but there are more than enough qualified conservative applicants to narrow the hiring disparity. True, the current university cultural climate isn't friendly to conservative dissenters. But that can be remedied by substantially increasing the number of conservative dissenters.

The Relentless Contortion
of the Constitution

The U.S. is a Republic, Not a Democracy
February 9, 1996

"A democracy cannot exist as a permanent form of government. It can only exist until the voters discover they can vote themselves largesse out of the public treasury. From that moment on, the majority always votes for the candidates promising the most benefits from the public treasury, with the result that a democracy always collapses over loose fiscal policy, always followed by a dictatorship."

These are the immortal words of Professor Alexander Fraser Tytler, a Scottish historian at Edinburgh (Scotland) University. Writing about the demise of Athenian democracy, he composed this passage more than 200 years ago, while our original 13 states were still colonies of England. Sounds like the current budget crisis, doesn't it? Hold this thought for a moment.

I recently read a draft of the new "Colorado Model Content Standards for Civics," as required by the state legislature for K-12 education. They were derived, in large part, from the national standards, drawn up by the Center for Civic Education in California. The Colorado educators who are writing the standards have asked for public input before they finalize their work. Good, here's mine.

Let me start by revealing my bias. After seeing the national American *history* standards, I was expecting the worst. Those have been roundly, and justifiably, criticized as a model of trendy, political correctness and leftist revisionism. After a public outcry, they've been sent back to the drawing board by Congress. In the wake of that debacle, I was pleasantly surprised by the first draft of the Colorado civics standards. The bulk of it is fair, relevant and worthwhile.

I have only one major problem with the civics draft. In it, our system of government is repeatedly referred to as a "constitutional democracy." (The word "republicanism" is mentioned in the glossary, but "democracy" is clearly the featured term.) James Madison must be

251

spinning in his grave. We are a republic, not a democracy. This is not a trivial distinction. In the *Federalist Papers*, Madison and Hamilton go on at length and with passion about the differences. They were of a mind with Alexander Tytler and scorned the political notion of a populist democracy. In *Federalist No. 10*, Madison says "...democracies have ever been spectacles of turbulence and contention; have ever been found incompatible with personal security or the rights of property; and have in general been as short in their lives as they are violent in their deaths." Consequently, our founders crafted a constitutional republic abundant with protections from the excesses of direct democracy, including representative and federal government, the separation of powers, checks and balances, judicial review, the presidential veto, the electoral college, indirect election of senators and equal representation of all the states in the Senate, to name just a few.

Supreme Court Chief Justice, John Marshall, proclaimed: "Between a balanced Republic and a Democracy, the difference is like that between order and chaos." Article IV, Section 4 of the U.S. Constitution reads: "The United States shall guarantee to every State in the union a republican Form of Government,..." The word "democracy" appears not once in the Constitution, Bill of Rights or Declaration of Independence. We pledge allegiance to the flag and to the *republic* for which it stands.

If the Colorado Civics Standards Task Force wants to describe our system as a constitutional republic with *democratic institutions*, that's OK with me. You might argue that we're more of a democracy today than we were 200 years ago, but we're not there yet. Let's not make it so by fiat. I had an enlightening discussion with Barbara Miller, a task force member. I expressed dismay when she told me that not one of the dozen or more members of her committee expressed a preference for "republic" over "democracy," especially because this debate has been raging for more than 200 years. She told me that in the absence of any dissent, the committee defaulted to the wording in the national standards: "constitutional democracy."

Well, I propose we exercise our prerogative to depart from the national standards on this matter. In Colorado, we can show how power, independence and freedom are devolved to the states. Let's teach our kids why we're a constitutional republic. Civics Task Force, the ball's in your court.

The Opposite of Activism
April 21, 2011

Justice Stephen Breyer, a stalwart of the liberal bloc on the U.S. Supreme Court, has written a new book, *Making Our Democracy Work*. Ironically, if our constitutional republic were in fact a true democracy, which it isn't, Breyer wouldn't have been appointed to the court for life, but rather elected by a majority of the voters. But that's another subject.

At a recent public appearance in Arkansas, Breyer cited his book while making the case for judicial activism. As *The Associated Press* described it, Breyer proclaimed that "the court should apply the Constitution's values with a pragmatic view toward present circumstances, rather than focusing only on the document's historical meaning."

Regarding historical meaning and intent as hindrances, judicial activists, like Breyer, have converted our foundational document into what they call a "living Constitution."

This is hardly a new idea. Conservative critic Thomas Sowell reminds us that this was a recurring theme a century ago among professors like Harvard Law School Dean Roscoe Pound who touted the notion of a "living Constitution" to put the law "in the hands of a progressive and enlightened caste whose conceptions are in advance of the public." That sentiment was shared by Justice Louis Brandeis, who called for a shift "from legal justice to social justice."

The competing school of judicial philosophy, still embraced by today's conservative bloc on the Supreme Court, has historically been known as "originalism," holding that the Constitution should be interpreted according to actual words and intent, not according to the personal beliefs of unelected philosopher-kings in black robes who have a different idea of how it ought to read.

Earlier this year, Federal District Court Judge Roger Vinson ruled Obamacare unconstitutional. He reasoned that mandating individuals to acquire private health insurance is an abuse of the commerce clause, which was never intended or applied to force people to buy something. When the Supreme Court has the last word on this matter, it has the potential to be a landmark case, reaching well beyond the issue of health care and addressing decades of congressional overreach, exploiting the commerce clause to justify all kinds of legislative mischief.

On the heels of Vinson's ruling, a *New York Times* editorial branded it "a breathtaking example of *judicial activism*" (italics mine). Whoa! Now, *The Times* is free to disagree with Vinson, but describing his ruling as "judicial activism," is both galling and laughable. That's exactly the opposite of what it was.

Judicial activism is what imperious liberal judges do when they refuse to be constrained by the Constitution or the law. It's what Breyer, Pound and Brandeis advocated, above. It's judicial fiat with judges usurping the role of legislators, conveniently and arbitrarily rewriting the Constitution to achieve their desired social or political ends. Vinson's ruling was a crowning example of judicial restraint. He didn't rewrite the Constitution; he protected the original intent of the commerce clause as understood by James Madison and other founders.

Justice Oliver Wendell Holmes Jr. concisely exposed judicial activism for what it is when he explained to an idealistic young lawyer in his courtroom, "This is a court of law, young man, not a court of justice." If you think a law is unjust, appeal to your legislators, not your judges. If you think the Constitution is unjust or out of date, then work to amend it in the prescribed manner.

Liberal proponents of judicial activism are defensive about that label, so they play a clever little word game. Like the *New York Times* editor, they misapply the term in order to neutralize it. They'll call it judicial activism when an originalist judge overturns an unconstitutional law or overrules an activist judge in a lower court. That's like equating a cure for cancer with the inducement of it.

Disdain for the Constitution
December 17, 2004

I've heard liberals express their dismay at all the fuss conservatives make over judicial activism. Some even claim to be unclear about the meaning of the term. Perhaps a recent remark of Sen. Harry Reid of Nevada, the incoming Senate minority leader, will serve as an illustration.

Appearing Dec. 6 on *Meet the Press*, Reid was asked to comment on Supreme Court Justice Clarence Thomas as a possible replacement for ailing Chief Justice William Rehnquist. "I think he (Thomas) has been an embarrassment to the Supreme Court. I think that his opinions are poorly written," said Reid.

Now, if Clarence Thomas were an African-American *liberal* Supreme Court justice, you can be sure Reid would never have "dissed" the man like that. (He might even have called him a "credit to his race.") A white Republican saying such a thing about a black jurist would have been accused of racism. But rare black *conservatives*, like Thomas and Condoleezza Rice, are apparently fair game.

I suspect it's not the *quality* of Thomas' opinions that Reid objects to; it's the *substance*. Thomas bases his decisions on the principles of limited government and strict constitutional constructionism. It's not like Thomas is a lone wolf, winging his opinions and jotting them down on the back of a napkin while watching NASCAR races on TV. He, and every other justice, is supported by the cream of the crop of law school graduates and brilliant staffers anxious to pad their resumes by clerking for the Supreme Court. The opinions they help their bosses write are painstakingly researched, crafted and vetted.

But Reid was just warming up. Here comes the best part and an insight into the mindset of judicial activists. Reid volunteered that he *could* support Thomas' fellow conservative on the high bench, Antonin Scalia, for chief justice. (It should be noted that Scalia and Thomas routinely vote on the same side employing similar reasoning. I guess Reid finds these decisions more palatable coming from a white conservative than from an uppity black who fails to vote like Thurgood

Marshall did.) Said Reid, "I cannot dispute the fact, as I have said, that (Scalia) is one smart guy. And I disagree with many of the results that he arrives at, *but his reasons for arriving at those results are very hard to dispute* [italics mine]." Aha!

When Reid says he disagrees with Scalia's results but finds it hard to argue with his reasoning, he lets the cat out of the bag, revealing his disdain for the rules of the game: the U.S. Constitution. In other words, Reid would prefer a tendentious approach, working backward from a predetermined political outcome and contriving a reinterpretation of the Constitution to get there. This, in a nutshell, is judicial activism.

Scalia (and Thomas and Rehnquist) plays by the rules and restricts his decisions to the boundaries established by the Constitution. Liberals refuse to be constrained by the Constitution. If they can't get a new law passed through the legislature, they circumvent that branch and shop for activist judges who will legislate from the bench. Their only standard is that the ends justify the means; to them the Constitution isn't our legal foundation – when it's inconvenient it's merely an obstacle.

The chief rationalization of judicial activists is that the Constitution is a "living document." By that they mean liberal judges, appointed for life, rewriting the Constitution at will to achieve contemporary political objectives. This is how the Massachusetts Supreme Court miraculously discovered, unnoticed by their predecessors for more than 200 years, a constitutional right to same-sex marriage.

This practice is not only anti-democratic, it's a violation of the fundamental principle of checks and balances among our three branches of government.

The founders didn't build an impenetrable force field around our basic governing document. They anticipated the need for modifications and additions to the Constitution. They provided a process for it and so far we've had 27 amendments. When there's compelling need, it requires ratification by three-quarters of the state legislatures. I know that's a more difficult task than enlisting the trendy political whims of five Supreme Court Justices, but it was designed that way for good reason. That blindfolded lady balancing the scales of justice wants a commitment, not just a one night stand.

Constitution Still Matters to Some
July 7, 2011

Just in time for Independence Day, *Time Magazine's* July 4 cover story displayed a shredded copy of the U.S. Constitution behind the superimposed question: "Does it Still Matter?" Inside, readers were treated to an absurdly stupid essay on this topic by managing editor Richard Stengel.

Time, established as the gold standard of news magazines by conservative Henry Luce in the 1920s, has been moving ever leftward for years. But this latest assault is embarrassing even by its biased standards.

According to Stengel: "The framers were not gods and were not infallible. Yes, they gave us, and the world, a blueprint for the protections of democratic freedoms – freedom of speech, assembly, religion – but they also gave us the idea that a black person was three-fifths of a human being, that women were not allowed to vote, and that South Dakota should have the same number of senators as California, which is kind of crazy ... If the Constitution was intended to limit the federal government, it sure doesn't say so."

Really? Let's take these specious criticisms in order:

1) Slavery was a contentious issue that couldn't be resolved when the Constitution was being written and ratified. Article I, Section 2 deals with the number of representatives for each state in the U.S. House. Blacks weren't mentioned by name. The phrase "three-fifths of all other persons" was a reference to slaves. Not all blacks were slaves. Free blacks in northern states were counted as one person. The southern states wanted all their black slaves to be counted as one person, giving them more seats in the House. The northern states disagreed. The "three-fifths" calculation was a numerical compromise, not a general denigration of blacks.

2) There's no specific wording in the Constitution prohibiting women from voting. It was silent on that subject, which is not surprising given the culture and customs of that age. The Founders were men of the 18th century, not the 20th. Women's suffrage wasn't on the political menu yet. That was remedied in

257

1920 through the amendment process, which the Founders had the foresight to provide. In this case the ratification of the 19th.

3) There's nothing "crazy" about each state, regardless of population, having an equal number of senators. The House of Representatives was regarded as the "people's house," with seats apportioned by population. The Senate was the "states' house," with two senators each. This was part of the Founders grand design, creating a republic, not a pure democracy. Article IV, Section 4 guarantees to every state a "republican form of government." The word "democracy" appears not at all in the Constitution or the Declaration of Independence.

4) Stengel's claim of unlimited federal power is dumbfounding. The main body of the Constitution overflows with limits on the federal government. Stengel should read it someday. And the first 10 Amendments, the Bill of Rights, is a litany of what the government can't do to individuals, along with an enumeration of the fundamental freedoms Americans enjoy about which "Congress shall make no law." The 10th Amendment reserves all the powers not specifically delegated to the federal government to the states or to the people.

If Stengel is unaware of these facts – which a schoolchild should know – he's remarkably ignorant. If he's willfully defaming and discrediting the Constitution, he's a rank demagogue. This is consistent with the left's pretense of a so-called "living Constitution," empowering liberal judges to act as unelected super-legislators, dictating public policy based on their notion of what the Constitution ought to say. As originally written and intended, the Constitution is a troublesome obstacle to their liberal political agenda, and amending it under the rules is inconvenient. Does the Constitution matter?

Not to them.

Empathy and the Supreme Court
May 22, 2009

During an Obama-McCain presidential debate in October, Barack Obama decried a Supreme Court ruling rejecting Lily Ledbetter's sex discrimination case against Goodyear. The court ruled narrowly and properly that she filed too late under the law and that her charges were, therefore, moot. Obama didn't like that outcome and declared that if someone "is being treated unfairly, then the court has to stand up, if nobody else will. And that's the kind of judge I want."

It was no surprise, then, that following the announcement of Supreme Court Justice David Souter's impending retirement, the president proclaimed that his replacement must be an individual endowed with "empathy," adding, "I will seek someone who understands that justice isn't about some abstract legal theory or footnote in a case book. It is also about how our laws affect the daily reality of people's lives." (Oprah, perhaps?) Compassionate and seductive as this pronouncement my sound to some, it represents a radical and dangerous departure from traditional American jurisprudence.

In fact, justice is very much about legal theory and case law. The principle of *stare decisis* holds that courts will generally honor the decisions of prior courts. This is what makes our system of justice predictable and consistent, rather than random and arbitrary.

When empathetic judges rule on their feelings, they are exceeding their authority. Perhaps the young Barack Obama was out "community organizing" on the day his Harvard law professor explained the reasoning of U.S. Supreme Court Justice Oliver Wendell Holmes Jr., when he instructed an idealistic young lawyer that, "This is a court of law, young man, not a court of justice." The point is that the role of the judicial branch of our government is to rule on the Constitution as written and the law as passed by congress and signed by the president. The courts are a co-equal branch of government, not a superior branch. Their job is not to rule on what they think the law ought to be. That's government by a presumptuous, unelected judiciary.

If changing times render some part of the Constitution outmoded, the remedy is to formally amend the Constitution, as we've done some 27 times, not to have judges rewrite it themselves. To use a sports metaphor, judges are referees, not rule makers. They're not there to represent or empathize with the fans or the players. They represent the rule book, and they aren't authorized to rewrite it or make it "fairer."

If a law is regarded as unjust, changing that law is the province of legislators, not judges acting arbitrarily as legislators. That's judicial activism, working backwards from a desired social or political outcome rationalized by a convenient reinterpretation of the Constitution or the law. The dispute between conservatives and liberals on judicial activism is philosophical and irreconcilable. The magic words, the *abracadabra* liberals use to justify such behavior, are a "living Constitution," which means, in effect, no *Constitution* at all. Conservatives are constitutional originalists. They believe that document is just what it says and that original intent is the overriding criterion. They believe the integrity of the *process* is paramount.

Liberals are inherent social engineers. Their overriding concern is with *outcomes*. If they can't get something straightforwardly, through the legislature via the democratic process, they would substitute sympathetic judges for lawmakers. Their disregard for original intent and the integrity of the process is rationalized by their belief that the ends justify the means. Recoiling defensively from charges of judicial activism, liberals have cynically attempted to redefine that term. They've turned it on its head, labeling conservative judges "judicial activists" when such judges oppose the judicial activism of liberal judges.

The Senate confirmation hearings over President Obama's empathetic nominee to the Supreme Court should make for an interesting debate on these principles.

The Case for the Death Penalty
June 7, 2015

Some people have been convicted of crimes they didn't commit, including capital crimes. An injustice can ultimately be mitigated if the penalty is imprisonment. If one is put to death for a crime he didn't commit, that's obviously irreversible.

While this is a legitimate theoretical argument against capital punishment, the chances of wrongful execution these days is near zero. In the cases of James Holmes and Dzhokhar Tsarnaev, the chance is *absolutely* zero.

Public opinion still overwhelmingly favors the death penalty for murder. According to the last Gallup Poll in October, 63 percent favor, 33 percent oppose. The gap has closed since 1994, when 80 percent favored it and 16 percent opposed. But support has remained in a consistent range of about 2-to-1 over the last decade.

There's certainly a legal case for capital punishment. The Constitution explicitly allows it. The Fifth Amendment specifies the process for holding someone "to answer for a capital or otherwise infamous crime." The 14th Amendment specifies that no person be deprived of *life*, liberty or property without due process of law. The courts have found no fundamental conflict with the Eighth Amendment's prohibition of cruel and unusual punishment.

Deterrence isn't the primary argument for the death penalty. The threat of execution clearly doesn't deter all. In the heat of the moment, crimes of passion trump reason. And professional contract killers have already discounted the risks vs. returns of their business. If it deters some, call that a bonus.

The religious and moral case is complicated. The Sixth Commandment doesn't prohibit killing, and certainly not those deserving it. The Old Testament is replete with the lawful killing of sinners by man and God. Translated from the original Hebrew, the key word accurately should read, "Thou shalt not *murder*." Murder is quite a different thing from justifiable killing, as in a just war, self-defense or a capital crime.

The overriding moral principle is "retribution." A fundamental tenet of the law is that one who commits a crime be made to forfeit something he values commensurate with the loss he inflicted on his victim. For property theft, financial restitution and imprisonment may be sufficient. For the theft of life under the most heinous and premeditated circumstances, equivalence requires the forfeiture of something the murderer equally values – his own life.

To disparage this as societal "revenge" misrepresents and debases the principle. Legal procedures, protections and consequences in capital cases proscribe rashness and torture. Due process is followed at every turn. On the calendar, it's certainly deliberative enough, arguably excessively so. Appeals can go on for decades.

Some opponents of capital punishment invoke humanitarian or religious objections. All lives matter and are equally valuable, they say. I disagree. Distinctions are made. Think of a natural disaster with thousands of casualties beyond the capacities of emergency medical providers, forcing them to practice triage. In that case, decisions are based not on the respective worth of individuals but on the severity of injuries and the probability of survival. Conversely, if the president is under attack, Secret Service agents are bound and committed to sacrifice their lives to protect his. Isn't that a judgment of relative value and importance if not just practicality?

Some lives have been more valuable to society than others based on the commendable deeds and accomplishments of one compared to the misdeeds and destruction perpetrated by another: Mother Teresa vs. Adolf Hitler and his worst agents of mass extermination executed after the Nuremburg Trials. In this life, society makes that judgment. If there's an afterlife, God can sort it out.

Our justice system isn't perfect, but it doesn't have to be to give Holmes and Tsarnaev what they deserve.

Border Control Our Right
November 17, 2006

It's said that a picture is worth a thousand words. I only have room for about 700 here so let me be more concise.

Just the other day, an editorial cartoon, set in the 1600s, depicted a rowboat full of pilgrims coming ashore in the New World and encountering a group of Indians constructing a log wall to keep them out. Standing next to a boulder marked "Plymouth Rock" (in case you didn't get it) on the shoreline, one of the Indians, with his arms folded in an unwelcoming position and a disapproving frown on his face, blocked their way. The caption conveyed the words of one of the would-be new arrivals reporting back to his fellow Pilgrims on the rowboat: "They say they're building a wall because too many of us enter illegally and won't learn their language or assimilate into their culture…"

Cute. I'm not sure what the cartoonist's intended message was. Perhaps he was accusing those who support border security and immigration control today of hypocrisy, since their ancestors may have once been invaders themselves. Of course the Indians didn't originate here either. The only real native Americans are dinosaurs and cockroaches. Whatever. But I took my own lesson from this cartoon.

If the Indians knew then what they know now, they'd have tried mightily to keep out the Pilgrims and all who followed. Over time, waves of immigrants overwhelmed the Indians, their societies and their culture. Early arrivals brought their own culture, religion, laws, language, system of political economy and technology with them. Later arrivals assimilated to the melting pot. It was the Indians who had to adapt.

I kind of like our culture, our customs and our language the way they are, and I'd like to preserve all that. I'm not opposed to immigration – legal immigration, that is – as long as it serves our interests. By controlling our borders and setting immigration limits and qualifications we can avoid the fate of the Indians and keep from being swamped by future waves of immigrants. Is this selfish? You bet. Just as every other nation in the world that behaves rationally is selfish.

Once upon a time, America thirsted for immigrants. That's when we were rapidly expanding our frontiers, heading west, homesteading, prospecting for gold and building railroads from sea to shining sea. We needed many skills, including an army of hearty laborers. That was then; this is now. We still need refined skills and manual labor, some of which can be supplied by immigrants and guest workers. But we don't need this in infinite quantities.

Another thing that's changed since the days of rugged individualism and Manifest Destiny is the creation of the welfare state. Now you don't have to necessarily carry your own weight. The government has woven an intricate safety net to support you. We don't need more net tax receivers.

A recent letter to the editor attempted to make some tortured point that those who oppose open borders are un-Christian, arguing that the Bible instructs us to "take in and help the stranger, the alien and the downtrodden," and that Jesus would not have said, "Go thou and build a wall" to keep out illegal immigrants. Advocates of liberation theology use similar arguments to paint Jesus as a socialist, which might have amused Lenin and Stalin. The distinction is that there is a vital difference between one's behavior toward an individual encountered on the street and the nation's public policy.

The Bible might envision the day when we could beat our swords into plowshares, but in the meantime there's nothing un-Christian about a nation defending itself from Islamofascist suicidal murderers. Similarly, sovereign states (like the Vatican, for example, which has boundaries and a protective wall) are entitled to secure their borders and establish their own immigration policies. If Christians, or anyone else, as individuals, want to assist the downtrodden, adopt a child from an impoverished nation or go on a mission abroad to help others, God bless them.

But that doesn't mean they can't also subscribe to reasonable and practical immigration and border security policies for their secular government at home.

The United States now has a population of 300 million. It's doubled in the last 50 years, increasingly from immigration. The world population is 6 billion today and projected to grow to 8 billion in 20 years. I don't doubt that half of them would love to come here if they could. That would be good for them but not so good for us. And that latter consideration should be the first criterion for our immigration policy. Remember what happened to the Indians.

Birth Rights and Wrongs
August 25, 2011

"Southern California has become a hub of so-called birthing tourism." So observed the *Los Angeles Times* in a story earlier this year about three townhouses in a residential neighborhood of San Gabriel that had been converted into maternity centers for upscale Chinese women, providing them with room, board and care before and after their babies are born.

The actual delivery, however, takes place in California hospitals. Why? Not primarily for the quality of medical services. The prize they seek is a very important document: a U.S. birth certificate. As the story noted, these Chinese women are "willing to pay handsomely to travel here to give birth to American citizens."

Unlike illegal immigrants who cross our southern border, these pregnant Chinese women don't enter our country illegally. They come on tourist visas, stay for a few months and then most go home to China with their newborns who have the option of returning someday as full-fledged American citizens, entitled to all the rights and benefits that includes.

I've written before about the current legal misinterpretation of birthright citizenship under the 14th Amendment. This case study in birthing tourism is a graphic example of its abuse. Here's a review.

The amendment was written in 1866 following the Civil War and ratified in 1868. In addition to punishing the confederate rebellion, it was intended to abolish the legacy of slavery. Section 1 effectively granted citizenship and all constitutional protections to former slaves "born or naturalized in the United States, and *subject to the jurisdiction thereof.*" That key phrase doesn't mean subject to our laws; it refers to persons who owe no allegiance to another country. That is, who were not citizens of another country or children of citizens of another country.

Consistent with that precise intent, the same Congress that wrote the 14th Amendment passed a civil rights law, also in 1866, restricting American citizenship to those born here "and not subject to any foreign power." Rep. John Bingham of Ohio, the author of the 14th Amendment, confirmed "that every human being born within the jurisdiction of the United States of parents not owing allegiance to any foreign sovereignty is, in the language of your Constitution itself, a natural born citizen."

It was this same concern about divided national loyalties that restricted presidential eligibility, in Article II, Section 1 of the Constitution, to "natural born citizens." In 1862, U.S. Attorney Edward Bates declared, "The Constitution does not make a citizen; it is in fact made by them." That means, to be a natural born citizen, a child must be born to a U.S. citizen not a non-citizen immigrant – legal or illegal. That's why children born in the U.S. to foreign diplomats are not regarded as citizens.

While on vacation and carrying a U.S. passport and visa, if you give birth to a baby in France, England or Mexico, your child is not granted citizenship by any of those governments – and certainly not if you're there illegally. As a sovereign nation, we have every right and prerogative to determine our immigration policies. That includes the number of immigrants we allow in, the selective qualifications they must satisfy, as well as limitations on how many from each country. Do you imagine France would allow 80 million German immigrants to overwhelm its sense of French culture?

Advocates of automatic birthright American citizenship for the children of illegal immigrants argue that children shouldn't be punished for their parents' crimes. That seems fair. But neither should they be rewarded for their parents' crimes. American citizenship isn't just another social program. While it's a fundamental right to those who are born to American citizens, to all others there should be nothing automatic about it. It's an honor and a privilege that must be first offered and then earned.

Political Factions Form Lumpy Stew
November 5, 1999

Election campaigns are a lot like the Christmas season. It's good that we have them, but by the time they're over you've had your fill of the whole thing.

Political ads on TV and radio are the worst part. They no doubt work; if they didn't, politicians wouldn't spend so much money on them. But it's a sad commentary on our society that, in this age of limitless information, so many people base their voting decisions on the superficial impressions they derive from a self-serving 30-second ad.

I'll admit I'm just grousing. I have no remedy for this state of affairs. I'm resigned to it as a consequence of a free society. But I don't have to like it. I'd prefer that Americans read copiously, fully research all the candidates and issues, and then cast their votes based on the recommendations I give right here in my column. This, of course, is not the way the world works.

Which is why I'm unmoved by hopeful but unrealistic proposals for campaign finance reform. The U.S. Supreme Court based its 1976 *Buckley v. Valeo* decision on the principle that in election campaigns, money equals free speech and, as such, is protected by the First Amendment.

To reinforce that, consider the following hypothetical scenario: Let's say a neo-Nazi is running for political office. A sympathetic and like-minded newspaper publisher goes to great lengths to promote the candidate's campaign in his paper. That's protected by the First Amendment.

On the other hand, a wealthy individual, who happens to be a Holocaust survivor, is determined to see the neo-Nazi candidate defeated, and is prepared to spend large sums on opposition TV ads to educate the public to that end. Imagine the anti-Nazi being silenced in the name of campaign finance reform. And then, adding insult to injury, seeing the neo-Nazi's TV ads paid for with tax dollars in a publicly funded election campaign. Count me out of that kind of reform.

To arrogant campaign-finance reformers, only their motives are pure. They'll say, for example, that if a senator accepts a contribution from the National Rifle Association, he's sold out to the gun lobby. This ignores the possibility that the senator honestly believes in Second Amendment rights as a matter of principle. An NRA contribution isn't necessarily the front end of a quid pro quo; it could just as well be the back end of an expression of support to someone who *already* shares their views. We might just as well suspect the motives of someone who accepts support from anti-gun groups.

James Madison had it right when he talked of a "saving multiplicity of factions," arguing that a pluralistic society with thousands of special interests competing against one another poses less of a danger than one where a few concentrated interests prevail. George Will has called it the Cuisinart theory of justice: "A good society is remarkably independent of individuals willing the social good. A good society is a lumpy stew of individuals and groups, each with its own inherent 'principle of motion.' This stew stirs itself, and in the fullness of time, comes out a creamy puree called 'the public interest'...This endless maelstrom of individuals pursuing private goods, produces, magically, the public good."

To protect the public interest, all we need is full disclosure. Under such a system, as contributions come in, candidates would post the names on the Internet. If they didn't want to post a name, they could return the check.

If I, as a candidate, cashed a check from, say, the Socialist Workers Party, I'd have to list it. In that unlikely case, I would explain that I'll take the party's money to keep it from going to anyone else, but will oppose it every step of the way. Voters can decide for themselves whether a candidate's funding sources are good or bad. That's the way it ought to work in a free society.

Cam(PAIN) and Suffering

October 25, 2012

Yes, the flood of campaign literature in your mailbox is annoying, as are the endless campaign ads on television and radio. And let's not forget the incessant phone calls at home from political pollsters, candidates' campaigns and activist groups.

While the problem may be clear, the remedy isn't. For better or worse, this is simply a consequence of a free society with free elections. You could pass a law to stop these kinds of things, except that it would run afoul of the Constitution. Think about it. That's why you can have the phone company block out commercial solicitors but not political messages.

And that's why the U.S. Supreme Court, in the landmark *Citizens United v. Federal Elections Commission*, struck down some of the restrictions in the McCain-Feingold campaign finance law. The Supremes declared political spending to be a form of protected speech under the First Amendment. That ruling also protected the rights of corporations and labor unions to seek to inform or influence the voting public via political advertising.

Of course, liberals and Democrats don't mind if unions get involved in politics; that's a major player in their political coalition. Corporations, conversely, are automatically suspect, as is most of private enterprise as compared to government enterprise which liberals see as fair, benevolent and untainted by profit. So they regard the *Citizens United* ruling as blasphemy.

But how could any private business – corporations, partnerships, LLCs, sole proprietorships – be reasonably banned from political involvement, financially or otherwise? That would be arbitrary discrimination. The bigger government gets and the more it seeks to control the private sector, the more businesses are justified in defending themselves and the producer interest in society; and the more essential that defense is to their survival.

Businesses are no more a "special interest" than unions, environmentalists, the ACLU, government employees, gays, feminists, illegal immigrants, the AARP, farmers, teachers, students or any other group that seeks favorable treatment from the government.

A simplistic argument for banning businesses or others from spending money to elect office-holders they favor is that it will enable them to "buy" such politicians. Not necessarily. It's more likely they're supporting a politician who already shares their views on a matter of public policy. For example, if I were to run for office, the National Rifle Association wouldn't be "buying" my vote with their support. I believe in Second Amendment rights of individuals to bear arms. They already have my sympathy.

Restrictions on campaign spending favor elected incumbents with advantages of public access and exposure over potential challengers who have to spend more money to be heard. Such restrictions would also leverage the political power and influence of liberal outlets that dominate the so-called "news" media. They're routinely biased in favor of leftist politicians, but their influence isn't counted as a campaign contribution.

Since they, too, are corporations, wouldn't it be consistent to have their content and budgets monitored and regulated by some government panel of objective wise men? Once again, not practical. But their influence can be mitigated by campaign spending on the other side.

It's a sad commentary on the civic engagement of our society that so many people base their votes on sensationalistic, distorted, even hysterical, 30-second political ads on TV or radio. But there's no practical remedy for that either.

Requiring a passing grade on a civics and current events exam, or an IQ test as a condition of voting, wouldn't pass Constitutional muster. The prerogative and lawful right of any voter – or non-voter – to be apathetic and ignorant is inherent in the mixed blessings of democracy.

So, you suck it up and endure the annoyances and distortions of political campaigns as part of the price of freedom. If it's any consolation, this isn't a problem in North Korea.

The Unfairness Doctrine
May 4, 2007

The Federal Radio Commission was established 80 years ago for the perfectly sensible purpose of regulating the radio spectrum so that competing broadcasters on a finite bandwidth wouldn't overlap each other's frequencies, creating an electronic Tower of Babel. Its successor, the Federal Communications Commission, later took on television as well.

When radio and television were in their infancies, there was a concern that the relatively small number of broadcast outlets would abuse their public trust. So the FCC created the Fairness Doctrine, requiring licensed radio and TV stations to address "vitally important controversial issues of interest in the community served by the broadcaster" while providing the "opportunity for the presentation of contrasting viewpoints on such issues."

Although this mandate was always unworkable and presumptuous, it might have made more sense back when radio and TV were a novelty. By 1987, when President Reagan put the Fairness Doctrine out of its misery, it made very little sense and makes absolutely none today. In the modern world of telecommunications, there are an infinite number of broadcast outlets, from cable and satellite TV and radio to the Internet. No one can hope to dictate public opinion.

So why is there a move by liberal democrats in Congress – including Bernie Sanders, the self-declared socialist senator from Vermont, and Dennis Kucinich, the Ohio representative from the left of Bernie Sanders – to bring back the Fairness Doctrine in 2007? It's all Rush Limbaugh's fault.

Liberal politicians hate the influence of conservative talk-show hosts on radio. They yearn for the good old days of Walter Cronkite and Dan Rather, when liberal spin on the news was broadcast exclusively by liberal anchors and reporters who pretended to be objective. At least when I broadcast my conservative views, there's no pretense. I advertise it as opinion and commentary, ditto for Rush.

Imagine in today's political universe, if broadcast outlets were required to present "contrasting viewpoints" on issues. It wouldn't be enough to present "both sides." You'd have to present *all* sides: liberals, conservatives, progressives, neo-conservatives, libertarians, anarchists, democratic socialists, communists (Trotskyites, Stalinists, Maoists), greens, gays, transgendered, extraterrestrials, etc., etc., etc.

Bring up a religious issue and you'd need to include Christians, Jews, Muslims, Buddhists, Scientologists, Zoroastrians, Wiccans, agnostics, atheists. Where would it end?

Easy. Given the impossibility of concocting this kind of balance, it would end with the elimination of opinion-oriented talk radio. Yes, the left would lose *Air America*, but hardly anyone listens to that anyway. In exchange, liberals would be rid of the army of conservatives who attract the big audiences. Bingo! There's the political motivation.

But what about the local and network news shows? Who would monitor them for content and balance? Presumably a panel of FCC judges, perfectly impartial philosopher-kings, above politics – although they'd be nominated and confirmed by politicians – who could be trusted to have the last word on what constitutes fairness.

Would Katie Couric's liberal spin on the *CBS Evening News* pass muster? How about the *Today* show or *60 Minutes*? Or Bill Moyers left-wing propaganda specials on *PBS*? *All Things Considered* on *NPR* is a liberal love-in. Would all these make the grade while Brit Hume is censored on the *Fox News Channel*? Can you see how arbitrary and unworkable this is?

Paranoid left-wingers like to posture about the conservative bias of the "corporate media." That, of course, is laughable. The *New York Times* and *The Washington Post* are corporations, as is *Time* magazine and *Newsweek*, all reliably liberal. *ABC, NBC, CBS, CNN, MSNBC, PBS* and *NPR* are all corporate entities that, likewise, spin the news in a liberal direction.

And, besides, what's the alternative to corporate (another way of saying private sector, an expletive for lefties) media? Government-run media? Wouldn't that be wonderful? Reminds me of the Soviet Union.

Reality

V. Culture

What we mean when we think of the "culture" of a society is what differentiates and distinguishes its people from those living in other countries or regions. The culture is the aggregation of those many traits, values, attributes, beliefs, religions, customs, attitudes and common social interactions which are generally shared by the citizens of the nation or state. This conceptualization can be extended in many directions to encompass the language we use to communicate, the food we eat, the products we produce, the art we create, the clothing we wear and the multitude of things we do in our work and leisure lives.

In particular, when we think of our own country, we can recognize a distinctively American culture. Certainly, our spirit of independence and devotion to the ideals of opportunity in a free society stem from the earliest days of founding the new republic. Our history has shown that our culture, along with our economy, politics and government has evolved considerably since those early days and continues to do so today.

Waves of new immigrant settlers, expansion to fill a continent and exploit its bountiful resources, and a civil war to reshape the union of disparate states have all been powerful influences in forming what the culture is now. Industrial, transportation, communication and information technologies have literally revolutionized the cultural landscape as well as the physical one in which we live.

Yes, Americans have established a cultural tradition that has been widely admired as a beacon of hope and strength to many around the world. Our sacrifices to turn back the horrors of Nazi Germany and ruthless regimes in the Cold War established us as leaders of the "free world." Our economic and technological innovations have similarly set us apart as leaders in those realms.

But the nature of immigration in recent decades has changed dramatically. The degree of illegal immigration is unprecedented, as is the concentration of immigration from one region, in this instance Latin America, especially Mexico, as compared to the diversity of geographical and ethnic immigration to America in the past. This is compounded by the reluctance of many new immigrants and their succeeding generations to willingly assimilate into the greater culture, preferring to maintain a separate identity as "hyphenated" Americans. What used to famously be called the American "melting pot" now increasingly resembles a "salad bowl." The challenge before us is to preserve our unique American culture.

Reality is Not an Abstraction

It's Hard to "Imagine" That
November 24, 2006

Elton John – make that *Sir* Elton John – recently declared in a magazine interview that "religion should be banned completely." At least he didn't say it should be banned *selectively*; that might smack of favoritism and discrimination. It seems his animus toward religion is driven largely by his status as a homosexual. He resents religiously based disapproval of his lifestyle and says that religion directs "hatred toward gay people." His ironic remedy is that religious intolerance, as he sees it, shouldn't be tolerated. He's also critical of religious leaders for not coming together to end war.

Elton John is a talented musician. But like so many right-brained artsy types, he's given more to emoting than reasoning or practicality. It's certainly true that throughout history religious differences have sometimes led to war. But he hasn't explained just how he'd "ban" religion or how the ban would be enforced. Would he have our armies go to war against religion? And would they first shoot their chaplains? What would Americans do with our First Amendment guarantee of religious freedom and those pesky references to "God" and the "Creator" in the Declaration of Independence?

Of course, Sir Elton John is not to be taken seriously. He's just venting. As long as the vast majority of humans believe in one form of deity or another, there will be religion – for better or worse.

In the midst of his ramblings, Elton John invoked the memory of John Lennon, saying that if he were alive today he'd be fighting for peace (my oxymoron, not his). Which reminded me of Lennon's epic song, *Imagine*. Baby boomer romantic nostalgia notwithstanding, the puerile lyrics of that tune sound like a collaboration of Karl Marx, Cindy Sheehan and Denis Kucinich.

Imagine there's no heaven / It's easy if you try / No hell below us / Above us only sky / Imagine all the people / Living for today

Even if you don't believe in rewards or punishment in the hereafter, responsible adults don't live just for today. They defer gratification and save for a rainy day and retirement. Think of the parable of the grasshopper and the ant.

Imagine there's no countries/It isn't hard to do/Nothing to kill or die for/And no religion, too/Imagine all the people/Living life in peace

No, I can't imagine that. It's anti-historical and contrary to human nature. People are inherently tribal and nationalistic. They band together, linked by common cultures, superstitions, beliefs, values and preferred systems of political economies.

You may say that I'm a dreamer/But I'm not the only one/I hope someday you'll join us/And the world will be as one

You're a dreamer. Never happen. The only way the world would be as one is under the guns of a militaristic, totalitarian regime. And even that would only be temporary. Empires invariably fall.

Imagine no possessions/I wonder if you can/No need for greed or hunger/A brotherhood of man/Imagine all the people/Sharing all the world

Good heavens, no! That is right out of *The Communist Manifesto*. No possessions? You mean no property rights? That means no rewards, no incentives, no creativity and very little production. Moochers living off a dwindling pool of hard workers. Who's going to harvest the crops while the "dreamers" are smoking dope and flashing peace signs with those silly grins on their faces? What everyone owns, no one owns. Think of the graffiti on the walls of community-owned property like a New York City subway station men's room. By comparison, have you ever seen graffiti on the walls of a bathroom in someone's private home?

You may say that I'm a dreamer/But I'm not the only one/I hope someday you'll join us/And the world will be as one

He's repeating himself. We've already covered that. Where's Mister Hold Button when I really need him?

End of song.

When I discussed this on my radio show recently, a well-meaning but hopelessly idealistic woman called in and defended Lennon's message as "aspirational," as in a lofty and hopeful goal. I responded that as an ambitious goal-setter myself, I've aspired to many things in my life and proudly accomplished some of them. But I don't believe in setting your sights on things that are impossible to achieve or counterproductive. That's a formula for wasted effort, failure and frustration.

Remarkably, the woman described herself as a devout Christian whose "aspirations" apparently didn't include renouncing her faith. Islamofascists also have no interest in discarding their predatory religious beliefs either. They just want you to give up yours. Imagine that.

Exposing "Falsisms"
June 13, 2008

If a "truism" is a statement, the truth of which is obvious and universally accepted, then there ought to be another term – let's call it a "falsism" – for statements we hear all the time that aren't true, even if widely accepted by people who've never given them much thought. Here are a few examples:

"Perception is reality." No. Reality is reality. If you perceive that you can fly like Superman and attempt to leap a tall building in a single bound, you'll go *splat!* against that building. Perhaps the falsism derives from the misapplication of the valid observation that perception is reality in *politics*. That is, people vote on the basis of their perceptions. And even if those perceptions are incorrect, enough people voting on incorrect perceptions can produce the reality of a politician winning an election, which may be the reality of prime importance to the victorious politician. Conversely, incorrect negative perceptions can defeat a politician.

It's another matter to say that perceptions can *create* realities, as with depositors who've lost confidence in the security of their savings – with justification or without – and stage a run on the bank. The run on the bank is very much a reality.

"Any publicity is good publicity." While it's true that, sometimes, bad publicity can be turned to one's advantage, it's absurd to apply this generalization to every situation. Just ask O.J. Simpson, Barry Bonds, Britney Spears, Elliot Spitzer or Larry Craig, to name a few.

"War achieves nothing." This may be an impassioned plea of pacifists but it doesn't hold up to rational scrutiny or the historical record. Sadly, war might wreak death and destruction, but the pertinent word here is *achieves*. If we define that as bringing about a desired outcome, wars have accomplished a great deal – for evil or good – from biblical times to the Roman Empire to the Middle East today. Some of those achievements have been transitory, but war has historically served to establish national boundaries, secure treasure and liberate or enslave multitudes.

The United States was born of the Revolutionary War. Our Civil War ended slavery and preserved the union. World War II rid the world of Nazi Germany. As Winston Churchill noted, "The only thing worse than war is losing one." And lest you believe you can ignore an aggressor and "boycott" a war, recall the warning of Leon Trotsky, "You may not be interested in war, but war is interested in you."

"Insanity is doing the same thing over and over and expecting a different result." You might call it stubbornness, but it's not called insanity by any accepted definition. Doctors don't even use that term any more. They prefer more specific variations of "psychopathology" to describe mental illness. In legal parlance, a lawyer might plead his client "not guilty by reason of insanity," arguing that he couldn't distinguish right from wrong. In general, there's nothing necessarily insane about perseverance. "If at first you don't succeed, try, try again," is a term of encouragement. On the 100th anniversary of their last World Series win, the Chicago Cubs might finally make it this year.

"You can't legislate morality." Of course you can, and all societies have done it from time immemorial. Think of Moses and the Ten Commandments. Prohibition under the 18th Amendment was the legislation of morality, as are laws against adultery, polygamy and doing business on the Sabbath. When Henry VIII found the pope's laws on marriage and divorce inconvenient, he made his own. What this bromide really means is that while you can *legislate* morality, passing such laws is no guarantee that they'll be followed. Even under the threat of punishment, human beings with free will sometimes do things of which others disapprove.

"It's not the things we don't know that get us in trouble. It's the things we know that ain't true." – Will Rogers (if he actually said it).

281

"We the People"
August 15, 2008

"We the people of the United States in Order to form a more perfect Union…do ordain and establish this Constitution." When those words, the Preamble to the Constitution, were crafted, the context was to introduce a document prescribing the foundation, organization and general rules of a new system of government based on a bottom-up model of government.

Power would derive from the people, not from the "divine right" of a king or from the condescending benevolence or superior wisdom of some ruling elite. Fortifying that document was the Bill of Rights, reinforcing the clear understanding that fundamental rights belonged naturally to *individuals* and were beyond the whims of government.

The phrase "We the people," it should be understood, does not imply that the United States is a commune, a homogenous collective of like-minded people who all agree on matters of public policy. When Democrats talk of their party as "the party of the people," they tend to apply that in just such a collective – or socialist – sense. As a Republican, I prefer to regard my party as "the party of the person" – the party that better respects and protects individual rights and prerogatives.

That doesn't mean I'm an anarchist or selfish or have no sense of community. I like to think I'm a good neighbor and a good citizen. But I also believe that voluntary, cooperative associations are more desirable and productive than mandatory ones. There have been times when Americans have forged a consensus on vital matters. But even during the American Revolution and World War II there were dissenters, to say nothing of the Civil War. Our motto, *E pluribus unum* – "Out of many, one" – is an ideal, not an absolute. I have no illusion that people in this nation or any other arc of one mind.

That wonderful, inspirational expression "We the people" has become, all too often, a meaningless cliché. It's repeatedly used by writers of letters to the editor or populist talk-show hosts – both liberal and conservative – who sanctimoniously utter platitudes like: "we must demand that those in our government follow the will of the people, since they work for us." But which people? The people who listen to left-wing *Air America* or agree with editorials in *The New York Times* are not the same people who support the conservative opinions of Rush Limbaugh or agree with free market editorials in *The Wall Street Journal*.

And politicians don't represent some abstract, unanimous "us." In the real world of politics, they tend to favor the agendas of the majority of voters and interest groups that put them in office. It's understandable that the minority of voters who supported a losing candidate feel poorly represented, but that's the way elections work. Boulder's "ins" are the "outs" in Colorado Springs.

It's not that "We the people" can't agree on anything, but it's certainly true that we won't agree on everything. Along with some areas of common ground, there are also irreconcilable differences between hawks and doves, seniors and juniors, protectionists and free traders, pro-lifers and pro-choicers, unions and business, big government and small, private and public, gays and straights, men and women, blacks and whites, urban and rural, nannyists and rugged individualists, rednecks and hippies, etc.

On most issues, grand and petty, and on the definition of the "common good," there is no monolithic "we." There's you and me and them. Always has been, always will be.

James Madison spoke of the offsetting *multiplicity* of factions as preferable to the inordinate influence of a few dominant interests. Minor political parties can be single-minded, purist and uncompromising. That's why they're minor parties with small followings. Major parties are the clearing houses of multiple factions, harboring their own internal disagreements while coming together to form a generally like-minded coalition. As Clinton Rossiter observed, "No America without democracy, no democracy without politics, no politics without parties." And, I'd add, no freedom without parties that disagree. And that, Rodney King, is why we can't all get along.

Biased "Critical Thinking"
December 1, 2006

Try a Google search for "critical thinking" and you'll come up with a flood of references. There's even a Foundation for Critical Thinking.

This is one of the more popular, trendy concepts in public education circles these days. In theory, it sounds like a wonderful idea. Teachers should lead students to suspend their beliefs, biases, preconceptions and conventional wisdom in order to evaluate information, ideas, theories, statements, propositions, historical events, political movements, individuals, etc., on the basis of facts, evidence, logic and reason. Who could disagree with this approach?

The world would surely be a better place if everyone, not just students, did this routinely. The problem is in the disconnect between the *theory* and *practice* of critical thinking as an educational discipline. Here are a couple of examples:

A recent article in *5280 Magazine* extolled the fine efforts of Denver Public Schools Superintendent Michael Bennet to turn around this underperforming district. As a demonstration of the difficulty of this task, we saw a paper submitted by a 10th grader at a DPS high school who was assigned to "write down five things the U.S. Government is currently doing that might be unconstitutional." The student offered two: "1. Bushe cold have help the Katrina people whin it hapin. 2. Bushe should't be tipin in to people's phone."

The student was given a grade of 40 percent for coming up with only two of five assigned items. Apparently, he got them both correct. If this is an example of critical thinking, there must not be any right or wrong answers, much less faulty reasoning.

Of course, this leading question just drips with political agenda. How would a student be graded if he concluded that the administration had not engaged in any unconstitutional acts? But even more troublesome is the obvious fact that this 10th grader is, at best, semi-literate. Do you really imagine that he has even the most basic understanding of the Constitution? Before he's ready to tackle higher-order critical thinking skills, shouldn't he have been taught how to read and write, and then introduced to the U.S. Constitution?

In a freshman geography class at East High School, students were instructed to "assume the personas of individuals in the next century or after, and write a letter to people in the 21st century, saying what they could and should have done to address global warming before its effects became so devastating." This is indoctrination. The question presumes an outcome that is debatable. Shouldn't a student have the option of questioning the premise? Isn't that a mainstay of critical thinking? How about writing a letter from the not-globally-warmed future thanking those in the early 21st century who had the foresight to resist unfounded claims of global-warming alarmists and avoid squandering trillions of dollars on a fool's errand? This is a possibility, too. How do you suppose that would be graded?

"Critical thinking" is just too often a catchall buzzword to justify blatant propagandizing and political activism. That was the lame excuse Overland High School teacher Jay Bennish used to shield himself from accountability when he abused his students with a political tirade denouncing capitalism and comparing President Bush to Adolf Hitler.

The problem with the critical thinking approach in practice is that too many of the teachers who employ it don't set aside *their* biases. We're all the product of our respective experiences, perspectives, perceptions, values, beliefs, ideologies and personal interests. Schoolteachers aren't some kind of detached philosopher-kings. The ones who dominate K-12 (and higher) education are inordinately Democrats, collectivists, liberals, union members, government employees, nannyists, politically correct social engineers, etc. With too few exceptions, I don't trust them to impartially referee exercises in critical thinking for idealistic, impressionable young minds. I believe in the power of ideas. So do activist liberal teachers. I'd just like equal treatment. I wonder if students are ever challenged with questions from the right, not just the left, such as:

- Name five ways teachers unions *might* be obstacles to improving the quality of public education.
- Critique Howard Zinn's *A People's History of the United States* and theorize about what motivates American leftists who obsess

about their nation's shortcomings while downplaying its greatness.

- Explain why the ideology of socialism is in direct conflict with human nature and, consequently, perpetually doomed to failure.
- Read Ayn Rand's *Atlas Shrugged* and give five examples of violations of individual rights in the name of the "common good."
- The liberal media largely ignore qualified global-warming skeptics. Name five scientists who dispute global-warming theory and explain their arguments.

I invite students, teachers and administrators to contact me with classroom examples.

If They Don't Like It, "Effem"
March 13, 1992

When I heard about the flap regarding Secretary of State James Baker's reported indiscretion, I immediately turned to Richard Iannelli's update of the *Devil's Dictionary,* where I found the following definition: "CANDID – See FRANK, but don't tell him who sent you."

The virtue of frankness is that it gets right to the point, saves time and lets you know exactly where someone stands. Because it refuses to compromise accuracy for diplomacy and makes no concession to civility, frankness is the natural enemy of popularity. We live in the age of the euphemism.

In his column in the *New York Post,* ex-Mayor of New York Ed Koch repeated a remark allegedly made by the secretary of state, in a private meeting, in the presence of Koch's unnamed source. Supposedly Baker responded to Jewish critics of the administration's policy toward Israel by saying something like: "F--- 'em. They didn't vote for us anyway."

To be sure, this is hearsay. And there are a lot of "allegedlies" and "supposedlies" in the account. Baker has flatly denied the remark, and a State Department spokeswoman has termed it "garbage." But they'd respond that way even if he had said it. Did he? Who knows? But he certainly could have, and it wouldn't necessarily have been anti-Semitic, just politically direct, although stylistically crude.

There's nothing offensive in the observation that most Jews vote for Democrats, in general, and voted for Dukakis over Bush, in particular. It's a fact. Jews tend to be liberal politically. Suppose Baker had said the following: "The president and I believe this administration's carefully formulated Middle East policy is morally justified and in the best strategic interests of the United States. We intend to continue it, regardless of the partisan criticism of some of our political opponents."

"F--- 'em!" is the shorthand version of that. Decorum dictates that you can't say it publicly. My point isn't to defend Bush administration Israeli policy; that's problematic. Let's put it aside. Rather, I'd like to strike a blow for candor.

Who are we kidding? "F--- 'em!" is an expression people use all the time. Powerful people, prominent people, ordinary people, even dignified people. Yes, it's coarse. But it's also a wonderfully concise expression. In just two syllables it speaks volumes. It conveys a wholly unambiguous meaning. Yes, it's insensitive, but it's supposed to be. It declares its target, "'em," to be totally without standing in one's political or social universe. Yes, it's ruthless, but at least it's honest. We need more of that today. Best of all, it's marvelously politically incorrect.

Remember the public reaction to Nixon's frequent use of *expletives* in the Watergate tapes. Come on. How many of the 535 members of Congress do you think don't talk like that in smoke-filled rooms? What do you think business executives say in private about their competitors? Or generals about the enemy? Or liberal media types about conservatives? How do you suppose they talk about men at NOW meetings? (Maybe that's a bad example.) What do you think Pat Schroeder's reaction is to a Mike Rosen criticism of her position on an issue? "F--- 'em," of course.

Yes, there are many legitimate grievances in our society. And some have practical remedies. But, increasingly, we've become a nation of special pleaders or, even worse, whiners. With all the really important items on the public and private policy agendas, there just isn't enough time available to waste on ceremonial courtesy for off-the-wall fringe groups. What's required is an expression that connotes summary dismissal of their bogus charges and demands.

Years ago, you couldn't use the word "damn" in polite company. Today, it's OK. Who knows? In 20 years, "F--- 'em" may be acceptable. In the meantime, we need a surrogate, a euphemism. I propose: "Effem!"

You're Offended? So?
March 21, 1997

A caller to my radio show recently took me to task over an opinion I had just expressed on some policy issue or another. She was angry and indignant. She wanted me to know that she was offended by my views. I don't think she was particularly comforted by my response when I said, "So?"

I wasn't just being ornery, nor was I going out of my way to bait her. There's a principle here that needs to be vigorously defended in these days of political correctness and hypersensitivity. If you're going to live in a society that allows free speech, you have to be willing to take the risk that someone else will listen. In spite of the contention of legions of professional "victims groups" with chips on their shoulders, Americans enjoy no such protection as "the right not to be offended."

Now, not everyone agrees with that assertion. Radical feminists have had some success on college campuses peddling the notion to weak-kneed administrations that sexual harassment is a purely subjective matter. That is, anything that offends a complainant is, by definition, offensive. By that reasoning, if someone feels sexually harassed – by a joke, a magazine photograph, a flirting gesture – then, Q.E.D., that person has been sexually harassed. This is reminiscent of the Salem witch trials. In such an environment, hypersensitivity or, even worse, politically motivated persecution reigns supreme.

The double standard is blatant. On the one hand, feminists contend that women are as capable as men of serving as two-fisted, fox-hole-dwelling, trained killers in the military. Then, they turn around and demand special protection for these delicate flowers who can be so devastated by a mere insensitive remark – that may not have even been objectively offensive. One can only hope that this, too, shall pass.

On the subject of my personal offensiveness, by today's standards I'm a pussycat. Have you heard Howard Stern, Don Imus, and any one of a thousand FM radio disk jockeys or low-brow talk radio wannabees? These are people who offend purely for the sake of offending. Stern pays his FCC fines on the express lane. In more than 15 years of radio broadcasting, I've never had a hint of an FCC violation.

What some people really resent about me are my beliefs, more than the forceful way I present them.

I don't like euphemisms. Squatters, whom the Denver City Council recently decided to evict from their shanties on the banks of the South Platte River, weren't simply "homeless people," they were mostly drunks, drifters and vagrants. A mother with three kids, deserted by her husband, is "homeless." The two different problems call for different remedies. If my directness in the use of terms offends someone's sensitivities, so be it. I'll stand on the facts.

Civility is one thing; mushiness of thought is another. I also don't like coyness and evasiveness. Say what you mean. And mean what you say.

My radio show often takes the form of debating and arguing (aggressive debating). I prefer to have guests who disagree with me. It helps listeners zero in on the fundamental differences and makes for more interesting radio. It annoys me when someone on the other side of an issue says something like: "*It's not clear to me* that we ought to have a balanced budget amendment."

What he means is: "I oppose a balanced budget amendment, and I disagree with your support of it." So why not say that?

I like to pursue my quarry relentlessly. I won't easily let a public official get away with a statement like: "I'd rather not comment on that." Of course, you'd rather not comment. You'd rather say as little as you can get away with. But *will* you comment; and if not, why not; and if not now, when? Some people don't like this kind of approach. They'd prefer a kinder and gentler format. They have a clear remedy. That's why God made radios with off and on switches, and buttons to change stations.

U.S. is No. 1 for Good Reason
October 12, 2001

Propagators of "multiculturalism" tell us that all cultures and societies have their virtues and vices; that it's beneficial to understand other peoples; and that we should be leery of making judgments about them. As a general principle, this idea has some merit. In practice, it's been taken to absurd extremes by guilt-ridden liberals who preach their own brand of moral relativism and self-flagellation in our schools. Impressionable young minds hear too much of America's vices and too little of our virtues, while exactly the opposite standard is applied to societies and cultures that have little to commend.

Former U.N. Ambassador Jeane Kirkpatrick put it well when she said of the U.S.: "We should not be afraid to admit the truth about ourselves, no matter how pleasant it is." To the extent that the terrorist war against America is a clash of cultures, and to the extent that it's being waged by dogmatists of a perverse brand of Islamic fundamentalism that would take the world back to the wonderful days of the Dark Ages, how can one avoid cultural comparisons and judgments?

Are we beyond reproach? Of course not. Who is? Are we "better" than the world of Osama bin Laden? Unquestionably. Can any rational being deny it? Pick your standards of justice and human decency: pluralism, free speech, freedom of religion, due process, women's rights, economic opportunity, social services, medical science, academic study, self-determination, etc. The list is inexhaustible.

Many Muslims have come to this country to seek a better life. They are here by choice. They can still embrace their religion and also enjoy the advantages of a free and prosperous society. I imagine some disapprove of elements of our pop culture. That's OK. So do I. But I much prefer it to the way of life in Afghanistan, Iran, Iraq or even Saudi Arabia. The difference between us and the deranged bin Ladens of this world is that we can disapprove of a people or culture without wanting to exterminate it. Why should we apologize for our preferences? Do you doubt that half the world's population would come here in an instant if we invited them?

What should we do to placate bin Laden and his soul mates, adopt their values? Perish the thought. George Will once observed that: "Part of our problem, today, in defending ourselves intellectually, is the notion that nations that are merely imperfect have no standing to despise nations that are atrocious." I despise what Afghanistan has become under the Taliban, and am thankful I will never live in a society remotely like that. I've spoken to Afghans in this country who agree and who tell me that the great majority of their countrymen, still under the iron rule of these fanatics, despise them as well.

Say what you will about America, but for all our imperfections there has never been a nation that has equaled our contribution to political freedom and economic achievement. Nor has there ever been a great power less imperialistic, more benevolent and as generous to its defeated enemies.

Earlier this week, after the first U.S. strikes on Taliban targets in Afghanistan, anti-American mobs in Pakistan set fire to movie theaters that show western films and banks that, presumably, exchange filthy Western lucre. These movie theaters and banks are there only because people in those countries choose to patronize them. Just as people, the world over, choose to accept U.S. foreign aid, U.S. medical technology and an endless parade of U.S. consumer products. Nobody is compelled to eat at a McDonald's restaurant.

We don't force American culture on anyone. Ours competes with every other culture in a global market. Apparently, billions are attracted to much of what we have to offer. Those who prefer bin Laden's and Saddam's alternatives can have them. I don't see the world beating a path to their door.

Lottery Win isn't American Dream
December 8, 2000

Fourteen co-workers in Albuquerque just hit the Powerball jackpot of $131 million. The figure is overstated marketing puffery, of course, just as it is in the Colorado lottery. The $131 million would be the sum total of a stream of payments stretched out over the life of a 25-year annuity. If the New Mexico winners want it all up front, however, they'd get a mere $70 million, the net present value of that annuity, which would leave each of them with about $2.5 million after taxes. Still, not a bad payday and a pretty good rate of return on a $10 investment.

Personally, I don't buy lottery tickets. As one who enjoys a game of chance, and as a student of the art of gambling, I'm opposed to sucker bets as a matter of principle. When you place a wager with a bookmaker, the percentage he takes as a handling fee is called the *vigorish*. (A good bookie isn't really in the business of taking risks on the outcome of sporting events. He seeks to lay off your wager against another person who's betting the opposite way.) Typically, the "vig" is something in the area of 10 percent.

By comparison, if you place a legal bet at the pari-mutuel window at a racetrack, the rake-off is twice that, more like 20 percent, including the government's hefty share of the action. The vig on lotteries is considerably worse, a gargantuan *50* percent, with most of the proceeds going to fund some government program like parks or schools. If you understand this and see it as a contribution to a good cause, that's fine. But I'd guess that the great majority of lottery players aren't buying tickets because they're public-spirited citizens. Rather, they're looking for the big hit. In that case, they're getting taken by the government playing the role of an exceedingly greedy bookie.

OK, so much for the mechanics. Now for the philosophy. And this isn't sour grapes. I don't begrudge the Powerball winners their spoils. They paid their money and took their chances. I wish them the best. What bothers me is the description of their good fortune, by some, as a classic example of "The American Dream." I don't think so. This is more like the Irish Sweepstakes.

The American Dream has to do with opportunity and hard work, not dumb luck and instant gratification. It's turning a pushcart into a chain of department stores. The American Dream isn't necessarily getting rich quick; it's usually getting moderately well-off slowly. Sometimes, a flighty idea like Pet Rocks or Beanie Babies comes along and pays what appear to be instant dividends. But even in those cases, it was more than the mindless act of buying a lottery ticket. Entrepreneurship was required. Capital was placed at risk. The factors of production were employed to turn an idea into a successful enterprise.

As the late John Houseman used to put it in those Smith Barney commercials, the American Dream is making money the old-fashioned way: you *earn* it.

When asked what they'll do with the loot, lottery winners typically talk of buying expensive cars, luxurious homes or taking lavish vacations. Rarely do you hear one say he's going to put it in a money market account while examining prudent investment alternatives. Perhaps that's why we've heard about so many lottery winners who turn their good fortune into bad. When it falls into your lap too easily, you're more inclined to squander it.

I'm not advocating banning the things. If you want to throw your money away, that's your business. So what's the harm in buying a little hope with a few bucks worth of lottery tickets? Just that it's a false hope, an exercise in self-delusion and a poor substitute for ambition. Don't tread water waiting for your ship to come in, swim out and meet it.

Photo IDs are a Must
March 8, 2012

Across the nation, Americans are routinely required to show a photo ID when they travel by air; operate a motor vehicle; buy alcohol at a liquor store, restaurant, bar or sporting event; write a check at a grocery store; get a job; rent a car; apply for a passport; make a credit card purchase; apply for a loan; get a marriage license; adopt a pet; open an account or cash a check at a bank; get medical care; fill a drug prescription; pick up tickets at the will-call window of a baseball park or theater; rent an apartment; close on a house; or get a hotel room, to mention just a few.

Under a new law in Illinois, you must now show photo ID to buy a can of Drano at a retail store (drain cleaner has been used as a weapon in an attack that scarred two Chicago women). Yet Illinois law does not require the showing of a photo ID – or any ID – to vote in state or federal elections.

According to the bipartisan National Conference of State Legislatures, there are only 31 states that require voter ID at polling places, and only 15 of those require photo ID. This is absurd.

In December 2011, the U.S. Justice department blocked a new law in South Carolina and is still withholding approval of a similar Texas law that would require photo ID for voting. Barack Obama's hand-picked attorney general, Eric Holder, claims these kinds of laws would suppress black voter turnout.

Nonsense. In 2008, after Georgia's photo ID law went into effect, voter turnout was up 6.1 percentage points from 2004, the fourth-largest increase of any state, including those without voter ID laws. The black share of the Georgia vote jumped to 30 percent in 2008 compared to 25 percent in the 2004 election.

How tough is it, really, to get a photo ID? There are 200 million licensed drivers in the U.S. with photo IDs. Non-drivers can secure general-purpose photo IDs at government offices. Obtaining one is much easier than a getting driver's license; there's no written exam, eye or road test.

And why would anyone want to suffer the inconvenience of going without a photo ID? Only a racist or political spinmeister could claim that blacks lack the common sense to accomplish this simple task. And you can be sure that anywhere photo ID laws are passed, Democratic community organizers will be out in force getting their core voters qualified. Yes, illegal immigrants and other lawbreakers might have trouble getting a valid photo ID, but why should that bother you, unless you're a Democrat who assumes most of these people would vote illegally for your party?

Naysayers claim there's no need for enhanced voter ID because there's only anecdotal evidence that voter fraud is a problem. Perhaps that's because there's never been a thorough government investigation. So, ignorance is bliss? And besides, on this matter, anecdotal evidence is quite enough. To paraphrase a common liberal plea, "even if it saves only one fraudulent vote, wouldn't it be worth it?"

Voting is one of the most important citizen rights and duties in our constitutional republic. It's our central democratic institution. It's far more important than cashing a check or buying beer.

There's no valid reason not to protect the integrity of our voting process with an inexpensive, basic technology like a photo ID. And contrary to the hollow, contrived, self-serving objections of the deniers, there's no reasonable downside.

A recent Rasmussen poll reports that 70 percent of Americans favor photo ID for voting. Others are rapidly joining those 15 states that already require it; Colorado should be among them.

Guns Don't Kill 13 Kids a Day
May 12, 2000

Typically, people who are moved to write letters to the editor disagree with a columnist. The ones who agree usually just nod in approval and move on. Recently, I wrote a column methodically debunking the claim that guns in the home are 43 times more likely to kill a family member or friend than an intruder. It actually drew an approving response from one letter writer who asked that I also address the assertion that 13 children are killed with guns every day. I'd be happy to.

This is an old saw, oft repeated by anti-gun types and enthusiastically broadcast by the liberal media. People have heard it so many times, most probably believe it's true. It's not. As you might suspect, the statistic is contrived and distorted. It was last cited in prominent statements by Bill and Hillary Clinton. Bill dusted it off and wheeled it out for an appearance on *NBC's Today* show on March 2 while lobbying for legislation to mandate trigger locks and smart guns. He insisted that "every single day there are 13 children who die from guns in this country." Hillary reprised the statistic on April 27 when she claimed that "every day in America we lose 13 precious children to gun-related violence."

Apparently, the original source is a 1997 study published by the National Center for Health Statistics (NCHS). It found that 4,205 persons up to and including the age of 19 were killed in that year in firearm-related fatalities. Divide that number by 365, and you get an average of 11.5 per day. Somehow the Clintons rounded that up to 13.

But the use of the term "children" is the most manipulative element of this emotionally charged claim. It conjures up images of thousands of 6-year-olds lying prostrate in a pool of blood, with a handgun alongside. My *American Heritage Dictionary* defines a "child" as a "person between birth and puberty...An infant; a baby."

According to Yale University researcher John R. Lott Jr., fewer than 3 percent of young people killed by guns are under the age of 10. The great majority are virtually adults between the ages of 17 and 19, and most of those are gang members, not young children who are victims of household mishaps. "Trigger locks would do nothing to stop gang members from using guns," says Lott.

According to the actual NCHS data, 86 percent of all firearm-related fatalities among young people was in the age group from 15-19. Of those, about a third – 1,135 of 3,576 – were suicides. Tougher gun laws wouldn't prevent those intent on committing suicide from using some other means.

If you confine the field to just those 14 years of age and younger – a more accurate notion of what we think of as "children" – the numbers are much less dramatic (which is why Bill, Hillary and gun-control advocates in general use the broader definition). Instead of 4,205 firearm-related fatalities in 1997, the number drops to 629. Eliminating suicides, it's down to 502. That comes to 1.4 per day, a far cry from 13. This is still disturbing, and every one of those deaths remains a personal tragedy, but it's not nearly as sensational a figure to throw around for purposes of inflaming public opinion.

The Second Amendment, like the other articles in our Bill of Rights, is not absolute. There are reasonable arguments to be made for some restrictions on the personal sale and possession of firearms and other weapons. A compromise will surely be struck between the intractable positions of gun-rights hard-liners and would-be gun-confiscating zealots. Some of the gun-rights people may tend toward paranoia, but at least they believe what they say. When anti-gun propagandists willfully spread bogus statistics, it undermines what remains of their credibility.

I recognize that gun-controllers instinctively seek to influence public opinion through appeals to emotions, but they shouldn't have to lie in the process.

Anti-gun Hysteria is No Solution
January 3, 2013

"Enough! Never again! We must put an end to this kind of gun violence!"

If intensity of moral outrage were sufficient to prevent the next slaughter of innocent children at a school like Sandy Hook or innocent shoppers at a mall in Oregon or firemen responding to an ambush at a fire in New York by yet another psychopathic suicidal-murderer, then we could all rest easy.

But irate sloganeering; simplistic, impractical, unconstitutional proposals; and wishful thinking driven by emotions offer little more than self-indulgent psychotherapy for those who utter them. The mentality of "we must do something, anything" is a poor prescription for rational public policy. Yet it's hard to compete with such people in an auction for desirable outcomes even though their desperate remedies won't produce the outcome they desire.

By some estimates, there are as many as 300 million privately owned firearms in the U.S. distributed among 50 percent of American households.

Let's get real. Despite the passions of anti-gunners, there will be no absolute ban or confiscation of guns. In addition to Second Amendment protections, there's widespread public opposition to any such thing. A 2011 Gallup poll found 73 percent opposed to a ban on handguns.

And spare me the demagoguery about the "all-powerful gun lobby." The National Rifle Association isn't a narrow special interest group. It's a huge general interest with half the households in the nation, about 50 million, possessing guns, including those who aren't dues paying members of the NRA. According to Gallup, 54 percent of Americans say they have a favorable opinion of the NRA. It's far less of a narrow special interest than labor unions, plaintiff's lawyers, farmers or gays. (Ironically, many members of these groups are gun owners.)

In reaction to the recent shootings, however, there could be a renewal of the 1994 assault weapons ban which expired in 2004. That would make automatic weapons and high-capacity magazines more difficult to come by but it won't eliminate them, nor will it put an end to mass public shootings.

If we can't stop millions of people from illegally crossing our borders or a flood of illegal drugs from circulating around the country, we certainly can't circumvent a vigorous black market in illegal weaponry. Criminals and psychopaths will still acquire them. (The 1999 Columbine massacre took place when the assault weapons ban was still in force.) How naïve does one have to be to believe that gang-bangers in Chicago will disarm themselves?

There are impassioned calls for universal mental-health screenings to ensure that no one who might ever be a threat to society will be able to legally own a gun. Should we mandate it like an annual emissions test on vehicles? Require everyone in the country to undergo psychiatric evaluations each year (you might be sane now, but demented next year)? Would five sessions, annually, with a shrink be enough? Never mind the cost and bureaucratic details.

Some are demanding censorship of violence in movies, TV and video games. There are pleas to reform the national culture and strengthen religion. Effecting these goals would be a daunting and long-range task.

The most doable and immediate action to protect schoolchildren is to fortify the nation's 132,000 K-12 schools with armed guards and weaponized teachers. That would reduce, but not eliminate, the risk. When the NRA's Wayne LaPierre proposed that tangible remedy, he was ridiculed by anti-gun zealots and wishful thinkers. But even if we fortified our schools, other public venues like malls, supermarkets, day care centers or churches would still be vulnerable.

The bottom line is, short of eliminating all guns from our society – an unachievable delusion – there's simply no "final solution" to this problem, only mitigations, all of which are rife with tradeoffs and unintended negative consequences that can't be eliminated – even if emotionally wrought idealists won't recognize or acknowledge them.

Props, Cops and Guns
April 18, 2013

President Obama last week did what he does best. The "Speaker of the White House" made yet another speech at a public media event. He long ago broke the all-time record for speechifying.

This time, it was to promote his gun control agenda at the University of Hartford, in front of a carefully selected, wildly supportive audience in the state that was the site of the Sandy Hook school massacre in Newtown.

The Obama team likes to use human props at such staged events. In Hartford, they were relatives of some of those killed at Sandy Hook, about a dozen of whom were then flown to Washington, D.C., on Air Force One to lobby members of Congress.

While there is unanimous public sympathy for the tragedy these folks suffered, the opinion of these Newtowners on the efficacy of gun control legislation is no more qualified than Diana DeGette's or anyone else's. In fact, there are relatives of Sandy Hook victims who have publicly expressed their opposition to some of these rush-to-judgment gun control measures. They weren't invited to ride along on Air Force One.

Speaking of human props, Obama played the same game on his recent visit to Denver, where uniformed city cops served as the backdrop for his gun control oratory and photo-op at the Denver Police Academy. This was designed to convey the impression that police officers generally favor the orgy of anti-gun laws rammed through by majority Democrats in the Colorado legislature – most notably the idiotic, unenforceable limit on magazine capacity that a number of county sheriffs said they would ignore.

Well, let's test that premise of police support. The pro-law-enforcement website www.PoliceOne.com recently released the results of its nationwide survey of more than 15,000 law-enforcement professionals. Here are some of the highlights:

Ninety-five percent of respondents say a federal ban on the manufacture and sale of magazines that hold more than 10 rounds would not reduce violent crime. Eighty-five percent said Obama's legislative proposals would have zero or negative effect on their safety. Eighty-six percent said legally armed citizens would have reduced the carnage at shootings like Newtown and Aurora. Seventy percent have a positive opinion of the public statements of law enforcement leaders who would refuse to enforce unreasonably restrictive gun laws in their jurisdictions, and 61 percent said they'd ignore such laws themselves if they were the chief or sheriff.

PoliceOne.com editor Doug Wylie summarized the survey: "Contrary to what the mainstream media and certain politicians would have us believe, police overwhelmingly favor an armed citizenry, would like to see more guns in the hands of responsible people, and are skeptical of any greater restrictions placed on gun purchase, ownership or accessibility."

Which brings us to another contradiction: Why do most rank and file police officers oppose these overreaching anti-gun laws while big-city chiefs of police support them? Perhaps the individual cops are practical and consider how these laws will affect them and their families personally, especially after they retire from the force and spend the rest of their lives as civilian gun owners. Police chiefs, on the other hand, are political animals and serve at the pleasure of elected mayors and city councils. In big cities like New York and Chicago, those politicians tend to be liberal Democrats whose constituents favor tough gun laws. That criminals and gang-bangers ignore those laws is obvious by the high crime rates in those cities in spite of the tough laws.

Elected sheriffs in rural and suburban counties who oppose these impractical or ineffective laws agree with the aforementioned cops and disagree with big-city police chiefs. Why? Because they're more likely to be Republicans or conservative Democrats with constituents who are comfortable around firearms and treasure their Second Amendment rights. Common sense is clearly on their side.

A Schism in World Views

Liberal Elitists aren't Elite
November 12, 2009

When it suits their purposes and advances their political agenda, liberals are unabashedly elitist. Nonetheless, they recoil from that term when conservatives label them as such. Their reasoning is positively schizophrenic, confusing private behavior with public policy.

A true elite is one whose talents place him, objectively, at or among the top in his field. Tiger Woods is an elite golfer, in fact, the best in the world. Albert Einstein was an elite scientist, a genius. Michelangelo, an elite artist. An "elitist," on the other hand, is one who is not necessarily talented or brilliant but who simply regards himself as such, and who would subordinate others to his will.

Al Gore, for example, is certainly not an elite scientist. In fact, he's not a scientist at all. He's not a physicist, climatologist or meteorologist. He's a politician, and when it comes to the highly debatable subject of climate change, he's just a guy with an opinion. As an advocate for a doomsday version of the theory of human-induced global warming, he selectively and misleadingly brokers the work of actual scientists and other polemicists in this field. To the extent that Gore would dictate how people, businesses and governments behave in the course of imposing environmental and economic policies, he's a pretentious elitist in the worst sense of that term.

Liberals profess to be the champions of the common man. But they don't trust the common man to make the right decisions. As inveterate busybodies and nannyists, they presume to protect us from ourselves through government mandates and regulations on everything from what we eat, to how we travel, to where we live, to what we say; all written by liberal elitists who know what's best for us.

If I'm having open-heart surgery, I'd certainly want to be operated on by an elite surgeon. I want an elite building contractor to construct my home. As a conservative and an individualist, I'm a firm believer in meritocracy. Excellence deserves to be suitably rewarded, and doing so breeds more of it. This is justice based on ability and performance. The liberal notion of "social justice" is based not on ability but on need. As Karl Marx put it: "From each according to his ability; to each, according to his need." In that sense, presumptuous liberal elitists would wield the heavy hand of government to downgrade those whose ability has earned them *truly* elite status while elevating those of lesser ability.

One liberal pontificated that he wants only the "best and brightest" in government to "run our country." I suspect he and I would disagree about who the best and brightest are and what qualities earn them that distinction. My list certainly wouldn't include Barney Frank, Nancy Pelosi, Harry Reid and Barrack Obama, to whom I don't defer as my intellectual superiors. His list probably wouldn't include Ronald Reagan. Moreover, I don't want government or politicians to "run our country." That's a statist view. The state is not society. It's a subset of society. It's the height of pretentious elitism to believe that any panel of bureaucrats is smart enough to "run" our intricate market economy. The Soviets tried that.

I'm no anarchist. I recognize the need for government but I believe in limited government. I want society to mostly run itself. And I'd extend the freedom of personal choice to others, within a reasonable body of laws, running the risk that some might make illiberal choices. That's the nature of a free society.

I agree with William F. Buckley Jr., who once declared that he'd rather be governed by the first 400 people in the Boston telephone book than by the faculty at Harvard.

In Defense of an Earned Elitism
March 14, 1997

Once upon a time in America, college seniors took great pride in being awarded a gold Phi Beta Kappa key. This is a symbol of extraordinary achievement in the liberal arts and sciences as conferred by the nation's oldest and most prestigious honor society, with a tradition going back some 220 years. As yet another sad commentary on the state of intellectual affairs in higher education, Phi Beta Kappa is becoming increasingly uncool, or at least politically incorrect.

At the University of Rhode Island last year, one out of five students offered the key turned it down. Some said the one-time membership fee of about $30 was too steep. Please. After a $100,000 four-year college education (subsidized or not), thirty bucks is too big a hit? They spend that much on beer over the weekend; ten times that on books each semester. The most common reason given was even more troubling: that the Phi Beta Kappa key smacks of "elitism."

Duh. Of course it's elitist. That's the point. The award goes to students who have distinguished themselves from their peers through superior academic performance over their college careers. Something tells me students shunning the PBK key are the same kind of young idealists who would accept the Lenin Peace Prize in a heartbeat.

Where do these impressionable students get such ideas? From their professors, of course, including all those aging hippies and flower children, veterans of the late 1960s and 1970s, who now hold court as the tenured left. Bradford Wilson, executive director of the National Association of Scholars – an academic alliance that speaks out against the leftist thought-police on campus – sums it up nicely: "In an intellectually charged environment, to belong to such an organization (Phi Beta Kappa) would be a high honor. In the climate we are in, academic accomplishment is secondary to social awareness, belonging to the politically correct organizations and being publicly identified as socially progressive."

Whether in higher education or lower education, our problem today is not an excess of elitism, it's a shortage of it. The alternative to elitism is ordinariness or mediocrity. We can see it in the current, trendy aversion to academic letter grades in the public schools, or the reluctance to award medals for athletic competition (anti-elitists prefer "participation ribbons" for one and all).

Frustrated parents call it lowering standards and "dumbing down." Collectivist educators call it "self-esteem" for under-achievers.

A society will always have an abundance of ordinary people. Since, by sheer force of numbers, they constitute a mathematical majority, a democratic political system will necessarily serve their purposes, marked by progressive income taxes and a multitude of programs to redistribute income. The trick is to restrain a society's basest instincts to drag down its most talented and productive, to kill the geese who lay the golden eggs. Whether it's Thomas Edison, Albert Einstein, Jonas Salk or Bill Gates, extraordinary ability in a minority of citizens has to be cultivated and rewarded if a society is to maximize its potential. You don't do this by hobbling budding geniuses in their most important developmental years.

Socialism is forever doomed to failure because it flies in the face of human nature. Human beings aren't worker ants or bees in a hive. They won't work as hard for someone else's benefit as they will for their own and their family's. Because socialism cannot sufficiently reward individual excellence, it gets much less of it. Egalitarians who confuse equality of opportunity (and even this ideal has its limitations) with equality of outcome make the same mistake.

William Henry put it succinctly in his book, *In Defense of Elitism* (Doubleday 1994): "We have foolishly embraced the unexamined notions that everyone is pretty much alike (and, worse, should be), that self-fulfillment is more important than objective achievement, that the common man is always right, that a good and just society should be far more concerned with succoring its losers than with honoring and encouraging its winners."

Flaws of the Kennedy Syndrome
September 3, 2009

The death of Sen. Ted Kennedy has most likely marked the end of the Kennedy dynasty. There's no apparent Kennedy currently positioned to pick up the baton of national political leadership. Liberalism as an ideology and political movement is alive and well, but it will have to find another "lion" with a different family name.

Jack and Bobby Kennedy were charismatic, larger-than-life political figures. Following their deaths, Ted, the last of the brothers, inherited the legacy. Following generations of Kennedys have been lesser figures. Several are lawyers. Some have dabbled in politics with modest results. Others entered the media, charitable foundations and the non-profit sector. There's hardly a secretary, insurance salesman, corporate executive, retailer, stock broker or soldier among them.

Ironically, this is the progeny of Joseph P. Kennedy, the family patriarch. The son of a humble Boston saloonkeeper, Joe was an ambitious, enterprising, hard-nosed scrapper who married well and amassed a fortune in banking and shipbuilding, to say nothing of bootlegging during Prohibition. Unlike most of us who are forced to deal with mundane necessities like earning a living, inheritors of wealth (like the Kennedys) are relieved of that concern. Of course they haven't taken a personal poverty oath, but their gratification comes not from producing income and wealth themselves but from redistributing the fruits of other people's production. I call this the Kennedy Syndrome.

I'm no opponent of wealth. I've tried to accumulate some of my own from what's left after the tax collector's cut. Perhaps, as one who started without any, I have a greater appreciation for those who earn it than for the Kennedys. And that's the fatal flaw of those afflicted with the Kennedy Syndrome. As compassionate do-gooders, they *sympathize* with the needy. That's commendable. But they have a blind spot in their inability to *empathize* with hardworking, industrious, risk-taking, entrepreneurial Americans who are the driving force behind our market economy and creators of new wealth.

The rich exist comfortably all over the world, even in the poorest countries. But dynamic, growing economies are marked by an ascendant middle-class, producing new generations of the rich and displacing much of the old. Eventually, Joe Kennedy's wealth will be dissipated and diluted by a growing legion of prodigal descendants who take it for granted.

The Kennedy Syndrome isn't wholly altruistic. It's also marked by a self-indulgent need to feel good about oneself and a compulsion to regulate and compel the behavior of others, infringing on their personal freedom in the process. As Mark Twain said, "To be good is noble. To tell other people to do good is even nobler and less trouble." And whatever its good intentions, the Kennedy Syndrome has things backwards. You can't consume or redistribute what hasn't first been produced. The creation of income and societal wealth must come first. Charity for the needy or social spending programs for the middle-class are derived from that. In its preoccupation with those in need, the Kennedy Syndrome neglects, penalizes and discourages those who produce.

The appetite of do-gooders to dispense public largesse with the property of others is insatiable. But piling one social program on another runs up government spending to unsustainable levels. There are limits to the taxes you can impose on productive citizens. After you've soaked the rich, the middle-class will get soaked as well. Government borrowing to finance budget deficits inescapably crowds out private sector investment, undermining the source of societal wealth.

In the words of William F. Buckley Jr., "Idealism is fine, but as it approaches reality, the costs become prohibitive."

Our Very Own America Haters

September 28, 2001

"Anyone who can blow up the Pentagon has my vote." So declared Richard Berthold, a University of New Mexico college professor, to his students while rescue crews were still searching for bodies in New York and Washington, D.C. Berthold is an old-line lefty, an aging hippie from the '60s. He claims immunity for that contemptible statement under the sanctuary of academic freedom and tenure.

Roger Lowenstein, described in a *Los Angeles Times* story as a 58-year-old educator, explains that his enmity for the American flag is rooted in his days as a Vietnam War protester: "It meant right-wing politics. It meant repression. It meant arrogance. It meant, 'We're the greatest'." Rep. Barbara Lee is the congresswoman from California's 9th Congressional District, encompassing Oakland, Alameda and the People's Republic of Berkeley. She was the only member of the U.S. House that voted against granting President Bush the authority to go after world-wide terrorists. Lee is objectively described as the most doctrinaire, radical leftist in Congress, the successor to, and a disciple of, Ron Dellums, who held that title before she did.

If you browse the Web, you'll find statements from all the usual suspects – Noam Chomsky, Ramsey Clark, Michael Moore, the War Resistors League, the Institute for Policy Studies, the Communist Party USA, etc.– professing perfunctory regret for this heinous act on America but, essentially, rationalizing the actions and sympathizing with the causes of these terrorists. Their familiar refrain is: "We brought this on ourselves." As if they'd be similarly understanding of a U.S. attack on civilians anywhere in the world.

These are the same people who vilify *us* for the hardships on children in Iraq resulting from the wholly justified economic sanctions on the murderous regime of Saddam Hussein. As always, they rehearse their list of U.S. foreign policy grievances in the Blame America First crowd. They demonize the CIA and the military, corporations, the wealthy, conservatives, and "the establishment."

The same party line is recited on college campuses from the Left Coast to the Midwest to the Ivy League. This isn't a rare form of propaganda, kept hidden under some secret rock. It is prevalent. This is what passes for conventional wisdom among the tenured left who dominate liberal arts faculties. This is what you're paying $40,000 a year to have your sons and daughters taught.

And what do these ideologues and fellow travelers have in common? They hate America. Don't expect them to admit that in so many words. Their language is rife with evasions, circumlocutions and outright lies. They may have some wispy notion of a socialist utopia that never was and never can be, their vision for a new America "after the revolution." But they hate most of our actual history, the heroes, institutions, values and lifestyles of bourgeois America. They hate what we are and what we've been.

They hate capitalism, consumerism, competition, the global economy, technology, SUVs, the military, the intelligence agencies, cops, nationalism, George W. Bush, Republicans, even the National Football League. They hate many of the very same things that Osama bin Laden hates about America. Their philosophical loyalty is not to America but to abstract ideas: their dreams of international socialism, world government, pacifism, humanism, radical environmentalism. They despise the petty, real America that stands in the way of that vision.

Domestic terrorism is nothing new to the radical left. Bin Laden is their protégé. To the bombers, arsonists, and cop-killing alumni of the '60s and '70s anti-war movement, it's a romantic stroll down memory lane. These days, they're joined by anarchists, Luddites and eco-saboteurs. Don't be deceived by their lip service to the victims of Sept. 11. To them, those individual deaths are an abstraction of far less importance than the cause of international "social justice." Deep down, they believe America deserved this. To paraphrase their mentor, Joseph Stalin, one death is a tragedy, 10,000 deaths is a statistic.

Patriotism and Dissent

January 16, 2004

> *"Dissent is the highest form of Patriotism."*
> *--Thomas Jefferson (?)*

Do a Web search and you'll find this questionable attribution heralded by every anti-war, anti-capitalist, Bush-hating, left-wing blogger on the planet. This is the way false rumors are spread on the internet. The Jefferson scholars I've checked with have no knowledge of his ever making that remark. If someone can substantiate this claim with a direct reference, i.e., a specific Jefferson writing or speech, I'd like to know about it.

We do know that Howard Zinn said, "Dissent is the highest form of patriotism," in a July 2002 interview with Sharon Basco, of the left-wing, populist Web site TomPaine.com. And we know that when he offered this simplistic, self-serving assertion he made no mention of Thomas Jefferson. Zinn, for the benefit of the unenlightened, is the leftist, America-bashing historian and author of *A People's History of the United States*, a 776-page "textbook" currently enjoying trendy popularity in liberal education circles. Your children may well be reading it in college or high school.

Zinn's view of the world is through the Marxist prism of class struggle. He has nothing but disdain for wealth and "private profit." He acknowledges that his book is a "biased account" and that "objectivity is impossible and undesirable" because, as he puts it, "I wanted my writing of history and my teaching of history to be part of a social struggle." If American history were a glass, Zinn obsesses only on the portion that's empty, diminishing or finessing the full body of American goodness and achievement.

Patriotism, very simply, is love of country. This doesn't mean blind love of country or mindless fealty to government. Of course you can love your country while also disagreeing with some of the things it does and is; the point is, patriots love it *on balance*. There's nothing inherently unpatriotic about dissent.

And, yes, dissenters can, indeed, be patriots. But it's just as true that some dissenters aren't patriots. Throughout most of the last century, many members of the Communist Party USA were dissenters but not patriots. Their principle loyalties were to their ideology and its home, the Soviet Union. Our own Founding Fathers were dissenters to British rule. They were surely the first *American* patriots, but they certainly weren't patriots to the crown. Benedict Arnold expressed his dissent to the American Revolution by treasonously betraying it. That wasn't the "highest form of patriotism," it was the lowest.

Dissent is alive and well in this country. Just listen to Howard Dean, *The New York Times* or the Hollywood left. Dissent is fine and is scrupulously protected as a fundamental right. It would be indefensible to persecute peaceful protesters.

But criticism and debate isn't persecution. Bush's critics seem to think that they should be above criticism themselves. While many America-hating one-worlders reflexively recoil from the very notion of patriotism, others brandish it as a mantle of immunity. By some tortured logic they argue that their dissent is patriotic but your disagreement with their arguments or uncivil behavior is not. The corollary to one's right to dissent is another's right to dissent from the substance of that dissent.

I love precisely the America that Zinn and his ilk abhor. When Samuel Johnson said "Patriotism is the last refuge of a scoundrel," he wasn't damning patriotism, per se; his ire was directed at *false* patriotism – the pretense of patriotism, à la Howard Zinn.

No, dissent isn't the highest form of patriotism. Brave and dedicated men and women in uniform are, right now, in Iraq and Afghanistan, serving their country and putting their lives on the line.

That's the highest form of patriotism.

So Dissent is No Longer American?
August 29, 2009

President Obama's health-care reform tour whistle-stopped in Grand Junction last Saturday. Yes, an important part of the job of the president is to communicate with the American public, but there's a point of overexposure. This guy is making a televised speech somewhere every day. He's the chief executive officer of the United States. You'd think a CEO would need more time behind his desk. There was nothing new in the Grand Junction session, just a re-hashing of the same old Obamacare talking points, which, as Democrats and liberal commentators define terms, are irrefutable truths while the counter-arguments of critics are simply "lies."

The *Denver Post* story described the event as one "marked by civility and a loudly applauding crowd," in which Obama's message "struck a chord in a conservative, mostly Republican area of western Colorado." If this is puzzling, here's an explanation, as reported to me by jilted Grand Junction Republicans: They weren't allowed in. Even those with tickets were denied admittance, while busloads of Democratic activists from the Front Range passed them by. The White House advance crew and local Democratic operatives were as proficient in stacking this audience with fawning Obama supporters as they were in Portsmouth, N.H., a few days earlier.

Of course, a sweeping restructuring of the nation's entire health care and insurance industry is an intensely controversial issue. But remarkably, the utterly predictable and appropriate national debate on the subject has been sanctimoniously cast by prominent Democrats as a conflict between good and evil – with their opponents, of course, on the side of evil.

During the eight years of George W. Bush's presidency, his raging critics repeatedly cited the pronouncement that "dissent is the highest form of patriotism." Liberals were conspicuously uncritical of gate-crashers at Bush events – militant anti-war demonstrators and hysterical cranks like Cindy Sheehan, ill-mannered MoveOn.org protesters, leftist college students shouting down conservative guest speakers, ACORN rabble-rousers, labor union thugs, militant Latinos opposing our immigration laws, etc. In 2003, then-Sen. Hillary Clinton declared: "I am sick and tired of people who say that if you debate and you disagree with (the Bush) administration somehow you're not patriotic. We should stand up and say we are Americans and we have a right to debate and disagree with any administration."

Now that the Democrats are in power, dissent has suddenly and conveniently become un-patriotic. Attacks on disenchanted citizens who speak up at town-hall meetings have ranged from the trivial to the outrageous. They've been ridiculed because of the way they dress, preferring Brooks Brothers to Birkenstocks. Nancy Pelosi has branded them as "un-American" and falsely accused them of brandishing Nazi swastikas. Rep. Brian Baird of Washington complains of "Brown Shirt" tactics. Rep. John Dingell of Michigan has compared them to the Ku Klux Klan. Sen. Barbara Boxer has even claimed they're guilty of "organizing." (Wasn't Obama a community organizer?)

Linda Douglass, a former *ABC-TV* correspondent, is the latest in a parade of liberal "journalists" to join the Obama team as paid flaks. Douglass, now the communications director for the White House's Health Reform Office, recently issued an official appeal to Obamacare supporters to serve as tattle-tales by reporting critics who dispense "misinformation" to a special email box. If George W. Bush had ever authorized something like this, Democrats and media liberals would be up in arms and calling for his impeachment, comparing it to Richard Nixon's "enemies list."

It's been said that behind every double standard is an unconfessed single standard. That would explain why, as cheerleaders for everything Obama, our noble journalistic watchdogs appear to have lost their bark.

Anarchists vs. Tea Partyers
October 1, 2009

There they go again. The latest stop on the world anarchist tour was Pittsburgh, site of last week's G20 summit of international finance ministers and governors of central banks.

While the grownups met indoors to discuss cooperation in the global economy, goons of various persuasions and incoherent causes did their thing on the streets. OK, they weren't all violent goons. There were also some better-behaved familiar goofballs like Cindy Sheehan and assorted greenies, pacifists and socialists.

But the anarchists were the most committed. They were a mostly youngish mob bedecked in standard revolutionary garb: faded jeans, black T-shirts, bandanas and ski masks to cover their faces. Their contribution to the world economy consisted of throwing rocks, bricks and trashcans at cops, breaking Starbucks windows and assaulting ATMs. Those whose faces were uncovered seemed to be smiling more than scowling. But, of course, this is what these people do for fun.

As anarchist festivals go, this one was relatively tame. Property damage was under $100,000 and fewer than 100 people were arrested. Small potatoes compared to the riot at the G8 summit in Genoa in 2001 and the violence in Montreal, Seattle and Turin, Italy, at other gatherings of world economic and political leaders.

One group of anarchists, apparently auditioning for *American Idol*, taunted police with a chorus of: "We all live in a fascist bully state," sung to the tune of the Beatles' *Yellow Submarine*. They probably missed the irony. It's only because of the civility and restraint of governments like the ones these sociopaths so revile that they can get away with their antics. If they actually lived in a fascist bully state they'd have been shot and carted off to a concentration camp or a reeducation center. Icons of the world's "People's Democratic Republics" like Stalin, Mao, Castro and Guevara (the guy on the anarchists' T-shirts) haven't been so tolerant of dissent.

Anarchists have only a childish concept of what they're against and not a clue about what they would have replace it. When better-armed anarchists break into their home, who are they going to call? Don't bother dialing 911; nobody will be there.

In the anarchist paradise of their dreams, do they imagine that mattresses will replace banks as financial intermediaries? Political economies come in only two forms: command and demand. In a command economy, government decides what gets produced, how it's done, who does it, and how it's distributed. In a demand economy, the capitalist alternative, those choices are made freely in the market – with varying degrees of government intrusion. The debate among rational adults is over the degree of government intrusion. Once set in motion, government intervention and control tends to expand, becoming ever more difficult to reverse until it metastasizes into a command economy. History has shown us repeatedly and dramatically that command economies don't work. They produce neither prosperity nor freedom.

By contrast, the tea party folks who have taken to the streets in the age of Obama understand the danger of excessively intrusive government and are trying to stand athwart it. They know what they're for. But they're rookies at protests and demonstrations. They're not quite sure what to do. They certainly don't want to break anything, and they even clean up after themselves. This is not what they do for fun. Most of them would rather spend weekends with their families and are too busy earning a productive living on weekdays. When they turn out there are no face masks, no confrontations with police and no violence.

Isn't it curious that the same Democrat politicians and liberal media types who condemned and ridiculed the law-abiding Tea Partyers haven't uttered a peep in disapproval of the nasty rabble that made a ruckus and dirtied their diapers in Pittsburgh?

Revolting Against Reality
December 9, 2010

California, Illinois, New Jersey, New York and Arizona are rapidly careening toward bankruptcy. Other states aren't far behind. In Colorado, Gov.-elect John Hickenlooper will be greeted with the prospect of a budget deficit as large as $1 billion. Tax revenues are sagging as a result of a weak economy and high unemployment.

But the heart of the problem is the unsustainable level of government spending and indebtedness driven by a cornucopia of entitlement, health care and welfare programs, along with overly generous government employee payrolls and lavish pension plans that have dwarfed growth in private sector compensation in recent years.

Our federal government is also upside down financially, only with more zeroes at the end of the numbers. Given its relative size, the feds count red ink in trillions of dollars rather than billions. The crisis is more imminent for the states, however, since states (like Colorado) are constitutionally prohibited from running deficits and don't have the option of printing money to make up the difference.

Overseas governments are in a similar pickle, and their citizens are doing something about it: They're revolting (double entendre intended). In France, labor unions and students have staged protests and general strikes, outraged over the government's perfectly reasonable proposal to raise the retirement age from 60 to 62. *Sacre bleu!* In London, student protesters expressed their opposition to college tuition increases by vandalizing the Milbank Tower skyscraper, breaking glass and throwing objects from the roof at police on the street below.

Last week in Spain, disgruntled air traffic controllers launched a wildcat strike, shutting down the airports. And their prime minister, Jose Luis Rodriguez Zapatero, is a socialist!

The prototype for all this was the rioting in Greece last spring when angry mobs of government workers, anarchists, communists and assorted rabble-rousers wreaked havoc over austerity measures forced by that nation's looming bankruptcy.

Is this a preview of coming attractions for the U.S.? If so, it will be an exercise in futility. This is a revolt against reality. These nations spend a much smaller share of their gross domestic product on defense than we do, and they're still going broke. This is about the inevitable collapse of the democratic socialist welfare state. In the name of "social justice," compassion knows no economic bounds. Well, the bounds are there whether or not democratic socialists know or care about them. In the prophetic words of Margaret Thatcher, "The problem with socialism is that you eventually run out of other people's money."

Our current spending levels exceed our practical tax capacity. No nation can tax itself rich. It can only produce itself rich. Excessive tax rates are the enemy of production and a barrier to the creation of societal wealth. You can soak the rich, spin-dry them and run them through a wringer, and you still won't come up with nearly enough revenue to close this runaway spending gap. And then who's left to soak?

The economic solution is obvious: Government must spend less – much less – on all kinds of things at the federal and state levels. The political solution is problematic. President Obama's federal deficit commission has poked some sacred cows but not nearly hard enough. For example, Americans are living longer, so they'll have to retire later. Commission co-chairs Alan Simpson and Erskine Bowles acknowledge this but can't bring themselves to bite the bullet. They recommend that the full retirement age be gradually raised from 67, under current law, to 69. That's reasonable, but they don't get all the way there until 2075. That's 65 years from now!

American colonists revolted against King George III because they were oppressed by an undemocratic government. The grievance today of revolting leftists worldwide is that they're not given enough by democratic governments. This is a formula for economic ruin.

A Bridge too Far (Left)
October 6, 2011

On a beautiful afternoon in the early fall with the leaves turning colors and a hint of approaching winter in the air, conservative college students as well as those not particularly involved in politics are often drawn to the campus stadium to enjoy the day and root for their football team.

Their liberal counterparts have a different idea of fun. They like to protest for lefty causes – or just protest for the sake of protest. It can be gratifying, morally self-indulgent, give life meaning and it's also a good way to hook up with liberal chicks (at least that was the case in the "free-love," turbulent 1960s.)

Last weekend, that latter group turned out in meager numbers in New York City as part of the Occupy Wall Street movement which has been limping along for a couple of weeks in the lower-Manhattan financial district. Having attracted little coverage, even from the sympathetic liberal media, the anti-Wall Streeters made a desperate attempt for attention. Emboldened by inspirational speakers such as Michael Moore and Susan Sarandon, in a coordinated maneuver, they engineered an eastward pivot in a daring attempt to "Take the (Brooklyn) bridge." Well, that's what they chanted when they got there. Hey, if they wanted it that badly, I'd have been happy to sell it to them. As it turned out, their mission was a bridge too far (left).

The NYPD, experienced in such matters, was ready for them, inviting the protesters to make their pilgrimage from Manhattan to Brooklyn over the bridge via the pedestrian walkway (or by taking the D train under the East River). Since that wouldn't have gotten them their protester battle ribbon for getting ceremoniously "arrested," they opted to block the vehicle traffic lanes instead. OK, they weren't actually arrested. Showered with chants of "The whole world is watching," the cops carried those who wouldn't move gently out of the thoroughfare, wrote them citations and let them go.

Incidentally, the whole world wasn't really watching. Most of its 7 billion inhabitants from Greece to Africa to Libya to Detroit have more serious problems to deal with and don't give a damn about these New York exhibitionists playing at repression.

A handful of copycat protesters also turned out in Denver and some other places, amid little more than yawns, to join the Wall Street occupiers in a smorgasbord of left-wing complaints. Among the things they're against are the legacy of George W. Bush, corporations (especially financial institutions), greed, capitalism, the global economy, global warming, inequality, home foreclosures, unemployment, war, unfair treatment of Muslims – and did I say George W. Bush?

One Wall Street protester, Jackie Fellner from New York's Westchester County, declared, "It's about big money dictating which politicians get elected and what programs get funded."

Really? I wonder if she's looked at the components of the federal budget that are driving our massive deficits. Has big corporate money been responsible for the more than two-thirds of federal spending on a cornucopia of social programs these protesters no doubt support? Programs like Social Security, Medicare, Medicaid, Supplemental Security Income, welfare, food stamps, housing subsidies, public education, student loans, etc., along with the interest on the national debt to service the deficits these programs generate.

For the most part, the Occupy Wall Street exercise in political street theater is a group therapy session. These aren't the kind of people who have a coherent understanding of what they're for, much less practical remedies. So they don't like capitalism or corporations.

What's their alternative, socialism and government control of the means of production? Would they prefer that the U.S. Postal Service take over Apple? They don't like investment houses or banks. So where would they have people put their savings, under their mattresses?

ACORNS and Wall Nuts

October 13, 2011

After a slow start, the liberal media have made up for lost time cheerleading for and promoting Occupy Wall Street demonstrators and their regional spawns, comparing the movement to the Arab Spring and describing it as the Tea Party of the left. Both of these allusions are absurd.

The popular revolutions in Egypt and Libya overthrew dictatorial regimes that repressed freedom and rigged elections. The current crowd of protesters is a hodgepodge of American lefties whose presidential and congressional candidates dominated a free and fair election in 2008. There's no dictatorship here. And the Obama administration has no need to control the media, most of whom are enthralled with his persona and liberal agenda.

What Occupy Wall Street really opposes is the outcome of democratic elections in 2010 when their side lost and the Republicans had the audacity to win a majority in the U.S. House, giving them merely one-half of one-third of our federal government.

The Tea Party movement is the exact opposite of Occupy Wall Street. Tea Partyers favor individual liberty, a free-market economy and limited government. The Occupy protesters are fundamentally collectivist, anti-capitalists, committed to unlimited government and cradle-to-grave welfarism.

The Tea Party movement was a spontaneous response to Democrat and Obama overreach. In the 2008 election, the left came to power riding a tide of anti-Bush sentiment compounded by the financial crash just before the election. Since 2010, the left has been on its heels defending the failed president they elected.

The idea to occupy Wall Street was hatched by *Adbusters*, an anti-consumerist, anti-capitalist Vancouver magazine. The protest is a strategy shift to retake the offensive via a contrived counterattack, diverting attention from the Obama disaster. This time the bogey man isn't George W. Bush, it's a cartoonish and bibulous characterization of "Wall Street, corporations and greed." This is right out of the Saul

Alinsky playbook. The short-term goal is to get Obama re-elected. The long-term goal is socialist utopia.

Check out the YouTube video featuring Nelini Stamp, a professional community organizer (just like Obama) for the Working Families Party, a front group for ACORN, the SEIU and other labor unions. She brags about her work in organizing, mobilizing and expanding the Occupy Wall Street movement. With recruiting help from MoveOn.org and unions joining the show, this is another variation of the staged "occupation" of the Wisconsin statehouse earlier this year. In the smart phone/social media era, spontaneity isn't what it used to be.

Demonstrators claim to speak for "99 percent" of Americans against the wealthy 1 percent. To buy that, you'd have to believe that 99 percent of Americans are Marxists and idiots. As measured by the dramatic GOP victory in 2010 and Obama's plunging approval numbers, swing-voting independents are abandoning him and the Democrats in droves.

The Occupy Wall Street collective is confused about what it wants but it wants it now! Some of the loonier demands from its independent thinkers: Striking all existing public and private debt from the books across the "entire planet"; elimination of all international borders; free college education; a guaranteed "living wage" for all regardless of employment; an end to free trade; trillions in additional spending for infrastructure and ecological restoration; and ending the fossil fuel economy.

Much like the violent demonstrations in Greece and London by unionists, government employees and leftist organizations, Occupy Wall Street is demonstrating against the collapse of runaway government spending and the welfare state in the face of economic reality. One of their many insipid signs declares, "We want our voices to be heard." They will be, along with everyone else's when the votes are counted in 2012. That's the way we do it in our constitutional republic, not through mobs engaging in political street theater. And that's when we'll find out if they really represent "99 percent" of Americans.

Bursting the Occupiers' Bubble
October 27, 2011

It's impossible to reason with the childish protesters who dominate the Occupy Wall Street charade. Their narrative is a collection of rants and slogans extracting a pound of lie from an ounce of truth.

The financial meltdown of 2008 is considerably more complicated than their simplistic notion of a conspiracy of greedy corporations and Wall Street bankers. To be sure, there were criminals, scoundrels and unethical opportunists in the financial sector, just as there are in every sector of our society. The reason only a few, like Ponzi-schemer Bernie Madoff and some inside traders, have gone to jail is that the bad judgment and stupidity of some others aren't prosecutable crimes.

The crash was the consequence of a market bubble. Market bubbles are as old as markets – from the Dutch tulip bubble of 1637, to the dot-com bubble of the 1990s, to this housing and mortgage-backed securities bubble. And as long as people are allowed to trade freely, we'll have more bubbles in the future. They're a consequence of human nature compounded by irrational exuberance or fear. Governments can't eliminate them without eliminating markets. And that would be worse than the occasional disease.

So what preconditions set the stage for the crash of 2008, and who set them in motion? The answer to the latter question is government. And the preconditions started with the Community Reinvestment Act of 1977 during the Carter administration. In the name of social justice, the left's ideological dogma, it was decreed that everyone has the right to own a home. Thus, mortgage lending was turned into yet another welfare program. Lenders were pressured by government to make loans to unqualified borrowers regardless of ability to pay. The crusade was expanded in the 1990s when the Clinton administration applied even more pressure through HUD.

The Federal Reserve was also culpable. In a misguided attempt to stimulate the economy, the Fed goosed the money supply, hoping to spur consumer spending. Normally, that would lead to the kind of general price inflation we've seen before. But consumers, already drowning in credit card debt, didn't take the bait. Instead, the flood of government-induced artificial demand for houses created a housing bubble, driving home prices up to ridiculous, unsustainable levels, founded on the false belief they would only go up in the future.

Financial sector intermediaries did what they're there to do. They make markets. As the housing bubble expanded, Wall Street made a market for investors who were nervous about stocks, unsatisfied with low interest rates on traditional fixed-income instruments and looking for a better rate of return on what they believed was a secure investment. The featured product was bundled, mortgage-backed securities.

For the most part, investment houses, brokers and investors were trying to make money for themselves and their clients, not lose it. It turned out to be a bad idea, except for the short sellers who anticipated the crash. When the housing bubble burst in 2008, the highly leveraged house of cards came down with it. Wall Street was popular when the Dow soared from 800 in 1982 to almost 14,000 in 2007, fattening individual 401(k) plans, and union and government worker pension plans. Now it's the villain.

The biggest bundlers of bad mortgages were Fannie Mae and Freddie Mac, the government-sponsored-enterprise twins. And Rep. Barney Frank and Sen. Chris Dodd were their biggest cheerleaders, denying there was a problem right up to the end – and beyond. They're not in jail either.

It's not surprising that leftists, who worship at the shrine of big government, ignore the foundational role of government in this fiasco. If they laid the blame at the feet of their savior, it would contradict their blind faith in statism.

Occupying a Cliché
January 26, 2012

Were it not for massive over-coverage by the liberal media, the Occupy-Wall-Street-and-Any-Other-Place-They-Can-Contrive movement would have faded away long ago. Those same media liberals who disdained the Tea Party movement relate to the "Occupiers" and sympathize with their agenda, politics and style. It shows in the comparative coverage.

In a front-page editorial masquerading as a news story on Martin Luther King Day, *The Denver Post* equated the Occupy movement with King's campaign for civil rights and an end to racial discrimination. This tortured comparison was a lame attempt to legitimize the Occupiers, elevate them to MLK's stature and resuscitate the movement, which the left had hoped would reach the strength of the Tea Party.

It's true that King's agenda went beyond civil rights. He talked of reparations for blacks denied equal treatment in the past, and called for racial preferences and hiring quotas. His colleagues and entourage included committed communists like Stanley Levinson, Bayard Rustin and Jack O'Dell (Bobby and Jack Kennedy cautioned him about these associations). He was an opponent of the Vietnam War.

But King's oratory is most remembered for his famous "I have a dream" speech, in which he expressed his hope that someday people would be "judged by the content of their character and not by the color of their skin." This suggested that all people should be afforded equal opportunities, not necessarily equal outcomes. But equal outcomes is what the Occupiers are all about. At their demonstrations, they complain about unequal and "unfair" rewards in our society. Their remedy is government intervention to control private enterprise and redistribute income and wealth. Their model is democratic socialism. It's not clear that MLK wanted to go quite that far.

The *Denver Post* story about MLK Day introduced us to some radical, contemporary bearers of King's torch who apparently do want to go that far, opportunistically hopping on the trendy Occupy

325

bandwagon and launching a campaign for economic justice which they're calling "Occupy the Dream."

"Economic justice" is another euphemism for socialism.

This occupy nonsense has become a cliché. First there was Occupy Wall Street, then Occupy _____ (fill in the name of a city), Occupy Congress, Occupy the Courts and, now, Occupy the Dream. Disruptive labor unions in Indianapolis are planning to Occupy the Super Bowl (they better have a deep strike fund; scalpers are getting big bucks for those tickets). In April; there's a planned Occupy the Federal Reserve. The original Occupy Wall Street organizers should charge a franchise fee for the use of the name (but that would be capitalism, wouldn't it?).

What's comically ironic about this is that none of these theatrical events actually "occupy" anything. After World War II, U.S. troops did indeed occupy Germany and Japan, rewrote the constitutions of those countries and ran their governments. We just ended our military occupation of Iraq. In the turbulent '60s, radical left-wing students protesting the Vietnam War (or anything else that disturbed them) really did occupy the dean's office. They "sat in" and shut the schools down. Occupy Wall Street merely camped out in a little park, trashed the place, stole from each other, flashed silly hand signals at meaningless meetings, and failed in a puny attempt to occupy the Brooklyn Bridge. They didn't invade the New York Stock Exchange or shut down Goldman Sachs. Business went on as usual there.

Locally, Occupy Denver was a minor nuisance. They didn't take over the City and County Building or the governor's office, and the state legislature wasn't even in session.

What these people ought to occupy is a job.

Of Comfort and Affliction
November 18, 2005

I gave a talk recently on one of my favorite topics: liberal bias in the media. In the course of my remarks I referred to a quote made famous by Finley Peter Dunne's fictional alter ego, Mr. Dooley, a caricature of an Irishman from the old country who once sarcastically declared that the job of the newspaper is to "comfort the afflicted and afflict the comfortable." Dunne, himself, was a one-time Progressive who saw the light and became a Teddy Roosevelt Republican and a critic of sanctimonious do-gooders. Contemporary journalists may be unaware that the context of the Dunne quote was critical of arrogant newspapers abusing their influence and power to "comfort and afflict."

Today, this bromide has become a credo of media liberals who proudly explain that it was taught as dogma in journalism school. Should you visit the Web site of the leftist Independent Press Association, you'll learn of its Campus Journalism Project, "a national network of progressive (*that's a euphemism for left-wing*) campus publications and journalists, founded to serve the thousands of students who are making social change through the media." They also tout their manual, *Afflict the Comfortable, Comfort the Afflicted: A Guide for Campus Alternative Journalism.*

Following my talk, I received a letter from a member of the audience who accused me of "seriously offending" Catholics, informing me that comforting the afflicted and afflicting the comfortable is the core message of Jesus, the pope and the Roman Catholic Church, and that I had "derided this theory."

Whoa! I wrote him back explaining how he had misinterpreted my point. While clergy and their flocks may choose to adopt this mission in their personal lives, supposedly objective journalists – reporters – are obliged to maintain their neutrality and not take sides or crusade for issues while on the job. Of course, they do. But it's unprofessional activism.

When it's convenient for them, journalists like to strut their objectivity and detachment by describing themselves as messengers rather than advocates. (They certainly cut terrorists a lot of slack, even shunning the use of that term.) But they're highly selective in the messages they choose to deliver. My mailman doesn't read my mail and edit it before he gives it to me. That's precisely what the media do as the gatekeepers of public information. And that's exactly why "old media" – the dominant liberal mass media – are so resentful of "new media" – the Internet, the blogosphere and guys like me on talk radio. Old media covet the monopoly they once enjoyed.

But let's go back to this notion of afflicting the comfortable and comforting the afflicted. Superficially, it has a noble ring but there's also a down side to it. For one thing, it sounds remarkably similar to the fundamental Marxist refrain: "From each according to his ability; to each according to his need."

The fatal flaw of socialism is its incompatibility with human nature. It's delusional to believe that one will work as hard for the benefit of a stranger as he would for his family and himself. Socialism penalizes excellence and rewards sloth. As such, it inevitably gets too little of the former and too much of the latter. One need only observe the economic failure of the Soviet Union, North Korea and Cuba vs. the resurgence of China, as capitalism increasingly takes hold there.

Afflicting the comfortable is another way of saying let's punish the successful. What's evil about success? If one is successful because of initiative, imagination, hard work, talent and risk taking, why should he be punished? This is how a free society creates wealth and capital for reinvestment, job creation and economic growth. It's why the United States is the most prosperous nation on Earth. It's also how we generate the means to help those in need.

Comforting the afflicted is a well-intended, kind and charitable thing to do if we define an affliction as a distressful situation caused by misfortune beyond one's control. But what about self-affliction? Is one equally entitled to someone else's property – afflict the comfortable – if his poor condition is the consequence of his own negligence, laziness or irresponsibility? Doesn't God help those who help themselves?

Journalists can't have it both ways. Objectivity and advocacy are contradictory, unless, that is, you're an advocate for objectivity. If journalists value their credibility, they shouldn't go around afflicting anyone. And if they want to comfort the afflicted, they should do it on their own time and their own nickel. Volunteer for a soup kitchen or write out a check to your favorite charity. But keep it out of your news reporting.

Reality

Liberal Guilt on Parade

Human Life Trumps Fish Life
August 10, 2001

The Endangered Species Act has long been the cause of unnecessary economic losses. Now it also appears to be responsible for the loss of human life. U.S. Rep. Scott McInnis has called for an investigation of the actions of U.S. Forest Service officials in response to a July wildfire in the Okanogan National Forest in the state of Washington. Four firefighters, two of which were teenage girls, died in that blaze while bureaucrats fiddled.

Initial reports have been attributed, in part, to unnamed sources, perhaps angry and frustrated whistle-blowers within the system. What seems to be emerging is a timeline in which urgent calls for helicopter water drops were placed on hold for as long as 10 hours while permission was sought to scoop water from the nearby Chewach River. Why was special permission required? Because, incredibly, fish protected under the ESA might be scooped up as well. By the time the water drops belatedly occurred, the fire had exploded out of control, and the four firefighters, according to *Fox News* reports, "burned to death while cowering under protective tents near the Chewach River."

The first concern in enviro-activist and liberal media circles was to come to the defense of the ESA. They cited the testimony of Dale Bosworth, the Forest Service's fire chief, who told Congress last week that the ESA shouldn't be a factor in such emergency situations and that the policy is to "get the water where we can get it and ask questions later." I doubt that it's much comfort to the family and friends of the dead firefighters that this is the way it's *supposed* to work. Obviously, it didn't work that way. The chain of command in the Okanogan fire reportedly included consultations with a fisheries biologist on the subject of the health and safety of bull trout fingerlings.

If it wasn't the letter of the ESA that led to the death of the firefighters, it was surely the political culture of it. Here's how the game is played: government bureaucrats, by their very nature, are risk averse. Enviros represent a fashionable and powerful political lobby. Complaints are their stock in trade, and they fire them off with a hair trigger. Routine forest fires are common in the summer; killer fires are uncommon. Hypersensitivity to environmental concerns is the order of the day. Regardless of the stated policy, bureaucrats make exceptions to the ESA at their own career peril.

The Okanogan fire was not initially diagnosed as a dire emergency. Bureaucratic prudence and the instinct to cover your derriere dictate that you err on the side of ESA hypersensitivity. So you touch all the enviro bases and place the welfare of the fishes first, while assuming this is a routine fire that poses no special danger to firefighters.

When it was created in 1973, the ESA sounded like a good idea. What patriotic American could object to saving the bald eagle from extinction? But, from its reasonable roots the ESA has morphed into a monster exploited by environmental radicals and technophobes to wage war on personal property rights, economic growth and development. Bald eagles are one thing; snail darters and Prebles meadow jumping mice are quite another. Obscure species have been conscripted by enviros as frontline troops in their cynical war against humanity. ESA reform is long overdue – 95 percent of all species that ever roamed the Earth are extinct and almost all that happened before humans came on the scene. The Earth is remarkably resilient and evolution is a never-ending process.

Earth First! terrorists and assorted animal-rights wackos, the kind of people who have described the human race as "a cancer on the planet," have a cockeyed agenda and perverse priorities. In a life or death situation, I'd opt for fried trout. Firefighters are the endangered species I care much more about.

PETA Tricks Take an Ominous Turn

June 14, 2002

In the midst of public policy debates about serious issues, People for the Ethical Treatment of Animals has not been wholly useless. It has often provided comic relief.

For example, PETA's recent protest of a cow patty bingo fundraiser for women's athletic teams at Florida Southern College. Squares on a field were sold to contestants, with the winner determined by the spot where Bessie planted a cow patty. Amy Rhodes, a PETA cruelty caseworker, complained that this event was an assault on the cow's dignity.

PETA regards the practice of humans keeping pets as the equivalent of slavery. PETA disapproves of fur and leather clothing, and certainly opposes the consumption of animals for human nourishment at McDonald's, Kentucky Fried Chicken, Red Lobster or Morton's.

No reasonable people condone animal cruelty. But we still make distinctions between animals and humans – and between animals and other animals. We employ some species to our use. We love our pets because they're domesticated, loyal and cute. We hate vermin such as rats, locusts, mosquitoes and cockroaches because they're disease-carrying, destructive, annoying and not cute. We do our best to eradicate harmful viruses and bacteria, while cultivating useful microorganisms.

We do these things because most rational people recognize that humans, by virtue of their superior intellect or, perhaps spirituality, sit at the top of the food chain. But PETA zealots are neither rational nor reasonable. They tend toward self-indulgent moral exhibitionism and they're intolerant of the dissent of the majority.

In a debate a few years ago, I implored Ingrid Newkirk, PETA's founder and fanatic-in-chief, to concede that it wasn't unethical for me to swat a mosquito sucking the blood out of my arm. She wouldn't.

Animals don't have rights, only people do. But people accord animals certain protections – up to a point. Going well beyond simple kindness to animals, PETA has embraced the ridiculous notion of animal *liberation*. Cows, chicken and pigs would be emancipated to roam free and form their own societies. I believe George Orwell meant *Animal Farm* as a metaphor. If it weren't for their utility to humans, these animals wouldn't have been bred in the first place.

Once content to conduct silly demonstrations and acts of intimidation and petty vandalism, PETA has grown increasingly radical, providing financial aid and comfort to individuals and groups involved in ecoterrorism – groups such as the Animal Liberation Front and Earth Liberation Front, which the FBI reports have been involved in more than 600 attacks, causing more than $43 million in damage since 1996.

PETA's tax-exempt status presumes that it operates exclusively for the charitable purpose of prevention of cruelty to animals. A recent congressional hearing, chaired by Rep. Scott McInnis of Colorado, looked into revoking that status. Taxpayers shouldn't be subsidizing this bunch.

With an annual budget of $17 million, PETA can't be dismissed as a menagerie of harmless kooks. Consider the recorded comments of their spokesman, Bruce Friedrich, at the Animal Rights 2001 conference last July:

"If these animals do have the same right to be free from pain and suffering at our hands, then, of course, we're going to be, as a movement, blowing stuff up and smashing windows. For the record, I don't do this stuff, but I advocate it. I think it's a great way to bring about animal liberation. And considering the level of the atrocity and the level of suffering, I think it would be a great thing if all these fast-food outlets, and these slaughterhouses, and these laboratories, and the banks that fund them exploded tomorrow. I think it's perfectly appropriate for people to take bricks and toss them through the windows. And, you know, everything else along the line. Hallelujah to the people who are willing to do it."

Are We a Sick Society?

August 9, 2012

Just two weeks after James Holmes' shooting rampage in Aurora, another armed madman struck a Sikh temple in Oak Creek, Wisc., killing six more innocent people.

After shooting a police officer multiple times, Wade Michael Page reportedly committed suicide. A year and a half ago, Jared Loughner attacked U.S. Rep. Gabrielle Giffords in Tucson, Ariz., killing six and wounding 13.

These incidents and others have stirred familiar declarations that America is a "sick society." We heard the same indictment 13 years ago after the killing spree by two deranged teenagers at Columbine High School.

That emotional cry of grief, anger and frustration is understandable, but I disagree. We're not a sick society; no more than any number of otherwise civilized nations on this planet where similar heinous acts occur.

Those who brand our society as sick presumably regard themselves as sufficiently healthy to make that judgment. How many of you reading these words would describe yourself as sick in the sense of shooting up a movie theater or high school? How many of your family members, friends or co-workers would you put in that category? How many of you regard yourself as a sociopath or fundamentally immoral? How many of you have ever committed a felony? So, you and I aren't sick but everyone else, except for those we know, is?

We're a nation of 315 million people, only an infinitesimal fraction of whom will ever commit these kinds of atrocities. But a relative few can do a great deal of damage in a free and open society which is especially vulnerable to domestic terrorism, whether committed by freelancers or organized groups.

We've spent hundreds of billions in recent years on heightened security precautions at airports, government buildings, schools and stadiums, but we're still vulnerable, and always will be. Welcome to the 21st century.

The intensity of our enemies, foreign and domestic, and the advancing technology of weaponry worldwide from automatic firearms to compact explosives to biological warfare, raises the level of the threat. New gun control laws will have little effect in protecting us from those intent on breaking the law. Neither will greater sensitivity to early signs of mental illness; there are just too few psychotherapists and too many potential psychotics.

For all our imperfections, the United States remains a beacon of freedom, justice, prosperity and relative benevolence. The market test of that: many more people want to come here, even illegally, than want to leave. No nation can match our historic achievements in science, technology or commerce. Students from around the world flock to our universities. American authors, scholars, musicians, athletes, filmmakers and entertainers dominate world culture. These are the measures of a healthy society – notwithstanding some sick people among us.

The world has always been a violent place. The United States is more violent than some societies and less violent than others. Our nation was born of violence in the American Revolution, multiplied by the Civil War and two world wars. There was violence in the days of the Wild West, Bonnie and Clyde, and Al Capone. America's strain of rugged individualism may be a factor, as well as having the world's most ethnically and racially diverse population.

We have a high crime rate, a high incarceration rate, and a great many deaths by firearms (two-thirds of which are suicides). Fortunately for civilization at large, America's ability to effectively channel violence was great enough to save the world from Nazi Germany and Imperial Japan in World War II. Random civil violence is a different matter, but would you feel safer in Syria, Egypt, Somalia, Afghanistan, Pakistan, Libya, Iraq or Mexico? It's all relative isn't it?

So, how can we end these horrible shootings once and for all? Sadly, we can't.

Big Brother and Big Screen TVs
April 24, 2009

Legislators and regulators in California don't trust residents to live their lives responsibly. Ironically, these are the same legislators and regulators staring at a more than $40 billion budget deficit. State spending in California, now $145 billion, has increased by 40 percent in just the last five years, dropping its credit rating to the lowest in the nation. Talk about irresponsibility!

California bureaucrats, greenies and nannyists are now targeting big-screen TVs as the latest culprit in their campaign against the delusion of man-made global warming. The California Energy Commission has proposed regulations that would prohibit the sale of big-screen TVs that don't meet the more stringent energy standards now on its drawing board. While the commission denies that it's actually "banning" big-screen TVs, that will be the practical effect of this policy. With manufacturers already voluntarily adopting the existing, heightened, federal government's Energy Star standards, there isn't much room for improvement. So, screens in excess of 40 inches, especially plasma screens, simply won't be able to meet the new California standard.

And that's just fine with California's anti-materialist tree-huggers, not content with simplifying their own lives but determined to impose regulations to simplify yours as well. Listen to one such zealot, Jaymi Heimbuch, writing from San Francisco (where else?) on www.treehugger.com (what else?): "State regulators are starting to draft the first set of rules that would give energy sucking LCDs and Plasmas the boot from California retail stores. The regulations are expected to pass in mid-2009. The new rules will go a long way in helping consumers make energy efficient choices – they'd be the only choices available." This is what's known as a Hobson's choice; that is, no choice at all. Having established the principle that bureaucrats can dictate the size of your TV set, you can expect their next move to limit your viewing choices to *PBS* and the *National Geographic Channel*.

If California goes ahead with this plan, they'll get a lesson in the law of unintended consequences in the real world. There'll be an instantaneous gray and black market for non-complying big-screen TVs. Consumers will buy them on the Internet from places where they're not illegal, or they'll cross borders to bring them in from neighboring states.

The Energy Commission defends the crackdown on big-screen TVs as a way to relieve strain on the power grid. That was the same justification offered for an earlier proposal, quickly withdrawn in the face of public outcry, which would have allowed power companies to use "smart meter" technology to reach into your home and remotely turn up the thermostat on your air conditioner if they judge that you're too comfortable on a hot day. A better alternative is to allow more power plants, especially nuclear, which emit no greenhouse gases. Fuhgeddaboutid! That's not on the public policy menu in the enviro-crazy state. Ironically, with so many people cutting back on their entertainment expenses during this recession, staying home and watching a movie on your big-screen TV uses less energy than driving to a theater.

I'm reminded of the two-way video screens in George Orwell's *1984*, through which Big Brother lectured you and observed you in the non-privacy of your austere, low-environmental-impact apartment. Given the mentality of the people who want to control your life to the point of dictating what kind of TV you can own, you'd think they'd like the idea of a bigger screen to better monitor your every move.

Nannyists and Chicken McNuggets
July 1, 2010

Ronald McDonald is a child abuser! That's the latest delusion of those nannyist, busybody scolds at the Center for Science in the Public Interest (CSPI), now threatening to sue McDonald's if the fast-food chain doesn't immediately desist in luring kids to their "un-nutritious" Happy Meals by bribing them with toys. Mickey D's offending promotion features Shrek-themed figures bundled with Big Macs, Chicken McNuggets and fries. Oh, the humanity!

In its sinister letter, CSPI berates McDonald's for seducing little kiddies with trinkets, inciting them to demand that their mommies and daddies deliver them unto the dietary hell of the Golden Arches. CSPI brands this as "pester power." How ironic. I can't think of a bigger pest than CSPI itself.

Commonly described by the left-stream media in reverential terms such as "non-profit watchdog" or "consumer advocacy group," CSPI is a Naderite offshoot with roots in the early '70s. Critics refer to it, unflatteringly, as the "food police." Some of its crusades have included attacks on ice cream, popcorn, potato chips and soda pop. You can only imagine what it thinks of cotton candy.

The sanctimony and arrogance of this group is reflected in its very name. Who gave these people the right to define and speak for the "public interest"? I'm part of the public and I have a different view of that interest. Personal responsibility – including parental responsibility – and consumer choice are the greater issues here. This is the kind of liberal mentality the Issacs had in mind when they wrote their 1983 book, *The Coercive Utopians*. There's nothing inherently harmful about eating at McDonald's as long as, like anything else, it isn't done to excess.

I feel sorry for the kid whose father runs CSPI if he takes him to a baseball game or the circus. "No hot dogs, Johnny. Eat your tofu and spinach."

In CSPI's press release, its litigation director, Stephen Gardener, hysterically characterizes McDonald's as a pedophile, "the stranger in the playground handing out candy to children...making parents' job nearly impossible." Nearly impossible? Any parent who can't manage this challenge has much greater problems. And McDonald's isn't giving their toys away. You have to buy the Happy Meal to get them. Unless your 5-year-old is independently wealthy and driving his own Mercedes to the mall, the money and transportation is coming from mommy and daddy.

Naderites have an instinctive animus for private enterprise and its evil spawn, *advertising*. If CSPI successfully bends McDonald's to its will, others that use toys in their marketing, like breakfast cereals and Cracker Jack, will surely be next. (Although the quality of Cracker Jack toys has significantly declined over the years; now, they're just boring paper foldouts. When I was a kid, they had serious prizes. I once found a 1957 Chevy in my box – full size.) Then they'll come for the Good Humor Man, the Pied Piper of ice cream, driving slowly through your neighborhood with his hypnotic bells. Ultimately, what child can be safe in his bed while Santa Claus remains at large?

But CSPI nannyists and their ilk aren't content to just raise your children. They don't like your lifestyle, either. You eat fatty foods, drink, smoke, don't exercise enough and refuse to pay attention to nutrition labels on boxes and containers.

You might think this is a consequence of a free society. Uh-uh. When their dream of government-provided health care is fully realized, your unhealthy choices will be their justification for controlling much more of your life.

Paternalistic bureaucrats will prescribe your diet, ban "junk food" and vices. Cigarettes, booze and Snickers bars will be relegated to the black market. And your mandatory morning exercise class will be led by Big Brother from your two-way view screen.

Homework Gets in the Way of Fun
March 23, 2001

Here's a news flash: schoolchildren don't like homework! It gets in the way of television viewing and social activities. And some parents don't like it either. When they try to help their kids, they discover they're just as bad at algebra now as they were in the seventh grade.

Joining the chorus are educrats who claim that homework favors smarter students and discriminates against not-so-smart ones who suffer irreparable damage to their *self-esteem*.

Stripped of the usual academic jargon and edubabble, these are in essence the conclusions of Etta Kralovec and John Buell, the authors of *The End of Homework: How Homework Disrupts Families, Overburdens Children and Limits Learning*.

Kralovec is a closed-loop functionary of the system, a product of a teachers college who then went on to teach new teachers. Buell has a similar background which includes a stint as associate editor of the left-wing monthly *The Progressive*. That, no doubt, explains the anti-capitalist, conspiratorial tone of the book, captured in passages like the following: "We would argue that the current stress on homework and the long school day may be another, and increasingly problematic, form of the preparation demanded by our corporate and consumer society – a way to accustom the student worker to long working hours. Not only is homework itself a form of psychological preparation, but both in its form and content seem designed to send the cardinal message of today's business civilization: *This is a competitive world whose purpose lies in endless production.*"

Not surprisingly, this book has been well received by the educratic establishment and often cited as vindication for their growing opposition to homework. The teachers unions don't like homework because it makes more work for their rank and file who have to grade it (if they can't lay it off on a teaching assistant).

The problem, we're told, is especially epidemic in the lower grades. Researchers at the University of Michigan report that 6-to-9-year-olds, who spent only 44 minutes a week on homework in 1981, now put in more than two hours' worth. If you do the math, that comes to a horrifying 17 minutes a day! Among 10-to-11-year-olds it's all the way up to 30 minutes a day. Outrageous!

In the words of George Orwell, "This is nonsense so bad only an intellectual would believe it." Listen, school isn't supposed to be fun all the time. Learning to do things that you don't want to is great training for life, which also isn't fun all the time. Homework teaches discipline, responsibility, organization, time management, and deferred gratification. Drilling helps reinforce new concepts and mechanics. If practice doesn't make perfect, it at least improves proficiency. To leftists this may be an exercise in capitalist indoctrination. To the rest of us, it's preparation for the real world.

The nations that are passing us in student knowledge and achievement are big on homework. The Michigan University researchers found that Japanese fifth graders do twice as much homework as their American counterparts, while Taiwanese students do twice as much, again, as the Japanese. Timothy Keith of the University of Iowa concludes that the power of graded homework to influence success ranks second only to ability, and ahead of race and family background. A study of British grammar school boys conducted by Holmes and Croll found working-class children benefitted even more from homework than did their wealthier schoolmates.

In this country, homework appears to be getting in the way of the activities to which soccer moms spend most of their waking hours ferrying their kids. Rather than cutting back on the homework, why not cut back on some of those activities? Dance, gymnastics, piano lessons, tae kwon do, involuntary community service, transcendental meditation, macramé, drivers ed. Enough already. Perhaps 15 minutes could be better spent by schoolchildren memorizing the multiplication tables so they can make change at the supermarket.

Day-Care Study of Limited Value
April 27, 2001

All things being equal, during their formative years, children are generally better served when their mothers stay home with them. This statement is so obvious as to defy contradiction. Unfortunately, all things are not always equal. And generalizations like this, while valid in a great number of cases, do not practically apply in the particular situations of many others.

That's why the findings of a recent study on the effects of day-care on young children are of limited value. Moreover, media accounts of the study were typically skewed and sensationalistic. While headlines blared dire warnings like: "Study faults day care," a careful reading of the stories that followed produced more ambiguous conclusions.

The lead of one wire-service story read: "Children who spend long hours in child care are more likely to be aggressive and disobedient when they reach kindergarten age." Several hundred words later, those who go beyond the headlines learn that there were offsetting benefits. Children enrolled in good day-care programs showed independence, assertiveness and superior performance in language, cognitive and memory skills.

One researcher warned that the report should not be taken to mean that day-care children are at risk to become psychopaths and "blow away other kids." His caveat fell on deaf ears. That's exactly how the study was interpreted by those predisposed to jump to that conclusion. Another of the study's contributors mused: "We started out with the simple question – 'Is day care good or bad for kids?' – and, I think the answer isn't that simple." Nonetheless, the usual alliance of social engineers and liberal activists immediately exploited the report to cry for more subsidies and government control of child-care programs.

The selective and tendentious reading of the study's findings provided ammunition for the holier-than-thou crowd to disparage career women and single moms. "They shouldn't have had children in the first place if they couldn't stay home with them," was the charge. Of course, such platitudes are of little value after the fact. People have kids for all kinds of reasons, some good and some bad. No training or license is required for parenting.

Certainly, the dedication and sacrifice of many stay-at-home moms is commendable. Most single moms have no choice. Married moms who choose to work, do so after considering the tradeoffs, and often make a perfectly defensible decision. Perhaps the extra income will enable the family to escape a terrible neighborhood, provide tuition to send the children to a quality private school, or build a fund to pay for a top college. Or maybe mom, after earning a graduate degree, also wants the gratification and fulfillment of a professional career. If she wants that and kids, too, that's her business and her husband's.

Managing a career and a family is a difficult task, to be sure, but many women handle it well and their kids turn out just fine. Others don't and come to regret their choices. Arguably, some kids are better off in day care than some other kids are with stay-at-home mothers. Who's to know and who's to judge? Generalizations cannot and should not dictate life choices for rational individuals with free will. There are too many exceptions in life.

For better or worse, this is no longer the era of Ozzie and Harriet, and, nostalgia notwithstanding, it's not likely we'll ever return to the family arrangements of those days. Women have career opportunities and options that June Cleaver couldn't have imagined.

A second income is often necessary just to meet the burden of taxation under an ever-expanding government. Economic and family considerations can't help but compete. In any event, there is no public policy prescription for this dilemma. It's a highly personal and private decision. And contrary to the pieties of moralizers, there is no right or wrong answer.

Freedom on Four Wheels
August 9, 2002

I love cars. I've always loved cars. When I was a little kid, 5 or 6 years old, my grandfather taught me to identify all the different makes by their logos above the grills and on the hubcaps.

What 15-year-old hasn't counted the days 'til he was old enough to get his license? So there's my bias.

Perhaps you saw a recent editorial cartoon in the *Rocky Mountain News* by Jim Borgman of *The Cincinnati Enquirer* who, apparently, doesn't love cars. It featured a stereotypical, middle-aged American male with thinning hair and a big potbelly wearing a T-shirt and jeans.

In successive frames, he talks to his SUV with exasperation:

"Because of you, the air is foul. The globe is warming."

"Because of you, I'm entangled in the affairs of countries that cause me headaches."

"Because of you, our cities are empty and I waste half my life in traffic to the burbs."

"Because of you, my family life is one big frantic snarl of hectic schedules."

"Because of you, I'm an obese drive-thru addict, a coronary just waiting to happen."

In the final frame he hugs his car, nonetheless, and says, "What would I do without you?"

If I'm not reading too much into this subtle message, I think Borgman disapproves of all of us fat-slob, self-indulgent, shortsighted, urban sprawling, soccer-momming, environment-despoiling, global-exploiting, bourgeois Americans so addicted to our cars that we refuse to alter our destructive ways even as we acknowledge the terrible consequences of our depravity. Whew!

You don't need my help to rebut Borgman's exaggerations, simplistic analysis, and false – or at best, debatable – assertions. Sure, motor vehicles and the internal combustion engine have their drawbacks, but I'd rather focus on the benefits side of the ledger. In keeping with Borgman's "because of you" theme, let's consider just a few of the wonderful things delivered (like Domino's Pizza) by the great American automobile.

Because of you:

- I have the freedom of the open road and the wind in my hair.
- I can tour America at leisure with my family.
- I can polish up my faithful chariot and pick up my date in style on a Saturday night to watch the submarine races at the shore – or cruise for babes on Main Street.
- I can go 0 to 60 in 5.9 seconds.
- I can enjoy the privacy of my personal vehicle on my own schedule in air-conditioned comfort, listening to my choice of music and singing along at will, sipping on a cup of coffee, munching on a doughnut and otherwise luxuriating.
- I can smoke while driving since it's illegal everywhere else.
- I can show off my shotgun rack through the rear window of my pickup.
- I can listen to Mike Rosen and Rush Limbaugh on my radio and call in on my cell phone.
- I can avoid waiting in the snow to strap-hang in a mass-transit cattle-car with strangers sneezing in my face and groping my body.
- I can conveniently carry my groceries home from the supermarket.
- I can transport my surfboard to the beach in my woody.
- I can drive my wife to the hospital in an emergency.
- I can display my bobble-head dog on the platform behind the back seat.
- I can stuff three other people in the trunk and we can all get into the drive-in movie for the price of one.
- I can have tailgate parties at Broncos games.
- I can pull out of the parking lot with a full load of fertilizer, power tools, floor tiles, lighting fixtures, and plumbing supplies at Home Depot.
- I can run errands on my lunch hour.
- My dog can know the pleasure of sticking his head out the window at 60 mph.
- I can keep my golf clubs in the trunk and play on the spur of the moment.

- I can freely express my views on bumper stickers, like "Nuke the whales," "Imagine whirled peas" and "My kid can beat up your honor student."
- And because of you, schools can save money by teaching drivers ed and sex ed in the same car.

Our Silly Little 'Addiction'
February 24, 2006

Sometimes you get great life lessons in unexpected places. Kudos to Scott Adams who writes the *Dilbert* comic strip. Adams cut through the fog and gave his readers a valuable insight into the real-world international politics and economics of the energy conundrum. In a recent strip, *Dilbert* readers were treated to the following exchange:

Dilbert: I'm thinking about buying a more fuel-efficient car.

Dogbert: Why?

Dilbert: It's my patriotic duty to reduce this country's dependence on foreign sources of oil.

Dogbert: Why?

Dilbert: Because then the countries that hate us will have less money to fund terrorists.

Dogbert: Actually, developing countries would buy the oil you saved. Thus adequately funding those same terrorists.

Dilbert: At least I wouldn't be funding them myself.

Dogbert: Oil is a *fungible* commodity. The capitalist system virtually guarantees that you'll end up buying the lowest cost oil from sources unknown to you.

Dilbert: Well, maybe, but I want my car to make a statement.

Dogbert: And the statement would be "Hey, everyone, I don't understand what fungible means."

Fungibility is the degree to which units of a given commodity are interchangeable. While there are different grades of petroleum in the overall world market, it's a basically fungible commodity. The same can be said of gold and silver. Money is fungible, too. So regardless of the source of government revenues – taxes, fees, debt, etc. – once the money is collected, it all goes into the same barrel to be spent.

To help explain that, a good example is the futile act of designating your United Way contribution to your favorite charity so some other one doesn't get the funds instead. Since United Way's collections are fungible, when you earmark dollars specifically to Charity A, it just means that other non-earmarked dollars, some fraction of which would have gone to Charity A, are now free to go to Charities B through Z.

Getting back to *Dilbert* and oil, the point is that all oil production becomes part of the world supply, and the price of oil is a function of aggregate demand for that finite supply. Changes in the amount supplied or the amount demanded cause the price to go up or down. It doesn't matter where the oil comes from or what it costs to extract it from the ground. So, lower cost producers, like Saudi Arabia, make more profit per unit of oil than higher cost producers like the United States. OPEC doesn't set the price of oil; the world market does that, although OPEC can influence the price by controlling its production.

It's silly to talk about our "addiction" to oil. We're no more *addicted* to it than we are to food or water. It's a commodity. We use it as an energy source and petrochemical raw material because it's abundant and a better value than other alternatives. We could have horses pull our cars but it wouldn't be as efficient – and you'd have to feed and house them, anyway.

It would be nice to find economical alternatives to petroleum and we no doubt will some day. Perhaps we'll solve the puzzle of nuclear fusion and figure out how to harvest water for its hydrogen power. General Motors and other automakers are working feverishly on developing fuel-cell technology. Conventional nuclear energy is a viable alternative for more power right now, but environmental extremists have succeeded in sufficiently demonizing it to scare much of the public and politicians away – at least for the time being.

Once upon a time, whale oil was a major energy source and people worried, then, about demand outpacing supply. Petroleum solved that problem – temporarily. In President Bush's State of the Union address he talked about accelerating the pace of technological research into energy alternatives. That's a necessary and obvious remedy.

The history of human progress is the history of solving today's problems with tomorrow's technology. And we will do just that once again. But don't kid yourself about kicking our oil "addiction" or ending our dependency on foreign petroleum anytime soon. For inescapable economic reasons, we're stuck with that for the foreseeable future and with all the international complications that go along with it.

Bread and Circuses
January 12, 2012

I was watching a movie the other day, one of those omnipresent action films replete with car chases and exploding structures. The cost of these productions often exceeds $100 million and the crashes and explosions are usually real, not computer generated images. While the action sequences may be entertaining, although overdone, it occurred to me that this is awfully wasteful.

Contrary to a popular misconception, destroying things is not good for the economy. French economist Frédéric Bastiat addressed this myth two centuries ago in his explanation of the Broken Windows Fallacy. While it might superficially appear that jobs are created in replacing what's been destroyed or broken, the resources and labor devoted to recreating that which already was would be more productively employed in adding to a society's wealth rather than just restoring it.

It also got me to thinking about our society's increasing obsession with entertainment, leisure and trivial pursuits. While the U.S., at more than $2 trillion annually, is still one of the top exporting nations in the world, in relative terms we don't manufacture as much as we used to. Our leading exports include aircraft, machinery, industrial supplies, military equipment, motor vehicles, replacement parts, agriculture, beverages, cigarettes, and services of many kinds. We also export a great deal of entertainment – films, TV, music, etc. – and drive the world's pop culture.

U.S. manufacturing output has declined as a share of our economy, and manufacturing employment has declined even more. That latter statistic is, ironically, good, not bad. High-tech manufacturing efficiencies and productivity enable us to do more with less labor, freeing that labor to the growing service sector. In the 18th century, before the industrial revolution, more than 90 percent of Americans worked on farms. Today, it's less than 5 percent, producing vastly more. Outlawing tractors, combines and other labor saving devices to create menial agricultural jobs would not be wise policy.

Some service-sector jobs productively leverage industrial efficiency while many others are simply a dividend of our prosperous society. Which brings us back to entertainment – ubiquitous entertainment: playgrounds for adults and kids from Las Vegas to Disney World; a universe of sporting events from football to cage fighting; hundreds of cable and satellite TV and radio stations; overpriced rock concerts for teeny boppers to aging baby boomers; zombie armies of Americans with permanently inserted ear buds perpetually plugged into the Internet, iPods, iPads, Kindles, smart phones, Facebook, Twitter, etc.

Sure, this is part and parcel of the enjoyment of life. All work and no play makes Jack a dull boy. And a wealthy society has more time for play. The Internet offers an abundance of worthwhile information, and social media serve a commercially useful purpose in advertising, marketing and promotion. But let's not kid ourselves; these media are also loaded with tons of crap.

Porn sites are more popular with the masses than intellectual treasure troves. Your teenage students spend a lot more time with online junk than academic substance. The bulk of non-business electronic conversations is just chatter. This is simply the high-tech equivalent and no more necessary or productive than two kids, in earlier days, talking to each other through tin cans connected by a length of string, or passing notes in grade school.

I don't mean to be a scold, and have no public policy remedy for overindulgent entertainment in a free society. I'm just observing a phenomenon and wondering how much better the general welfare would be served if some of the time, energy and creativity frittered away on facilitating and participating in frivolous entertainment were redirected toward productive enterprise.

An overdose of bread and circuses preceded the fall of the Roman Empire. In the immortal words of Mark Twain, "History doesn't repeat itself, but it does rhyme."

A Medley of Rosenosophy

Does God Grade on a Curve?
August 3, 1990

Niccolò Machiavelli – the famed Italian diplomat of the Renaissance, advisor to princes, and poster boy for political pragmatism – lay on his deathbed, the story goes, with his father confessor at his side. Machiavelli was not known for his religious devoutness.

Nonetheless, the priest implored him, "Machiavelli, Machiavelli, I beseech thee, renounce the devil."

Seeking to keep his options open, even at death's doorstep, Machiavelli replied, "Father, Father, this is no time to be making enemies."

The eternal question of life's final reward – or penalty, as the case may be – was the central theme in Woody Allen's most recent and arguably best movie, *Crimes and Misdemeanors*. A man is faced with the moral dilemma of having to commit a murder in order to save his life's work. He recalls from his youth, the admonition of his father, "The eyes of God see everything," but goes ahead with the crime anyway.

It's the kind of movie that gives one pause for thought.

Let's assume there is a God and that he holds each one of us accountable for our earthly acts.

Let's also assume that there's a heaven and a hell.

The big question, then, is just what are the respective admission standards? How good do you have to be to get into heaven?

I think it's fair to assume that Hitler won't be there, and that Mother Teresa will. But what about the rest of us? Clearly, it's not the nature of human beings to be perfectly moral. If it were, there would be no need for churches, temples, confessions, repentance – or prisons.

Most of us, during a normal lifetime, are going to commit a sin or two here and there.

Christians believe that sincere repentance and the acceptance of Jesus as Lord bestows forgiveness for almost all sins and opens the gates to heaven for true believers. Those of us who aren't Christians – and perhaps some who are – find themselves looking for another answer.

If Mother Teresa gets an "A" in life, and Hitler gets an "F," most of the rest of us fall somewhere in between, hopefully closer to the good mother than to the fuehrer. Is a "B" good enough to get you into heaven? How about a high "C?" Do we really have to compete with Mother Teresa? Is that fair? Personally, as much as I admire her works, I couldn't live my life the way she does. And I wouldn't want to.

Most people lead a reasonably moral life. Not saint-like, but reasonably moral. If the eyes of God do, in fact, see everything, it's all there on a record. You can't get away with adultery by hiding under the sheets. He even knows when you've improved your lie in the rough.

What keeps most people from becoming obsessed with the prospect of burning in hell for eternity is the belief that the demerits you've recorded will be weighed against the greater body of good things you've done – even when no one was watching.

All sins are not created equal. If heaven is only open to those who have never taken the Lord's name in vain, it must surely be a very exclusive place. Filching a hotel towel or playing golf on the Sabbath are not the equivalent of murder. There has to be a sliding scale, and a way of balancing debits with credits. Sending flowers on Mother's Day and rooting for Notre Dame have to be worth something.

When it comes to salvation, it's difficult to compete with the practitioners of organized religion. These people are in the business of getting into heaven. They get wholesale rates. When you're a sole (soul?) proprietor, you have to take some things on faith. Maybe it's wishful thinking, but I'd like to believe that God grades on a curve.

Just Answer the #!*&% Question

May 25, 2001

In response to a number of recent emails on this theme, here's the inside skinny on an aspect of talk radio. As popular and ubiquitous as talk radio is today, it's hard to believe that prior to the 1970s there was relatively little of it. Yes, there were a handful of notable radio-talkers, like Barry Gray, Jean Shepherd and Barry Farber, but the programs did not include listeners calling in to participate. These days, callers are a vital part of the show – even more so than guests. But it's also important to understand that successful talk-show hosts do not target their program primarily to callers.

That isn't a contradiction; it's simple mathematics. Shows with good audience ratings have many times more listeners than callers. For example, with 200,000 people in the area *listening* to my show in a given week, fewer than one in 1,000 (fewer than 200) will *call in* and get on the air. There are, no doubt, 200 people who would love to talk about the finer points of bird watching, but probably not 200,000 others who would care to listen. Full telephone lines aren't the same as large listening audiences.

A talk show host's first responsibility is to his listeners. Good caller-radio is not necessarily good listener-radio. Case in point: it might fascinate an individual caller to have a psychic guest tell his fortune, and while other callers might be lined up behind him to have their fortunes read, why would most listeners care? In a typical week, I get my share of great callers, average callers and terrible callers. But I never lose sight that I'm playing to a much larger audience of listeners who will never call in. When engaged in a heated debate with a politically committed caller, I have no illusions that I'll change his opinion; rather, I'm hoping to entertain and influence the greater body of listeners.

There is also no reason to assume that callers are representative of listeners. An overly polite and pandering talk-show host, while indulging one caller, can frustrate thousands of listeners or drive them away out of boredom. No one's ever accused me of being overly polite. I do a show with an edge and I like to keep it moving. I'm sometimes feisty although generally civil with civil and reasonable people. But there's one thing in particular that gets my goat; people who refuse to give a direct and honest answer to a fair question.

Perhaps talk-radio callers learned this device from politicians who do it all the time. When a straightforward answer to a question would embarrass them, undermine their argument, or expose the inconsistency or illogic of their position, some people simply ignore the question. Or even worse, answer a question with a question. That's not an answer, it's a question. Stop tap dancing and just answer the #!*&% question! As a tactic this is wholly transparent, rude, cowardly and intellectually dishonest. It's not even effective. A debate is like a tennis match. You don't have to win every point, just most of them. Sometimes your best strategy is to concede a point, cut your losses, and move on.

Put me to the test on the air sometime. I'll always answer a fair question directly, while reserving the option of explaining. Obviously, I can't force people in the world at large to play by the same rules, but I can, and do, hold their feet to the fire in the confines of my radio show. I hope I've helped others to recognize this ploy when they encounter it in other venues. One final note. I've observed that liberals play this game of dodging questions far more than conservatives. Perhaps it's because, as Whitaker Chambers once observed, the left realizes it can only take power through deception.

A Wonderful but Risky Life
June 23, 2006

In last Sunday's *Denver Post*, the bulk of the front page was devoted to a story about the current spate of home foreclosures. Over a photo of duplexes on a serene residential block in Brighton was the title, "Heartbreak along Mockingbird Lane." Below was the headline, "Foreclosures Send Homeowners Down Uneasy Street."

What followed was mostly a human interest story labeled "Foreclosing on the American Dream." You get the point. There were many sad personal accounts of people who had lost their homes. There was also a critical explanation of lending and real estate development practices that have contributed to this predicament, along with helpful tips about what you might do to avoid this fate.

The Denver Post is on the case and feels your pain. We see a lot of this in the mass media. It's good business to make yourself liked by readers, viewers or listeners. Katie Couric has leveraged folksy popularity and perkiness to catapult herself from the *Today* show to the Dan Rather Chair at *CBS*. It's why liberal positions on issues and policies are more attractive to most of those in the media whose job it is to deliver messages to the public. As hopeless utopians, liberals can promise more desirable outcomes to more people at someone else's expense. They can't necessarily deliver on those promises, but they sure sound nice.

The populist urge is irresistible to such people. By populism, I mean a heartfelt appeal to "the people." And I say "heartfelt" advisedly, an appeal to the heart rather than to reason. It's also commonly an appeal to simplistic and uninformed frustration, anger, jealousy, bias, and paranoid victimhood. If you want to be liked by the masses, side with the "little guys." Do the math. They greatly outnumber the "oppressors," those traditional populist bogeymen like big corporations, bankers, the Federal Reserve, Wall Street, oil companies, insurance companies, The Pentagon, the rich, etc., etc.

My thankless task over the past quarter-century, since I made the crossover from my business career to the media, has been to take the more difficult, less superficially popular side of the argument. It's been said that a politician will ask you what you want while a free market economist will ask you what you want *most*.

The real world is a choice among imperfect trade-offs, with utopia not on the menu. So let's deal with the thorny problem of home foreclosures. No, my hero isn't Mr. Potter, the avaricious banker in Frank Capra's *It's a Wonderful Life*. I don't relish foreclosures and I'm not unsympathetic, but I'm also aware of the potential consequences of economic decisions in a market economy.

The American dream, contrary to the contemporary belief of some, is not to hit the lottery and get rich quick. It's to take advantage of the ample opportunities available in our society, work hard, save some money and earn the rewards. Owning your own home has traditionally been a part of that. Real-estate markets are historically subject to ups and downs in the short run, but are a good store of value over the long haul if you can stick it out.

It's common for young marrieds and singles to financially stretch when buying their first or second home. They make optimistic assumptions about their career and income prospects, and figure to grow into their mortgage payment. In most cases that's exactly what happens.

But some gamble and lose. During the go-go '90s many people stretched too far or gambled unwisely on adjustable rate mortgages and got caught short. Nobody forced them to do this. When you reach for the brass ring, there's always the risk you'll fall off the horse. The opportunity to succeed in this country is one side of the coin; on the other is the opportunity to fail. It's not the end of the world. You dust yourself off, lick your wounds, maybe rent for a few years and take another shot at it later. The bank or mortgage company might well get stuck for the negative equity in your home. Is anyone taking up a collection for them?

If you don't like this system, here's a remedy: Let's add another level of government. Before you can buy a home, you'll have to appear before a panel of bureaucrats who will decide just how far you'll be able to reach for that brass ring. They'll appraise your career prospects, dictate the number of children you can afford, mandate a budget, limit your square footage, design a floor plan and select the appropriate neighborhood for you. Even if it would save only one foreclosure, wouldn't it be worth it?

'Listen Up, Jellyfish: We Have Met the Enemy and Sold Them Cookies'
September 8, 1989

Sister Peg Maloney, who identifies herself as the associate director of the Justice and Peace Office of the Catholic Archdiocese of Denver, has been venting public outrage at a scene captured in a photograph taken recently during Basic Cadet training (BCT) at the Air Force Academy.

Pictured was a bare-chested cadet in a black hood, holding an executioner's ax over his head. He was standing alongside a column of marching recruits in combat fatigues.

The good sister likened this image to the training of Middle-Eastern terrorists. She decried the use of billions of dollars for defense each year at the expense of social programs, especially when those defense dollars are used to fund this kind of symbolism.

She went on to pray for the day when the Air Force would have to hold a bake sale to buy missiles. Unless military cuisine has improved markedly since I was in the service, the Air Force might think twice before adopting the sister's approach to ICBM procurement.

I checked with the Air Force Academy for an explanation of the executioner scene. Sister Maloney, it turns out, hadn't bothered. Anyone who's ever been to a Falcon's football game would understand. The "Executioner" is a BCT squadron mascot. There are ten of them, in all. Each squadron has a nickname, starting with a letter of the alphabet from A-J.

I remember when I was in Army basic training. They told me I would be molded into a trained killer. When we weren't learning to make beds, fold underwear and buff linoleum floors, this seemed to make some sense since the tools of my newly found trade included things like rifles, bayonets and hand grenades. The idea of bake sales never came up. Consequently, we were taught to be aggressive and to learn how to defend ourselves, a skill which might come in handy if someone in a different uniform were trying to kill you.

I imagine it's in keeping with this general philosophy that the current crop of BCT squadrons at the Academy bear the following ferocious names. There are, from A-J:

The Aggressors, Barbarians, Cobras, Demons, Executioners, Flying Tigers, Guts, Hell Cats, Interceptors, and *Jaguars*. There should be something in this lineup to offend almost anyone who wants to be, from animal rights activists to anti-Satanists.

Perhaps the sister is right. Names and mascots suggesting this kind of pugnaciousness could only hurt cookie sales in the future. In the interest of a kinder and gentler Air Force, maybe they should rename the BCT squadrons. We could have, for example: *The Altruists, Butterflies, Cupcakes, Dandelions, Existentialists, Flower Children, Gay Caballeros, Holistics* and the *Jellyfish*. You may have noticed I left one out, in the unlikely event that we needed someone who could fight. (Suppose, heaven forbid, some rowdies tried to disrupt the bake sale.) With apologies to Sister Maloney, we might call those rough and tumble guys in the I-squadron the *Ill-Mannered*.

I called the Denver Archdiocese to ask whether Sister Maloney was speaking for it. I was told that she wasn't, that she was speaking for herself and, perhaps, for the Justice and Peace Office which apparently speaks for itself, not the church. From the Catholics I know, the Office certainly doesn't speak for them. Since I have no reason to believe Sister Maloney knows God any better than I do, I doubt she speaks for Him, either.

Justice and Peace are lovely values, although frequently difficult to define. But I notice the conspicuous absence in that duo of another value: Freedom. It's people like Sister Maloney who either devalue that one or take it for granted. I don't, and that's why I appreciate the need for a strong and – perish the thought – potentially tenacious defense.

Of course it would be nice if we didn't need a military, and could spend all that money on the social programs the sister favors (or even better, give it back to the taxpayers.) It would also be nice if we didn't need a police force, courts and jails. It would be nice if we didn't need referees in football games, or to take a number at the deli-counter. But that's not the world we live in, and the prayers of our well-intentioned Sister Maloneys notwithstanding, never will be.

I hope the Air Force hangs tough on this one. I have this recurring nightmare that I'd hate to see come true. I'm at a Falcons game this fall when the cadet squadrons march in. And there's Sister Maloney, sitting next to me, leading the crowd in a cheer of "Give 'Em Hell, *Jellyfish*."

The Genders Simply aren't Identical
August 13, 1993

Men and Women are fundamentally different. That's the conclusion Chris Evatt, a certified woman, draws in her book, *He and She*, in which Evatt highlights no less than 60 significant differences. Such as:

Men are more competitive, women are more cooperative. Women tend to be other-focused, men self-focused. Being right is more important to men than women. Women apologize more than men. Women are emotionally jealous; men are sexually jealous. Women's language is more circumspect, men's more direct. Men fear engulfment; women fear abandonment.

Although I concur with these generalizations, I'd nonetheless acknowledge that individuals ought to be treated as individuals. Some women may be better suited to traditional male roles and some men to female ones. But that's about as "enlightened" – in the Phil Donahue sense – as I'm going to get. I am not an androgynist. I agree with Evatt that there are fundamental differences between the male and female genders, and that these differences are natural, desirable and immutable.

Sigmund Freud coined the term "penis envy," which has since taken on a meaning that might encompass women who would really prefer to be men, possessing the male sex organ and all that goes with it. In addition to exchanging estrogen for testosterone, being able to relieve themselves from a standing position, no longer having to suffer the ordeal of menstrual cycles and enjoying enhanced physical strength, such women would also acquire the advantages of living in a "man's world" – a societal bias that has traditionally afforded men more opportunities than women.

For those women who have vehemently resented what they have regarded as a second-class status in society, and who have been willing to forego the gratification of exclusively female prerogatives like childbirth and motherhood, you might understand why the prospect of a gender exchange could be appealing. I can empathize with them – I'd rather be a man than a woman, too.

But with the onslaught of modern feminism, penis envy seems to have gone out of fashion. The strategy of "If you can't beat them, join them" appears to have given way to "If you can't beat them, dismember them," so to speak.

Modern feminists have replaced (or, perhaps suppressed) envy with a crusade to remake the male of the species, in their image. Traditional male virtues like aggressiveness, control of emotions and competitiveness have been stigmatized as defects. Traditional female characteristics, on the other hand, like compassion, emotionalism, nurturing and domestication have been declared superior and more desirable. The woman's touch, feminists tell us, is the one best suited to modern-day corporate management, civic affairs and world leadership. Men should get in touch with their "feminine side" and become more like the girls. This might be described as the evolution of feminism from penis *envy* to penis*ectomy*.

So where will it all lead? I suppose one of two things will eventually happen. Either this trend will flower, and the male of the species will come to resemble the Phil Donahue and Richard Simmons prototypes, or there will be a backlash.

I'm not envisioning a retrogression to the age of the caveman and his club, or even to bare feet and pregnancy, just a reassertion of common sense. It's hard to gauge the extent of overall male resistance to feminization since the dominant media culture that seeks to shape public opinion speaks, on this issue, with a feminist voice, but I do see a counterrevolution in the making.

What we need is a champion and a catalyzing act: The symbolic equivalent of James Cagney reaching across the table in *Public Enemy* and shoving a grapefruit in Molly Yard's face.

Defending 'Islamofascist'
September 22, 2006

What I like about the term Islamofacism is that it calls a spade a spade. It's not some wishy-washy euphemism. It pinpoints and accurately describes this century's greatest threat to humanity. It combines intolerant religious zealotry, that's the "Islamo" part, with ruthless totalitarianism, that's the "fascist" part.

The enemy isn't terrorism, per se. That's a tactic, not a cause, and a universal one at that. Timothy McVeigh, the Oklahoma City bomber, was a terrorist, but he wasn't an Islamofascist. Klebold and Harris, the Columbine killers, were terrorists, but not Islamofascists.

A *Rocky Mountain News* letter to the editor from a Boulderite (where else?) took issue with my defense of the term in a recent column. I'll stand by it. The letter writer argued that fascism is best used to describe Hitler's brand of "authoritarianism" and his "support" of "private enterprise" (aka "corporatism" as the Boulderite termed it, a buzz word for anti-capitalist lefties with an affection for socialism). I'd say that Hitler was more of a totalitarian than an authoritarian, and that he wasn't content to "support" private enterprise, he wanted to control it — along with everything else.

Intellectually lazy leftists tend to throw around the term "fascist" gratuitously. They use it childishly as an epithet for people or policies they just don't like. Ronald Reagan was an advocate of limited government. He said government was the problem, not the solution. He didn't want to control business; he wanted to *decontrol* it. Nonetheless, irrational leftists called him a fascist.

Perhaps reserving the term fascist for American conservatives that he doesn't like, the aforementioned letter writer offered his personal preference for the term "theocracy" rather than Islamofascism. He then went on to outrageously equate the likes of Osama bin Laden with James Dobson and conservative Christians.

James Dobson never flew an airplane into the World Trade Center. And his Focus on the Family organization doesn't train suicide bombers to kill innocent Muslim women and children. I've never heard Dobson call for the death of non-Christians, simply because they're non-

Christians, nor does he want to outlaw other religions in this country or change the Constitution to make the president subservient to the church.

The comparison is absurd. Christian missionaries seek to convert others through persuasion and good deeds. Islamofascists force conversion at the point of a sword.

Theocracy is a legitimate term in some contexts, but an insufficient one to describe Islamofascists. The Vatican, for example, is a theocracy, but a benign one, not an intolerant, militant, aggressive force. Christians may believe that those who don't accept Jesus will be denied entrance to heaven, but they don't also want to kill them – not these days anyway. The current generation of Islamofascists are wholesale murderers.

Along with 9/11, examples of Islamofascist acts include the murder of Dutch filmmaker Theo Van Gogh, attacks on Danish embassies in response to newspaper cartoons of Muhammad, the ritual slaughter of *Wall Street Journal* reporter Daniel Pearl in Pakistan, and the recent calls for the assassination of Pope Benedict XVI because of remarks he made at a scholarly conference in Germany to which some Muslims took offense. In the 21st century, civilized people don't murder others for what they say. Islamofascists do.

President Bush and others have made it abundantly clear on repeated occasions that Islamofascism is not synonymous with Islam. Islamofascism is a radical subset of Islam. Just as Earth First! terrorists are a radical subset of environmentalists. Not all Muslims are Islamofascists, but all Islamofascists are Muslims. Al-Qaida is Islamofascist, as are the Taliban and the extreme Wahhabi sect.

An essential question is just how widespread is Islamofascism within the Muslim world of more than a billion followers? Is it 500 million? Is it 100 million? Is it only a small minority, but one that has cowed the Muslim "silent majority" into submission or acquiescence? If so, that "minority" may be large enough, and committed and destructive enough to instigate a world war.

Which takes us to the other essential question: What, if anything, is the respectable Islamic world going to do about cleaning up its own house? Where's the modern-day Martin Luther of Islam? Who will lead the Islamic Reformation and avert a worldwide confrontation that could kill tens of millions? If there are any prominent, powerful candidates, they've certainly been keeping a low profile for the last couple of decades.

The Paranoids are after Us
November 15, 1996

Prior to last Sunday's game with Chicago, I was beginning to believe that National Football League officials were involved in a conspiracy against the Broncos. It just seemed that we had been victimized by a flurry of bad calls in recent weeks. Then, on a key drive late in the third quarter of the Bears game, an official ruled that Rashaan Salaam had fumbled deep in Denver territory. It was a bad call that, for once, went in our favor. So much for my conspiracy theory.

Some others, however, survive. Just a couple of months ago, one conspiracy theory making the rounds alleged that the CIA had introduced crack cocaine to inner-city Los Angeles for the dual purpose of funding the Nicaraguan Contras and debilitating the black community. The story was heralded by the *San Jose Mercury News* and embraced by disgruntled Sandinista sympathizers and Louis Farrakhan followers. The initial charges got big headlines across the country. The *L.A. Times* put ten staffers on the story, investigated all the allegations and recently ran a series exposing it as a fraud. The *Times* discovered that L.A.'s leading pusher was dealing in crack three years before the Sandinista revolution, and five years before the Contra army was ever formed. At most, $50,000 was funneled to the Contras by two Nicaraguan exiles during a couple of months in 1981. There was no evidence linking the CIA to anything. The debunking of the conspiracy theory got scant attention in the national media.

Last week, Pierre Salinger emerged from hibernation in France proclaiming that TWA Flight 800 was really shot down by a U.S. Naval vessel during target practice. How did he know this? Well, he had a *document* in his possession proving it. That's a wonderful word, "document." It conveys an air of authority. Did he have a notarized statement signed by the head of the FBI authorizing the cover up? A deposition from the captain of the naval vessel that fired the missile? No, what Salinger originally claimed was a secret communiqué from an intelligence source turns out to be nothing more than someone's rantings that have been kicking around on the Internet for the last month or two. The FBI and the Navy Department say the charge is preposterous. I believe them.

It's implausible that the Navy would be conducting missile target practice at night just a few miles off the coast of Long Island so close to a major commercial airport. If an accident like this had happened, do you really believe that knowledge of it by a naval crew of several hundred, the entire chain of command, the FBI, the National Transportation Safety Board and, presumably, the president of the United States could be contained? This is a lot bigger than some Clinton sexual tryst. In this day and age, you can't keep a secret like that. (Or maybe it wasn't an accident; maybe the Navy thought Pat Schroeder was on the plane and shot it down on purpose as an act of revenge for her exploitation of the Tailhook incident. If you're going to concoct a conspiracy, why not create a doozy?)

Conspiracy theories dispel life's uncertainties. They resolve confounding and frustrating mysteries, providing ready solutions for questions that otherwise have no apparent answers – kind of like religion. They're enjoyed, equally, by lefties like Oliver Stone hallucinating about the Kennedy assassination, and right-wing paranoids suspecting Bilderbergers and Trilateralists under every bed. I like the Navy, I have fond memories of my experiences there. I wouldn't want it to be true that a Navy vessel shot down a civilian airliner and then covered it up. I recognize my bias, but I also recognize an absurd scenario when I hear one.

Conspiracy theories are believed mostly by people who desperately want to believe them. Those who hate the military, the CIA, the FBI and any symbols of authority, want to believe the worst about them. Another school of conspiracy theorists – who want capitalism's rewards but who aren't up to its rigors and don't understand its workings – attribute their lack of economic success to a cabal of shadowy corporate figures, international bankers and Jews.

Pierre Salinger is probably just an old fool. When this latest conspiratorial fantasy is debunked, I hope he gets the heavy dose of scorn and ridicule he so roundly deserves.

Debunking ANWR Hysteria

August 24, 2001

A tiny slice of the Alaskan National Wildlife Refuge (ANWR) has been proposed for oil drilling. To hear environmental absolutists and those taken in by their propaganda sing its praises, you'd think this place is an idyllic retreat for nature lovers. Well, you'd think wrong. After returning from a recent trip to the precise site, Jonah Goldberg, editor of *National Review Online*, observed that the area would do nicely if "you wanted a picture to go with the word 'Godforsaken' in the dictionary." He described a dismal, treeless coastal plain where winters last for nine months, punctuated by 58 consecutive days of total darkness and temperatures dropping to 70 degrees below zero. The highlight of the all-too-brief summer is the infestation of frenzied, caribou-eating mosquitoes spawned from puddles of freestanding water in the flat tundra as far as the eye can see. If you'd prefer a description from a liberal source, here's how the *Washington Post* described it 14 years ago before the cause became fashionable: "[T]hat part of the [ANWR] is one of the bleakest, most remote places on this continent, and there is hardly any other area where drilling would have less impact on surrounding life."

99% of Alaska is owned by government, including 192 million acres of parks, wilderness areas and preserves. ANWR comprises 19.6 million acres, much of it (when it's light) the stuff of picture postcards. Nobody's talking about messing with that. 92% of ANWR can't legally be touched. In 1980, Congress set aside 1.5 million acres of already-populated coastal plain, known as the 1002 (Ten-0-2) Area, for potential oil and gas development. That's what the debate is all about. The U.S. Geological Survey has estimated that ANWR could yield 16 billion barrels of oil, the equivalent of 30 years of oil imports from Saudi Arabia. In a May 2000 report, the Energy Information Administration called this "the largest unexplored, potentially productive onshore basin in the United States."

If energy exploration and development were allowed to proceed, it would be conducted under stringent environmental protections. And, thanks to new technologies like directional drilling and multilateral wells, only a scant 2,000 acres would be affected by oil operations, one-hundredth of one percent of the refuge. ANWR is about the size of the state of South Carolina. By comparison, the oil drilling area is about the size of Denver International Airport. Interior Secretary Gail Norton has helped put this in a reasonable perspective with some profoundly graphic comparisons:

** If the state of Alaska were a football field, all of ANWR would fill the space between the goal line and the six-yard line, the 1002 Area would extend only to the one-half yard line, and the actual area of energy production within ANWR would equal less than the length of one link on the 10-yard first down chain.

** If the state of Alaska were the front page of a daily newspaper like the *New York Times*, ANWR would be seven column inches of text, the 1002 Area would be one-half inch of text, and the area of energy production would equal the size of less than one character of text.

** If the state of Alaska were a 1,000 page phone book like in New York City, ANWR would be equal to 52 pages, the 1002 Area would be four pages, and the area of energy production would be equal to one-half square inch on one page.

** If the state of Alaska were a two-hour movie, ANWR would represent six minutes and 24 seconds, the 1002 Area would be equal to one-half minute, and the area of energy production would be four-hundredths of a second, about the time it takes to blink your eye.

New sources of oil and gas are essential. We'll develop the 1002 Area prudently. In rebuttal, enviro ideologues offer only their usual brand of hysteria and demonology.

Global Warming Hysteria
April 25, 2008

A growing contingent of scientists has been brave enough to stand athwart the politically fashionable global warming steamroller. More than 500 such skeptics convened in New York at the 2008 International Conference on Climate Change last month. They argue factually and persuasively that what warming the world has seen in the last hundred years is at best minimal and at worst exaggerated.

Conversely, radical increases in global temperatures or rising sea levels proclaimed by Al Gore and his ilk aren't facts. They're merely guesses, some of them hysterical, about conditions decades or centuries into the future and based on assumptions about innumerable variables, many of which are beyond our scientific comprehension or expertise.

Climate change is a natural and age-old phenomenon on this planet, recurring in roughly 1,500 year cycles and predating humanity by millions of years. Ice ages have come and gone. Compared to the overwhelming influence of the sun and the impact of nonhuman influences on this planet – ocean-generated water vapor, animal life, vegetation, etc. – the notion that the puny contribution of mankind is the principal cause of climate change is a grand conceit.

Human activity constitutes a small fraction of the myriad influences on climate. Marginal changes in human activity within our technological and practical economic means represent an even smaller fraction of that small fraction. The trillions of dollars the world would spend on wasteful schemes to avert a delusional global warming doomsday is the greatest fool's errand in history. Count me among the global warming skeptics. If I'm still around in a hundred years, I'll delight in saying, "I told you so."

Global warming hysteria is steeped in politics and a strange collection of bedfellows. Along with sincere environmentalist true-believers are the camp followers who embrace this as a quasi-religious calling.

Then there are the watermelons – green on the outside, red on the inside. They embrace ecological arguments to achieve ideological goals, exploiting fears of enviro-Armageddon to regulate and control evil capitalists and redistribute world income and wealth. Václav Klaus, president of the Czech Republic, recognizes the signs. "As someone who lived under communism for most of (my) life," he warned, "I feel obliged to say that I see the biggest threat to freedom, democracy, the market economy and prosperity now in ambitious environmentalism, not communism. This ideology wants to replace the free and spontaneous evolution of mankind by a sort of central (now global) planning."

Add to the mix political opportunists seeking election and economic opportunists seeking a quick buck from government grants, subsidies and market manipulation, and you have an irresistible coalition.

In this time of runaway oil prices and surging world demand for energy it's only sensible to marshal creative technological resources and capital to use energy, from whatever source, as efficiently as possible. That's precisely why government-driven boondoggles like ethanol are worse than wasteful, especially as this misallocation of agricultural resources has driven up the world price of foodstuffs. Justifying a wrongheaded policy by simply asserting it's "for the environment" is just as stupid as justifying a wasteful government-spending program with the magic words "it's for the children."

It's currently fashionable for politicians to brag about their policies for a "new energy economy" and the jobs created by it. Economically productive energy programs are wonderful. Just spending taxpayer money for humbug isn't. The market is a much better judge and taskmaster than government for what makes economic sense. Imagine your tax dollars at work hiring 10,000 people to generate turbine electricity by climbing a perpetual wheel like hamsters in a cage. Wouldn't that be a great way to create jobs in a new energy economy?

I've got a better idea. While we're waiting for the breakthrough in hydrogen fusion technology that will make water a cheap and plentiful energy source, why not put Americans to work developing our known natural gas and petroleum resources offshore and in the Arctic National Wildlife Refuge?

ADDENDUM: The following illustration demonstrates the miniscule impact that the activities of mankind actually have on the earth relative to CO_2 emissions:

The U.S. Impact on Greenhouse Gases and CO_2 Levels

All greenhouse gases account for only 2% of the total atmosphere

- o   3.62% of greenhouse gases are CO_2
- o   3.4% of CO_2 is caused by human activity
- o   22% of world CO_2 emissions come from the U.S.
- o   Cap & Trade would reduce U.S. man-made CO_2 output by 15%

  (Source: National Center for Policy Analysis)

So, do the math:

- ➢   0.02*0.036*0.034*0.22 = 0.0000053856 or about five ten thousandths of one percent. That's the U.S. human-activity contribution to worldwide CO_2 levels.

- ➢   Next, if you multiply that by the effect of U.S. Cap & Trade policies, worldwide CO_2 emissions would be reduced by: 0.02*0.036*0.034*0.22*0.15 = 0.000000807840 or about eight-one-hundred thousandths of one percent.

- ➢   This example puts in perspective the contribution of CO_2 caused by U.S. human activity to the worldwide level of CO_2 in the atmosphere, and then the impact of U.S. Cap and Trade policies on worldwide CO_2 levels:

To illustrate the relative magnitude of this, consider the following comparison to a typical human being:

- ➢   A 200 pound man is made up of about 130 lbs., or 15.6 gallons of water.
- ➢   Those 15.6 gallons of water represent the entire atmosphere.
- ➢   Of those 15.6 gallons of atmosphere, 2%, or 0.3 gallons, represents the greenhouse gas portion of the atmosphere.
- ➢   Of that one third gallon of greenhouse gases, 3.6%, or 2.9 tablespoons, represents the CO_2 portion of the greenhouse gases worldwide.
- ➢   Of those 2.9 tablespoons of CO_2, 3.4%, or 0.3 teaspoon, represents the portion of the CO_2 attributable to worldwide human activity.
- ➢   Of that one third teaspoon of worldwide CO_2 contribution, 22%, or 0.3 gram, is attributable to American activity.
- ➢   Of that one third gram of American CO_2 contribution, 15%, or 0.05 gram, might be eliminated by cap and trade and other governmental mandates.
- ➢   This is approximately equal to a single drop of water from an eyedropper.

Forcing a Greener Mankind
June 14, 2012

"Nonsense so great only an intellectual could believe it." When George Orwell offered that description, what he no doubt had in mind was academic tripe of the kind recently presented in a paper, *Human Engineering and Climate Change*. The authors are S. Matthew Liao, a philosophy professor at New York University, and two colleagues, Anders Sandberg and Rebecca Roche, from Oxford.

They start with the premise that human activity is a major contributor to climate change. Although I don't subscribe to that alarmist theory, at least it's debatable. What's positively absurd is their remedy. They worry that market solutions (like carbon taxation), diplomacy (like the Kyoto Protocol), and "ordinary behavioral solutions" (like education and encouragement) may not be enough to make people drive less, recycle more, and generally adopt greener lifestyles.

"The fact that many people lack the motivation to alter their behavior in the required ways" to sufficiently reduce greenhouse gas emissions calls for a new kind of solution, they argue. What they propose is biomedical re-engineering of human beings to mitigate climate change. If people won't change, they would change people.

Some of these changes include adding an "emetic" (something that induces vomiting) to red meat to discourage its consumption, or developing a "meat patch" (like a nicotine patch) that people would wear so that "henceforth eating eco-unfriendly food would induce unpleasant experiences."

They say "larger people consume more energy." The examples they give include greater consumption of food; more fuel to transport heavier persons in a car; more fabric needed for clothing and; more wear and tear on shoes, carpets and furniture. (I'm not kidding; it's in their paper.) So, they propose reducing birth weight and making people smaller and shorter through genetic engineering and hormone treatments.

Another of their creative ventures in human engineering is to "enhance and improve our moral decisions by making us more altruistic and empathetic." This would be accomplished through interventions

374

affecting the sensitivity of neural systems. They note that "test subjects given the prosocial hormone oxytocin were more willing to share money with strangers." Also, that testosterone decreases empathy. (Yet another reason women are better than men.)

Lest you assume this paper was scorned even by the liberal intelligentsia, it's slated for publication in a greenie journal, *Ethics, Policy & Environment*, whose field of issues includes "environmental ethics, animal welfare, environmental justice, sustainability, and cultural values relevant to environmental concerns." On March 12, the *Atlantic* featured a lengthy, softball interview of Liao by Ross Anderson, its technology guy, who treated all this as reasonable.

Responding to an online barrage of outrage and ridicule, Liao objected that critics had grossly misrepresented his paper. He referred to a disclaimer in the text explaining that the authors weren't necessarily endorsing these solutions and that if they were available they should only voluntarily be adopted by individuals.

Well, *that's* a relief. So we won't all be subject to altruistic lobotomies, only those who want to be. For a moment, I envisioned a society of human-engineered Elois like those depicted in H.G. Wells' *The Time Machine*. In which case, who would protect us from the Morlocks? As Woody Allen once remarked, "The lion shall lie down with the lamb, but the lamb won't get much sleep."

One wonders then, what the purpose of their paper was. Was it just a pointless, abstract exercise by puckish, tenured academics with nothing better to do? I read every word of it, including Liao's convenient, perfunctory disclaimer. I assure you that I'm not misrepresenting it. This crew is deadly serious about these crackpot ideas. It's just another stage in the evolution of anthropogenic global warming hysteria, now justifying the biological greening of humans.

It may already be happening. When I wasn't snickering, their paper did, indeed, nauseate me.

Jesus and Santa Coexist
December 31, 2009

Now that Christmas is over and we're approaching a new year, let's finally dispatch the tiresome debate over whether to greet people with "Merry Christmas" or "happy holidays." It's a free country, so take your pick. Personally, I prefer "Merry Christmas."

The de-Christmasization of the season with contrived substitutes like "winter festival" is an affront to common sense and an unnecessary surrender to the forces of secularization, political correctness and hypersensitivity.

Can you spell A-C-L-U?

Christmas has two dimensions, one secular and one religious, that have overlapped and peacefully coexisted for centuries. Some people celebrate Santa Claus Christmas, some Jesus Christ Christmas and most people in this country, including the majority of Christians, celebrate both. It's unlikely that Jesus ever said "Merry Christmas" around his birthday, and it certainly wasn't an official government holiday in his time. Today, "Merry Christmas" is a decidedly joint concept.

Some Christians strongly resent the commercialization of Santa Claus Christmas. It's their prerogative to boycott that and focus on the birth of Christ and his teachings. (Although I suspect that most 6-year-old Christian kids go to bed on Christmas Eve eagerly awaiting Santa's arrival.) On the other hand, some atheists grouse about the religiosity of Christmas and the comingling of church and state. That's their prerogative, just as it is everyone else's to reject these complaints if they choose.

I'm not a Christian. I'm not even religious. But I've always loved Christmas: the spirit of the season, the music – secular and religious – the sights, smells, food, fellowship, parties and the exchange of gifts. I'm not offended by the commercialization. Personally, I like commerce.

Retailers clearly celebrate Santa Claus Christmas. You don't see images of the Virgin Mary when they herald their Christmas sales. It's all about Santa, the elves, Rudolph and Frosty the Snowman. We have federally recognized legal holidays throughout the year but, among them, the exchanging of gifts is unique to Christmas. Excited children don't have trouble falling asleep on Presidents' Day Eve.

There's no need to euphemize "Christmas." Hanukkah comes at about the same time, but it's not a legal holiday, and Jews make up only about 2 percent of the population. If Hanukkah were in July, it would fly under the general public radar just as Purim does.

Kwanzaa? Be serious. That was the fabrication of Ron Karenga, a violent ex-con and Marxist black supremacist who, in 1966, pulled the holiday out of thin air because he thought Christmas was too white. (Someone should have told him that Bing Crosby's immortal *White Christmas* referred to snow, not race.) They had never heard of Kwanzaa in Africa. The vast majority of American blacks are Christians, and celebrate Christmas along with everyone else. The same for Latinos. (In the spirit of the season, I can even forgive Jose Feliciano for the maddeningly repetitive lyrics of *Feliz Navidad*.)

Yes, you might say Thanksgiving kicks off the "holiday season," but it's a relative newcomer. Long before that, it was all about Christmas. And prior to the birth of Christ, pagans celebrated the winter solstice at this time of year (when they discovered that daylight was making a comeback) with Christmas trees that were obviously called something else then. Not to be left out, Christians strategically scheduled the celebration of Christ's birth as a competitive event. We're no more likely to see Jesus' original birth certificate than Barack Obama's.

We're a nation of 300 million people, the vast majority of whom are just fine with Merry Christmas. Even a reformed Ebenezer Scrooge exclaimed it. It's been Merry Christmas for centuries. How in the world have we been bullied into being defensive about it? Shout it out! No one will arrest you.

Reality

Acknowledgements

The task of reducing a collection of some 1,600 columns composed over more than 30 years down to fewer than 200 was daunting. That required more painful cuts than the Denver Broncos coaching staff faces each year in getting its opening-day roster down to about 50. I owe a debt of gratitude in that effort to Mark Swanson for his assistance and hard work as the editor of this book, and to his wife, Jane, for her assistance as a proofreader. John Fund, an old friend, who made his mark for over two decades on the outstanding editorial pages of *The Wall Street Journal,* now writes for *National Review Online* and *The American Spectator,* along with being a prolific author of his own books, offered some outstanding guidance in this project. Rick Bieber does a great job as the manager of my Facebook page. It wouldn't exist without him. I spend at least 2-3 hours a day just reading and responding to as many as I can of the hundreds of emails I get from my *KOA Radio* listeners. Rick does the heavy lifting for me on Facebook.

At *KOA*, Dave Lauer has been the faithful producer of my radio show for 25 years. That means putting up with someone like me who's been described as everything from a perfectionist to obsessive compulsive to anal retentive. Dave is a dedicated, loyal and essential part of the team. Lee Larsen was the big boss for most of my 30 years at *KOA* before he retired several years ago. I'd say he was the best executive in the entire industry, instrumental in my success and always supportive of my work. Succeeding Lee was Pat Connor who worked under Lee with distinction for all those years in a variety of management capacities. Pat is a friend and colleague who's also been very helpful to me. He's earned the top post and is doing a fine job steering the ship. Greg Foster, our vice president of programming, has a positive and gracious management style; it has been a pleasure working with him.

Ross Kaminsky is an up and coming talk show host at *KOA* whom I recommended to station management and who frequently fills in for me. He's also a prolific opinion writer, appearing in numerous national publications and online. He's a kindred spirit on matters of economics, finance and politics who is able to channel his libertarian instincts with a greater measure of practicality than most others of that persuasion. His feedback has been invaluable to me in this project.

Proofing and fact checking a book is painstaking work. My two talented and literate daughters, Lynn and Jill, have helped out in this area and offered many creative suggestions for the book, for which I am grateful. And even more so, to Nancy Baker Stump, who applied her advanced skills in spelling, grammar and vocabulary acquired at Susquehanna University and her experience as a top-notch corporate executive assistant. Nancy also screened my *Denver Post* columns going back more than thirty years. All of this has made her an extraordinary proofreader. Additionally, she's my former wife, the mother of our children and still a good friend.

Finally, a word of gratitude to thousands of loyal radio listeners who have followed me since 1980. Radio is not like the U.S. Postal Service or a tenured position in the education establishment. Holding a job for 30 years on a premier radio property like *KOA* in a highly competitive industry is no easy feat. It's been a great ride and an extremely gratifying one.

CPSIA information can be obtained
at www.ICGtesting.com
Printed in the USA
LVHW030333111218
600023LV00001B/241/P